D1566265

Financial Decision Making and Retirement Security in an Aging World

Financial Decision Making and Retirement Security in an Aging World

EDITED BY

Olivia S. Mitchell,
P. Brett Hammond, and
Stephen P. Utkus

OXFORD
UNIVERSITY PRESS

OXFORD
UNIVERSITY PRESS

Great Clarendon Street, Oxford, OX2 6DP,
United Kingdom

Oxford University Press is a department of the University of Oxford.
It furthers the University's objective of excellence in research, scholarship,
and education by publishing worldwide. Oxford is a registered trade mark of
Oxford University Press in the UK and in certain other countries

First Edition published in 2017

Impression: 1

Published in the United States of America by Oxford University Press
198 Madison Avenue, New York, NY 10016, United States of America

British Library Cataloguing in Publication Data
Data available

Library of Congress Control Number: 2017935043

ISBN 978–0–19–880803–9

Printed and bound by
CPI Group (UK) Ltd, Croydon, CR0 4YY

Links to third party websites are provided by Oxford in good faith and
for information only. Oxford disclaims any responsibility for the materials
contained in any third party website referenced in this work.

Preface

As the world's population lives longer, it will become increasingly important for plan sponsors, retirement advisors, regulators, and financial firms to focus closely on how older persons fare in the face of rising difficulties with cognition and financial management. This book offers state-of-the-art research and recommendations on how to evaluate when older persons need financial advice, help them make better financial decisions, and to identify policy options for handling these individual and social challenges efficiently and fairly. This, our newest volume in the Pension Research Council/Oxford University Press series, draws lessons from theory and practice, and we are confident that the book will interest employees and retirees, consumers and researchers, and financial institutions working to design better retirement plan offerings.

In the process of preparing this book, many people and institutions played key roles. Co-editors P. Brett Hammond and Stephen P. Utkus provided numerous excellent suggestions as we organized and edited the analysis herein. We also thank our Advisory Board and Members of the Pension Research Council for intellectual and financial support. Additional support was received from the Pension Research Council, the Boettner Center for Pensions and Retirement Research, and the Ralph H. Blanchard Memorial Endowment at the Wharton School of the University of Pennsylvania. We greatly appreciate the Oxford University Press which publishes our series on global retirement security. The manuscript was expertly prepared and carefully edited by Joseph Brucker.

Our work at the Pension Research Council and the Boettner Center for Pensions and Retirement Research of the Wharton School of the University of Pennsylvania has been dedicated to furthering pensions and retiree well-being for more than 60 years. We are delighted that this volume continues our effort to produce excellent new research and disseminate it to all who seek to learn.

Olivia S. Mitchell
Executive Director, Pension Research Council
Director, Boettner Center for Pensions and Retirement Research
The Wharton School, University of Pennsylvania

Contents

List of Figures   ix
List of Tables   xi
Notes on Contributors   xiii

1. Introduction: Financial Decision Making and Retirement
   Security in an Aging World   1
   Brett Hammond, Olivia S. Mitchell, and Stephen P. Utkus

Part I. The Aging Brain and Financial Decision Making

2. Aging and Competence in Decision Making   15
   Wändi Bruine de Bruin

3. Challenges for Financial Decision Making at Older Ages   33
   Keith Jacks Gamble

4. Retirement and Cognitive Functioning: International Evidence   46
   Raquel Fonseca, Arie Kapteyn, and Gema Zamarro

Part II. Tools for Retirement Planning and Decision Making

5. Choosing a Financial Advisor: When and How to Delegate?   85
   Hugh Hoikwang Kim, Raimond Maurer, and Olivia S. Mitchell

6. Advice in Defined Contribution Plans   96
   Gordon L. Clark, Maurizio Fiaschetti, and Peter Tufano

7. Seven Life Priorities in Retirement   115
   Surya Kolluri and Cynthia Hutchins

8. Worker Choices About Payouts in Public Pensions   130
   Robert L. Clark and Janet Raye Cowell

Part III. Solutions and Opportunities

9. Aging and Exploitation: How Should the Financial Service
   Industry Respond?   153
   Marguerite DeLiema and Martha Deevy

10. Understanding and Combating Investment Fraud   185
    Christine N. Kieffer and Gary R. Mottola

The Pension Research Council   213
Index   217

List of Figures

2.1	Age differences in judgment and decision tasks	16
2.2	Overview of skills relevant to understanding age differences in decision making competence	17
4.1	Cognitive functioning and gender differences	59
5.1	Life cycle profiles of key variables from a baseline model	87
6.1	Australian rates of retirement by age and sex	103
6.2	Proportion of topics raised on calls by category over time	106
6.3	Frequency of calls by category and age over time	108
7.1	Percentage identifying the most frightening disabling prospect in later life	118
7.2	Reasons for moving in retirement	119
7.3	Percentage of older respondents providing financial support to family members in the last five years	121
7.4	Financial support provided by people age 50+ to family members in the last five years, by investable assets	123
7.5	Percentage of working retirees who agree to each statement on working in retirement	125
7.6	Percentage by age of respondents who give money/goods to charities, non-profits, or other causes	125
8.1	Annuity options in state-managed retirement plans: number of plans with each option	132
9.1	Increase in SAR filings containing the phrase 'elder financial exploitation' following FinCEN Advisory FIN-2011-A003 (August 2010–August 2011)	166
9.2	Increase in SARs filings containing the phrase 'elder financial exploitation' from 2012 to 2015 by type of financial service institution	167
9.3	Regulatory oversight of select financial service providers	172
10.1	Number of different fraudulent investments that survey respondents were targeted to participate in	195
10.2	Number of times identified influence tactics appeared in analysis of fraud pitch transcripts	198

List of Tables

2.1   Applying decision rules: an experimental presentation   18
2.2   Resistance to sunk costs: an experimental presentation   19
2.3   Credit card repayment decision: an experimental presentation   20
2.4   Numeracy: an experimental presentation   21
4.1   Dataset, samples, dependent and independent variables in
    the reviewed papers   50
4.2   Instrument and different instrumental approaches: results   54
4.3   Effects of retirement on cognition for all countries   58
4.4   Effect of retirement on cognition for all countries by gender   60
4.5   Effect of retirement on cognition for all countries by skill
    education   62
4.6   Effect of retirement on cognition for all countries by
    physically demanding job   63
4A.1 Descriptive statistics   67
4A.2 Early and full retirement ages across the OECD nations   69
4A.3 First-stage results, pooled data   70
4A.4 First-stage results by skill group, pooled data   71
4A.5 First-stage results by physically demanding jobs groups,
    pooled data   72
4A.6 First-stage results by blue-collar jobs and white-collar jobs,
    pooled data   73
4A.7 Effect of retirement on cognition by survey   74
4A.8 Effect of retirement on cognition, pooled data by occupation   76
5.1   Impact of introducing a delegation option at alternative ages:
    investor gains in well-being   89
5.2   Welfare consequences of financial advice provision for
    alternative minimum fees   90
5.3   Impact of introducing plain-vanilla portfolios in lieu of
    investor inertia: how the change in investor well-being
    compares to benchmark, for alternative management fees
    and equity glide paths   91
5A.1 Summary of calibrated parameters for the baseline model   93
6.1   Relationship between call volume by topics and
    macroeconomic factors   104
8.1   Percentage of state retirees selecting annuity options   135
8.2   Impact of deferred annuity on annual payouts and pension
    present values (PV)   138

8A.1   Percentage of state plan retirees selecting annuity options   142
8A.2   Annuity payout options offered by state retirement plans   143
 9.1   Mandatory reporting laws for financial service institutions
        and employees by state (2015)   169
10.1   Sample characteristics for data analysis   191
10.2   Factors associated with investment fraud victimization   193
10.3   Factors associated with investment fraud targeting   196

Notes on Contributors

Wändi Bruine de Bruin holds a University Leadership Chair in Behavioural Decision Making at the Leeds University Business School, where she co-directs the Centre for Decision Research. She is also affiliated with Carnegie Mellon University's Department of Engineering and Public Policy, the University of California Dornsife Centre for Economic and Social Research, and the RAND Corporation. Her research focuses on individual differences in decision making competence across the lifespan, as well as consumer decisions about topics such as household finances, health, energy, and climate change. Her work with the Federal Reserve Bank of New York contributed to the design of a new Survey of Consumer Expectations. She holds a PhD in Behavioral Decision Making and Psychology from Carnegie Mellon University, an MSc in Cognitive Psychology, and a BSc in Psychology from the Free University Amsterdam.

Gordon L. Clark is Professor and Director of the Smith School of Enterprise and Environment at Oxford University, holds a Professorial Fellowship at St Edmund Hall, is the Sir Louis Matheson Distinguishing Visiting Professor at Monash University, and is a Visiting Professor at Stanford University. His research focuses on the governance and management of beneficial organizations and the behavior of participants in pension and retirement income funds. He holds a DSc and an MA in Economic Geography from the University of Oxford, as well as a PhD in Economics and an MA in Economic Geography from McMaster University. He also holds a BEcon and an MA in Economics from Monash University.

Robert L. Clark is Stephen Zelnak Professor of Economics and Professor of Management, Innovation and Entrepreneurship in the Poole College of Management, North Carolina State University. He is also Research Associate at the National Bureau of Economic Research and a member of the Pension Research Council Advisory Board. He has conducted research examining retirement decisions, the choice between defined benefit and defined contribution plans, the impact of pension conversions to defined contribution and cash balance plans, the role of information and communications on 401(k) contributions, and government regulation of pensions. He received a PhD and an MA in Economics from Duke University, as well as a BA in Economics from Millsaps College. He also holds an AA in Mathematics from Hinds Junior College.

Janet Raye Cowell is North Carolina's popularly-elected Treasurer and is the first woman to hold the office. She oversees pension investments for North Carolina's teachers, firefighters, and public employees. As Treasurer, she manages the 32nd largest public pension in the world and the second most solid in the nation. Under her executive leadership, North Carolina is one of only ten states in the country to earn an AAA bond rating by all three rating agencies. She was twice named one of the top 25 public pension executives in the world by Sovereign Wealth Fund Institute. She holds a BA and an MBA from the University of Pennsylvania.

Martha Deevy is a Senior Research Scholar and Director of the Financial Security Division at the Stanford Center on Longevity, where she focuses on defining new solutions that help insure long-term financial security in retirement; solutions that help individuals work longer, save more and avoid financial pitfalls. She joined the Stanford Center on Longevity after senior management positions at Apple, Charles Schwab, and Intuit. She has also served on the boards of directors of a number of publicly traded and non-profit organizations. Martha received an MBA in Finance and Management Information Systems from the University of Minnesota and a BA in Economics from the University of Illinois.

Marguerite (Marti) DeLiema is a postdoctoral researcher at the Stanford Center on Longevity in the Financial Security Division. Her work focuses on identifying the socio-demographic, cognitive, and contextual factors related to elder financial exploitation using qualitative and quantitative research methods. Along with collaborators at Stanford and federal regulatory agencies, she is developing a categorization scheme for financial fraud that will inform a national victimization survey. Her prior research focused on elder abuse and neglect in community settings, and the tactics scam artists use to deceive older victims. She received her PhD in Gerontology from the University of Southern California and a BS in biological psychology from UCLA.

Maurizio Fiaschetti is Lecturer in Banking and Finance at the School of Oriental and African Studies and Visiting Research Associate at the Smith School of Enterprise and the Environment, Oxford University. His research focuses on decision making and strategic interactions in the financial sector, applied econometrics, and financial economics. He holds a PhD and an MSc in International Economics; an MSc in Economics, Management, and Corporate Governance; a Diploma in Finance and Private Banking; and a BSc (Hons) in Economics of Financial Markets and Institutions, all from the University of Rome—Tor Vergata.

Raquel Fonseca is an Associate Professor at Université du Québec à Montréal, an affiliated adjunct Economist at RAND Corporation, and a fellow at the Center for Interuniversity Research and Analysis of Organizations. Her research focuses on the welfare effects of social security reforms as well as on the interaction between health, savings, and retirement patterns over the life cycle. Previously she worked as an economist at the RAND Corporation and as a Professor at the Pardee RAND Graduate School of Public Policy. She received her MA in economics from Université Catholique de Louvain, and her PhD in Economics from UCL and attended the European Doctoral Program from CORE-UCL, Belgium.

Keith Jacks Gamble is an Assistant Professor of Finance at DePaul University. Previously he was a Lecturer of Economics and Whitebox Post-Doctoral Fellow at the Yale School of Management. His research interests include financial decision making, investor behavior, and behavioral finance. His PhD in Economics is from the University of California, Berkeley and his BA in Economics from Harvard.

Brett Hammond is Research Leader at the American Funds for Capital Group. Previously he directed applied index and modeling research teams at MSCI, and he served as Chief Investment Strategist at TIAA-CREF. He was also a member of the senior management team at the National Academies (the National Research Council) and Adjunct Professor at the Wharton School. He also served as Board member for the Q Group. His expertise includes target-date funds, inflation-linked bonds, and individual financial advice. His BSc in economics and political science is from the University of California at Santa Cruz and PhD from the Massachusetts Institute of Technology.

Cynthia Hutchins is the Director of Financial Gerontology for Bank of America Merrill Lynch, where she works to educate financial advisors on gerontological issues such as aging, retirement, and legacy planning. She has also worked to help pre-retirees and retirees prepare for retirement across seven life priorities including work, leisure, health, finance, family, giving, and home. Her degree in Business and Finance is from Towson State University and her Masters in Gerontology from the University of Southern California.

Arie Kapteyn is a Professor of Economics and the Executive Director of the Dornsife College of Letters, Arts and Sciences Center for Economic and Social Research at the University of Southern California. Previously he was a Senior Economist and Director of the Labor & Population division of the RAND Corporation. He is a pioneer in the development of new methods of data collection, using the Internet and mobile devices. His current research focuses on aging and economic decision making. His MA in econometrics is from Erasmus University Rotterdam, his MA in agricultural economics from Wageningen University, and his PhD from Leiden University, all in the Netherlands.

Christine N. Kieffer is Senior Director of the FINRA Investor Education Foundation where she manages national, state, and grassroots partnerships, and she also develops tools and programs for law enforcement, victim advocates, and consumers to advance investor protection and fraud prevention initiatives. Her research focuses on investor attitudes and behaviors, primarily related to financial fraud, and she oversees financial readiness programs for military families and other underserved audiences, and participates in implementation of the National Financial Capability Study. Her BSc is from Vanderbilt University with double majors in Economics and Mathematics.

Hugh Hoikwang Kim is an Assistant Professor of Finance in the Department of Finance at the University of South Carolina. His research focuses on understanding investor behavior in a range of market settings. He previously taught at the SKK University in Korea. He received MSc and PhD degrees in Applied Economics from the Wharton School, University of Pennsylvania and a BA in Economics from Seoul National University.

Surya Kolluri manages Policy and Market Planning for the Merrill Lynch BAC-ML Global Wealth and Retirement Solutions Business, where he oversees the incubation and commercialization of social impact and environmental programs. He also manages external relationships with regard to research and policy development in the areas of aging and longevity. Previously he worked at Bain & Company. He serves on the boards of Rebuilding Together Boston, the CEO Initiative for Alzheimer's, and the Global Coalition on Aging. His MBA is from the Wharton School at the University of Pennsylvania and his MSc from Drexel University, Philadelphia.

Raimond Maurer is the Chair of Investment, Portfolio Management, and Pension Finance at the Finance Department of Goethe University Frankfurt. His research focuses on asset management, lifetime portfolio choice, real estate, and pension finance. He also serves on the Advisory Board of the Pension Research Council, and on the boards of the Union Real Estate Investment group, the Society of Actuaries, the Association of Certified International Investment Analysts, and the Faculty Senate of Goethe University. Previously he was Visiting Professor and Metzler Exchange Professor at the Wharton School. He earned his Habilitation, PhD, and Diploma in business administration from Mannheim University, and he received an honorary doctorate from the State University of Finance and Economics of St. Petersburg.

Olivia S. Mitchell is the International Foundation of Employee Benefit Plans Professor, as well as Professor of Insurance/Risk Management and Business Economics/Policy; Executive Director of the Pension Research Council; and Director of the Boettner Center for Pensions and Retirement Research, all at the Wharton School of the University of Pennsylvania. Concurrently she serves as a Research Associate at the NBER; Independent Director on the Wells Fargo Advantage Fund Trusts Board; Co-Investigator for the Health and Retirement Study at the University of Michigan; Member of the Executive Board for the Michigan Retirement Research Center; and Senior Scholar at the Centre for Research on the Economics of Aging at Singapore Management University. She received MA and PhD degrees in Economics from the University of Wisconsin-Madison, and a BA in Economics from Harvard University.

Gary R. Mottola is Research Director of the FINRA Investor Education Foundation and a social psychologist with expertise in the financial services industry. His research projects seek to better understand financial capability in America, protect investors from financial fraud, and improve financial disclosure statements. He is also an Adjunct Professor of Statistics in Villanova University's Economics Department. He received his BA from the University at Albany, his MA from Brooklyn College, and his PhD from the University of Delaware.

Peter Tufano is the Peter Moores Dean and Professor of Finance at the University of Oxford's Said Business School. He is also a Research Associate at the NBER, where he co-founded the Household Finance Working Group, and a Research Fellow of the CEPR. His research focuses on household finance issues, especially savings decisions of low-to-moderate income households, and he has also worked on tax-time savings and removing legal barriers to prize-linked savings. Previously he was taught at Harvard Business School. He received his BA in economics, MBA, and PhD in Business Economics from Harvard University.

Stephen P. Utkus is Principal and Director of the Vanguard Center for Retirement Research, where he is also a member of Vanguard's institutional retirement and investment business senior leadership team in the US. He also serves on the company's Strategic Asset Allocation Committee, and on the Advisory Board of Wharton's Pension Research Council. Concurrently he serves as Visiting Scholar at the Wharton School of the University of Pennsylvania, and on the Board of Trustees of the Employee Benefit Research Institute. He earned his MBA in Finance from the University of Pennsylvania and his BSc in Computer Science from MIT.

Gema Zamarro is an Associate Professor and holds the 21st Century Endowed Chair in Teacher Quality at the Department of Education Reform at the University of Arkansas. She also directs Charassein: The Character Assessment Initiative, a research group for the study of measures and development of character skills; and she is adjunct Senior Economist at the USC Dornsife Center for Economic and Social Research and adjunct

Economist at the RAND Corporation. Previously she worked as an economist at the RAND Corporation and Professor of Econometrics at the Pardee RAND Graduate School of Public Policy; she also taught econometrics at Tilburg University in the Netherlands. Her research explores the causal effect of retirement on health, the gender gap, and financial literacy, and the relationship between financial literacy and food security. Her PhD in Economics is from CEMFI and UNED, her MSc in Economics and Finance from CEMFI, and her BA in Economics from Universidad Carlos III de Madrid.

Chapter 1

Introduction: Financial Decision Making and Retirement Security in an Aging World

Brett Hammond, Olivia S. Mitchell, and Stephen P. Utkus

The World Health Organization reports that by 2050, two billion people will be age 60 and older, up from 605 million in 2000—and the proportion age 60 and older will jump from 11 percent to 22 percent (WHO 2014). These older generations are healthier, better educated, and wealthier than their predecessors in most countries. Nevertheless, while people are living longer, one point of vulnerability remains cognition and cognitive ability, particularly at advanced ages. In fact, it has been estimated that today half of all adults in their 80s either have dementia or some milder form of cognitive impairment without dementia (Bernard 2015). Meanwhile, as we grow older, we remain responsible for managing our own wealth, health, and insurance arrangements, sometimes successfully, and other times to our detriment. The goal of this volume is to review emerging research on the changing capacity of aging households to manage their own finances, to assess the implications for financial decision making and behavior later in life, and to draw out options for addressing key concerns.

With the rise of individual responsibility for lifetime financial security, a wide range of institutions—regulators and public agencies, employers, financial institutions, and advisors—is developing ways to educate, guide, and advise savers as they navigate key decisions about their financial futures. In the course of creating informative new programs and exhorting individuals to take notice, these efforts have often relied on individuals' ability and willingness to listen and take appropriate action, often with regard to unfamiliar decisions for which the consequences are seemingly uncertain and in many cases not immediate. Yet evidence from the accumulation phase of retirement illustrates the limits of education and advice programs to change behavior. Younger savers tend to be subject to inertia, and many make seemingly poor choices without more explicit guidance. The response has been the growth of automatic savings and investment programs, whether mandatory or automatic-enrollment based, designed to simplify or streamline complex financial choices.

To date, however, much less attention has been paid to the questions pertaining to retirees—and those approaching retirement—and their capacity to make effective financial decisions. This is the case despite the fact that older persons confront additional and perhaps more daunting challenges than their pre-retirement counterparts. As they approach and enter retirement, households must aggregate a lifetime of savings and benefit programs, both public and private, while developing a practical overview of their resources. They must also navigate a number of new risks, particularly longevity risk, as well as the costs of health care and long-term care. Meanwhile, government pensions, workplace retirement programs, and financial advisors are only recently coming to grips with these complex issues and the help that older individuals will need.

It is also becoming clear that regulators and financial service providers will need to account for the changing cognitive capacity of older individuals. Older decision makers benefit from accumulated experience and better emotional regulation, as compared to younger individuals. Yet some people do struggle with making complex financial choices due to a general decline in cognitive skill. Yet others are subject to severe impairment, due to the rise of dementia at older ages. So even if the content of financial advice is good and the delivery compelling, some older persons will find it difficult to arrive at appropriate decisions and stick to them. Additionally, although there is some question whether older individuals are more prone to act on poor advice or accept fraudulent offers, it is often true that older individuals hold more wealth and hence are potentially at greater risk.

In this introductory chapter, we provide an overview of the problem and tie together the findings and implications raised in the subsequent chapters authored by experts in this field. We conclude that a key policy issue is how all entities involved in serving older households—regulators, employers, pension providers, financial institutions, and advisors—will cope under these circumstances. This is critical to the protection of retiree financial security in an aging world.

Financial Decision Making at Older Ages

A growing body of evidence on household financial literacy has shown that many individuals of all ages lack certain critical financial skills, and that older individuals may be particularly deficient (Lusardi and Mitchell 2014; Lusardi et al. 2013). There is no single reason for this falloff in performance, but it may have to do with the nature of the decisions themselves, the skills of the individuals making them, and the tools and assistance available to help.

No matter how one might try to simplify, it will always be the case that decisions involving major purchases (such as a car or home), education, job and career, and health care are some of the most complex and multifaceted that any households confront. Assuring lifetime financial security can be on par with, or in some cases more complex than, decisions about education, work, and health. In the case of retirement security, this involves deciding how much to save (versus spend on other financial demands), where to invest among a variety of choices, how often to monitor and adjust investments, when and how much to spend from an accumulated nest egg, and how to make the money last as long as one lives. These decisions must be made repeatedly, over long horizons, and amid significant risk and uncertainty about future income, investment returns, spending needs, and life expectancy.

Only some of these risks in the retirement phase are readily mitigated. Government-run pensions like US Social Security do pay inflation-adjusted, lifetime benefits for eligible retired workers and their spouses. But in the US and other countries, these programs can provide only partial income replacement, and many face solvency challenges in view of population aging. Additionally, benefit-claiming decisions can be complex. For instance, several recent authors have provided analyses explaining how people should think about Social Security retirement benefit options (e.g., Shoven and Slavov 2014; Kotlikoff et al. 2015; Maurer et al. forthcoming). Defined benefit retirement plans also traditionally provided retirement income based on years of work and pre-retirement income, but few younger workers will have access to these plans in the future, outside the public sector. Moreover, some pension plans face an uncertain future due to poor funding, while even in well-funded plans, workers face a loss of future pension accruals in the event of a job change or job termination, especially later in life. Further, in the US and other countries, defined contribution plans are increasingly the norm, and these rarely provide retirees with guaranteed income streams.

In sum, older persons now face increased responsibility for later life risk management and decision making responsibilities. They will need to navigate these choices on their own, or seek help from government agencies, workplace retirement programs, and financial advisors, in order to make better choices. In the US defined contribution retirement system, for example, government policymakers and employers have started enhancing decision making assistance in a number of ways. Regulators are introducing new policies to encourage lifetime income programs and to govern the quality of advice for rollovers from workplace programs to personal pension accounts. Meanwhile, plan sponsors and providers are creating new programs of information about retirement options and risks, and introducing systems of advice for managing investment portfolios, claiming Social Security benefits, or drawing down retirement savings.

Even with these elements, however, the retirement system remains complex and can generate dysfunctional decision making. One reason is the variety of behavioral beliefs and preferences associated with decisions that make it hard for people to achieve long-term financial security. For instance, over-optimism, over-confidence, extrapolation bias, and 'gambler's fallacy' all affect people's perceived (versus 'actual') probability of an event such as achieving an investment return or adequate retirement income (e.g., Shefrin 2010).[1] In addition, behavioral preferences such as prospect theory, along with regret and self-control issues, can affect not just the perceived probability of an event, but also the 'utility' a person receives from that event.[2] In other words, people tend to overweight the *probability* of extreme (small-probability) events *and* to over/underweight the *value* of some events versus others (Kahneman and Tversky 1979). In particular, future orientation ('impatience') can vary significantly among people, affecting the value they place on forgoing consumption now to fund future spending (Burks et al. 2009; Chabris et al. 2008; Schreiber and Weber 2016). Other perception errors, such as how personal financial choices are framed (Tversky and Kahneman 1981) and accounted for (Thaler 1999), can exacerbate these effects.

To date, empirical studies of behavioral biases in decision making have mainly focused on younger people and the choices they confront. While older people encounter many of the same budgeting and investing challenges as their younger colleagues, they can also face additional difficulties along several dimensions. Younger people have more time to 'get it right': that is, due to having a longer remaining work life, they have more potential for forgoing current consumption in order to fund future spending. By contrast, for retirees the scope of new action is smaller, especially given that their human capital (the present value of their future work earnings) is declining rapidly. In short, young people have human capital to draw on and more time to make midcourse corrections (e.g., increase their savings rates, reallocate investments, etc.). Older individuals have fewer degrees of freedom, and are delimited by previous irreversible decisions they have made on wealth, health, education, work, and other factors.

Older persons also confront a series of consequential, often irreversible decisions that will affect the remainder of their lives. Examples include when to claim Social Security and pension benefits, how much to invest in health and health insurance, how to draw down savings, whether and how much to invest in guaranteed income products, whether to sell one's home and move, and how to navigate the transition to old-age care. And the most difficult element of the decision is that they must do this with uncertain knowledge of their health prospects and longevity. Many of these factors are typically not within younger persons' calculus.

Additional Considerations in the Older Population

Three other issues are especially important for older people: capabilities, context, and tools. The first has to do with older persons' capabilities to manage complex financial decisions. We know that younger people are subject to behavioral challenges when it comes to financial decision making. What is of interest in this volume is to understand whether older people face similar or different challenges. For example, it is well known that older people are better at regulating their emotional state than younger individuals. Yet they also tend to suffer progressive cognitive declines that make it more difficult to process new information with age (Hartshorne and Germine 2015), even for those without severe maladies such as Alzheimer's, dementia, and Parkinson's disease. At the same time, recent research shows that few elderly experience a commensurate decline in confidence in their own financial abilities (Gamble et al. 2015; Finke et al. 2016).

Beyond information-processing, the character of decision making can also change. For example, many individuals have personal discount rates that are above market discount rates, suggesting impulsivity. In the cross-section, older people have personal discount rates higher than younger people and these rise significantly after age 70 (Huffman et al. 2016). Impatience at these ages may be associated with lower net wealth, poorer health, and less adequate end-of-life planning. Other relevant changes in capabilities among older people include increased anxiety, reduced mobility, vision and hearing loss, depression, and effects of prescription regimens, all of which can affect behavior, even among those with otherwise 'normal' cognitive functioning (Lachs and Han 2015).

Such cognitive changes may be at least partially offset by experiential judgment based on accumulated knowledge of financial matters (Li et al. 2016). This is evident in research showing that financial 'mistakes' follow a U-shaped pattern, with middle-age people performing better than those younger or older (Agarwal et al. 2009).

It is worth noting, of course, that people do not age mentally and physically at the same rate. Differences among older people can exceed the differences between older and younger people (Huffman et al. 2016). Consequently, while efforts to assist older people might start by identifying those with more reduced financial abilities, little attention has been given to systematic approaches for doing so (an exception is Moye et al. 2013).

A second set of factors that can affect financial decision making at older ages is contextual and social. Not only do the elderly face numerous and complex challenges, but older people often have more money than younger people and experience more social isolation. This is a troubling combination since it can make them prone to receive as well as accept advances from people offering 'assistance' on financial matters (Lachs and Han 2015).

A consequence is that older people can be both more exposed to and less able to spot ruses or scams.

The third set of factors affecting financial decisions at older ages has to do with the tools, content, and default options available to older people as they age. Customized advice, sophisticated tools, and planning options are available to those with significant wealth, but for the less affluent, the mismatch between financial planning, decision needs, and the resources to support them may be more meaningful. For example, many forms of automated or 'robo' advice, versions of which are proliferating, have focused on pre-retirement investing outside of retirement plans. Automated income services for defined contribution plans are a relatively new addition to the landscape. Moreover, though some investment service providers have spent large sums on tools and programs for retirement planning, take-up rates have been higher for younger individuals than for older ones (Cornehlsen and Schwarz 2015).

More generally, older people are urged to seek financial advice; reduce swings in the value of accumulated wealth; draw a modest proportion of that wealth each year for spending needs; and reduce spending if wealth is inadequate or falls. They might also be offered long-term care insurance, annuities for guaranteed income, or reverse home mortgages, but use of these risk mitigation products is quite low. Improving outcomes with respect to these choices is a challenging task for research and policy discussions around older people's financial management, taking into account decision complexity, declining capabilities, changes in context, and resource limits.

Recognizing special concerns associated with financial security for older people, both academic and public discussion has begun to examine the underlying issues and options for addressing them. A wide range of options for financial planning and decisions for older people include increased financial literacy education (Lusardi et al. 2015) that continues through life (Joint Academy Initiative on Aging 2010); nudges to encourage positive action, as well as a focus on decision choice architecture (Thaler and Sunstein 2008); required financial drivers' licenses; required use of advance directives; changes in fiduciary responsibilities and compliance (CFPB 2016); investment safe harbors (Agarwal et al. 2009; Antolin et al. 2008); and increased *ex ante* regulatory oversight for financial products and advice.

Nevertheless, if the financial decision making and management challenges facing older people are complex and uncertain, the advice and tools available to them have gaps, and the ability of some older people to process information and make decisions is a challenge, what are we to make of all of this?

In what follows, we provide an overview of research from three lines of inquiry pertinent to our topic: the aging brain and financial decision making; the use of advice and other options for setting and achieving financial goals; and the policy landscape for improving financial outcomes for older people. Our effort is to assess the special characteristics and needs of older people in the financial context, and to review new policy and program developments for the elderly as they navigate the financial aspects of retirement. The chapters that follow take the discussion further, focusing on age and decision making; financial goals, advice, and options; and the policy landscape.

The Aging Brain and Financial Decision Making

Accurately assessing decision making competence among older people is important for at least two reasons. First, in the large, it can lay the groundwork for understanding the older population's needs, and for building policies and programs that reflect any special needs. Second, at the micro level, accurate assessments of capabilities can help us adjust policies and programs and actions to variations among individuals.

Taken together, the chapters by Wändi Bruine de Bruin, Keith Jacks Gamble, and Raquel Fonseca, Arie Kapteyn, and Gema Zamarro (this volume) look at advances in measuring decision making competence for older people as well as sorting through the range of available types of interventions available. Overall, they find that cognitive performance is nonlinear, varying considerably across individuals of the same age, and can be difficult to track. One explanation is that performance is informed by both 'fluid intelligence' (roughly, the ability to solve abstract problems), which peaks about age 20, as well as 'crystallized intelligence' (wisdom and experience), which continues to grow and then level off at about age 65. Cognitive performance as a whole tends to peak in about the mid-50s, an ideal time to make specific retirement plans.

Fortunately, it is possible to assess practical abilities using hypothetical or proxy task tests. Research using such tests documents declining cognitive performance with older age and shows that older people are more likely to misapply financial decision rules and not apply expected value calculations. While older people may make more financial mistakes, they can be less stubborn than younger people in sticking with bad decisions. They also respond better to positive motivators and reinforcement and tend to be more optimistic.

Using these findings, research points to interventions that may be more likely to work and others to avoid. Financial education and experience that starts early in life and continues throughout may bear fruit in improved abilities and outcomes later in life. Among older people, continued cognitive training may help offset a portion of inevitable decline, but it can also be taxing so best limited to shorter periods and smaller choice sets. In addition, personalizing these exercises is likely to be more fruitful than abstract maxims, and training can fruitfully focus on imagining how to set and achieve financial goals and seek advice. Nudges, rather than requirements, may therefore be productive.

Financial Goals, Advice, and Product Options

The volume next turns to work showing that it is especially important to understand older persons' priorities as well as the tools and products available to them for setting goals and achieving them. According to Kolluri and Hutchins (this volume), today's older Americans are thinking more broadly than their predecessors about retirement in light of seven priorities: health, home, family, work, giving, finances, and leisure. With a multifaceted set of priorities, it is no surprise that the options available to many people are proliferating as well as concerns about how to assess, choose between, and manage them.

Of special interest is the question of when financial advice will be most valuable and for whom. Kim, Maurer, and Mitchell's chapter (this volume) points out that most people exhibit considerable inertia in managing their financial assets, partly because it costs them time and money to manage their own portfolios. The authors simulate the wealth effects of self-management, investing in a target-date fund, or using a financial advisor, and they show substantial benefits of turning to competent financial advice early in one's working years and continuing the relationship. While well-timed advice may be valuable, few people seek it. In their chapter, Clark, Fiaschetti, and Tufano study advice-seekers in the Australian pension system and they conclude that only a small proportion of people contact their providers. Of those, younger people tend to ask about administrative matters. Older persons are somewhat more likely to ask about retirement matters, but usually well after the age when there is much they can do to affect wealth outcomes. Clark and Cowell's chapter (this volume) considers the options available for public defined benefit (DB) participants at retirement. They conclude that public DB plans, rather than eliminating annuities with their automated and guaranteed features, would do better to consider including deferred annuities and options that would integrate with Social Security.

Policy Responses for the Older Population

Part III of this volume takes into account the findings on cognitive challenges and the complex nature of financial planning for retirement by focusing on options for improving protections for older people. A conclusion that can be drawn from this work is that people in general, and older ones in particular, may benefit from advice—but they may not be inclined to seek it or to be particularly good at managing complicated investments and income streams themselves. Consequently, packaged and/or automatic defaults for investments and income in retirement may deserve a hard look.

Chapters by DeLiema and Deevy, and Kieffer and Mottola (this volume), examine the dynamics of fraud, exploitation, and poor decision making as well as programs and policies used in the private sector and by public agencies to protect older people. Fraud alone directed at older Americans is estimated to cost around $50 billion per year, with additional ancillary effects. And as we have noted, older people are more likely to have wealth than younger people, and to experience financial 'events' (retirement, house sale, health expenditure), so they are more likely to be targeted for exploitation and fraud. With technology, new cohorts of older Americans are less likely to have a personal relationship with a financial institution, something that is not reducing but certainly is altering the challenges in this area.

Firms, trade organizations, financial regulators, and several US agencies have stepped up fraud and exploitation awareness as well as other programs, including hotlines, call centers, and marketing campaigns. In addition, the new US Department of Labor regulation expanding the fiduciary duty of brokers to individual investors has altered the relationship between financial institutions and older people with qualified investments. Moreover, several other state and federal regulations are being considered to shield firms who work to protect clients from financial exploitation.

Beyond current research on older people, behavior, and programs, each of the chapters in this section suggest areas where additional knowledge is needed. For instance, much of the current research is cross-sectional rather than longitudinal, making it difficult to tease out the distinct effects of aging, the passage of time, and one's birth cohort on the results. Following people through time will be likely to improve understanding of changes in decision making and the effects of interventions on behavior. In addition, within-group variations in competence and capabilities may be significant, and researchers still face the challenge of understanding just how policies and programs to assist older people need to be adjusted for these variations.

Conclusions

The growth in aged households continues around the world, both in absolute numbers and as a proportion of the total population. The collected wisdom of contributors to this volume has helped us understand what programs and interventions would likely improve financial outcomes for older people. Nevertheless they also point out that much remains to be done. Additional features and programs such as automatic defaults and safe harbors, new advice programs, a 'financial driver's license,' wider use of advanced directives, and targeted training programs, may prove effective given further testing. It is also important to explore the costs and benefits of additional customization in light of older persons' different capabilities and attitudes. These may be knotty problems to solve, but their importance and the potential consequences of inaction or misdirected action are likely to be substantial.

Notes

1. These types of beliefs can shift the probability density function of an expected event by a change in mean, variance, or shape (linear to nonlinear). An exception is 'ambiguity aversion' which does not necessarily shift the perceived probability function.
2. Preference biases can shift the shape of the utility function as well as the event probability function. The classic shift is, in prospect theory, a kinked utility function where people are more fearful of bad outcomes than they are pleased about positive outcomes.

References

Agarwal, S., J. C. Driscoll, X. Gabaix, and D. Laibson (2009). 'The Age of Reason: Financial Decisions over the Life Cycle and Implications for Regulation'. In D. H. Romer and J. Wolfers (eds.), *Brookings Papers on Economic Activity.* Washington, DC: Brookings Institution, pp. 51–111.

Antolin, P., C. Pugh, and F. Stewart (2008). 'Forms of Benefit Payment at Retirement'. OECD Working Papers on Insurance and Private Pensions No. 26. Paris: OECD Publishing.

Bernard, T. S. (2015). 'As Cognition Slips, Financial Skills Are Often the First to Go'. *New York Times*, April 24.

Burks, S. V., J. P. Carpenter, L. Goette, and A. Rustichini (2009). 'Cognitive Skills Affect Economic Preferences, Strategic Behavior, and Job Attachment'. *Proceedings of the National Academy of Sciences* 106(19): 7745–50.

Chabris, C. F., D. Laibson, C. L. Morris, J. P. Schuldt, and D. Taubinsky (2008). 'Individual Laboratory-Measured Discount Rates Predict Field Behavior'. *Journal of Risk and Uncertainty* 37(2–3): 237–69.

Consumer Financial Protection Bureau (CFPB) (2016). 'Recommendations and Report for Financial Institutions on Preventing and Responding to Elder Financial Exploitation'. Washington, DC: CFPB. <http://files.consumerfinance.gov/f/201603_cfpb_recommendations-and-report-for-financial-institutions-on-preventing-and-responding-to-elder-financial-exploitation.pdf>.

Cornehlsen, J. and T. Schwarz (2015). 'Rise of Robo-Advisors Brings Challenges, Opportunities for Consumers'. New York: ABC News. <http://abcnews.go.com/Business/rise-robo-advisors-brings-challenges-opportunities-consumers/story?id=33692949>.

Finke, M. S., J. S. Howe, and S. J. Huston (2016). 'Old Age and the Decline in Financial Literacy'. *Management Science* 60(8): 1861–83.

Gamble, K. J., P. A. Boyle, L. Yu, and D. A. Bennett (2015). 'Aging and Financial Decision Making'. *Management Science* 61(11): 2603–10.

Hartshorne, J. K. and L. T. Germine (2015). 'When Does Cognitive Functioning Peak? The Asynchronous Rise and Fall of Different Cognitive Abilities across the Life Span'. *Psychological Science* 26(4): 433–43.

Huffman, D., R. Maurer, and O. S. Mitchell (2016). 'Time Discounting and Economic Decision Making Among the Elderly'. NBER Working Paper No. 22438. Cambridge, MA: National Bureau of Economic Research.

Joint Academy Initiative on Aging (2010). 'More Years, More Life'. Hamburg: Academy of Sciences Leopoldina and German Academy of Science and Engineering. <https://www.leopoldina.org/uploads/tx_leopublication/2009_NatEmpf_Altern_in_D-EN.pdf>.

Kahneman, D. and A. Tversky (1979). 'Prospect Theory: An Analysis of Decision Making under Risk'. *Econometrica* 47(2): 263–91.

Kotlikoff, L. J., P. Moeller, and P. Solman (2015). *Get What's Yours: The Secrets to Maxing Out Your Social Security.* New York: Simon & Schuster.

Lachs, M. S. and S. D. Han (2015). 'Age-Associated Financial Vulnerability: An Emerging Public Health Issue'. *Annals of Internal Medicine* 163(11): 877–8.

Li, Y., J. Gao, A. Zeynep Enkavi, L. Zaval, E. U. Weber, and E. J. Johnson (2016). 'Sound Credit Scores and Financial Decisions Despite Cognitive Aging'. *Proceedings of the National Academy of Sciences* 21(1): 65–9.

Lusardi, A. and O. S. Mitchell (2014). 'The Economic Importance of Financial Literacy: Theory and Evidence'. *Journal of Economic Literature* 52(1): 5–44.

Lusardi, A., O. S. Mitchell, and V. Curto (2013). 'Financial Literacy and Financial Sophistication among Older Americans'. *Journal of Pension Economics and Finance* 13(4): 347–66.

Lusardi, A., A. S. Samek, A. Kapteyn, L. Glinert, A. Hung, and A. Heinberg (2015). 'Visual Tools and Narratives: New Ways to Improve Financial Literacy'. NBER Working Paper 20229. Cambridge, MA: National Bureau of Economic Research.

Maurer, R., O. S. Mitchell, R. Rogalla, and T. Schimetschek (Forthcoming). 'Will They Take the Money and Work? An Empirical Analysis of People's Willingness to Delay Claiming Social Security Benefits for a Lump Sum'. *Journal of Risk and Insurance.*

Moye, J., D. C. Marson, and B. Edelstein (2013). 'Assessment of Capacity in an Aging Society'. *American Psychologist* 68(3): 158–71.

Schreiber, P. and M. Weber (2016). 'The Influence of Time Preferences on Retirement Timing'. University of Mannheim Discussion Paper. Mannheim: University of Mannheim.

Shefrin, H. (2010). 'Behavioralizing Finance'. *Foundations and Trends in Finance* 4(10): 1–184.

Shoven, J. B. and S. N. Slavov. (2014). 'Does it Pay to Delay Social Security?' *Journal of Pension Economics and Finance* 13(2): 121–44.

Thaler, R. H. (1999). 'Mental Accounting Matters'. *Journal of Behavioral Decision Making* 12(3): 183–206.

Thaler, R. H. and C. R. Sunstein (2008). *Nudge: Improving Decisions about Health, Wealth, and Happiness.* New Haven, CT: Yale University Press.

Tversky, A. and D. Kahneman (1981). 'The Framing of Decisions and the Psychology of Choice Science'. *Science* 211(4481): 453–8.

World Health Organization (WHO) (2014). *Facts about Aging.* Geneva: WHO. <http://www.who.int/ageing/about/facts/en/>.

Part I

The Aging Brain and Financial Decision Making

Chapter 2

Aging and Competence in Decision Making

Wändi Bruine de Bruin

People are living longer, implying that they must make important life decisions affecting their finances, health, and overall well-being. As policy-makers in different countries give people increasing responsibility for their health care and retirement, older adults are confronted with more compli-cated decisions about these topics. As a result, older persons' decision making competence is of rising importance.

Unfortunately, relatively little is known about aging and decision making competence. Researchers on judgment and decision making traditionally recruited college students who participated in studies for course credit. Because these studies aimed to identify when people experience problems in making their decisions, the assumption was that findings would gener-alize to the general population. For instance, if college students experi-enced difficulties in making decisions then it was thought that individuals with lower educational attainment or other disadvantages would also face those problems.

Recent improvements in sampling and recruitment have spurred new research with age-diverse participants. Initial studies of adult age differences in decision making competence have reported mixed findings. For example, Figure 2.1 shows age differences in six tasks that have been studied in the judgment and decision making literature.

The six tasks comprise the Adult Decision Making Competence battery which measures individual differences in decision making competence. The tasks are reliable, in terms of correlations across items and test–retest performance (Bruine de Bruin et al. 2007). The tasks also have demon-strated validity, in terms of correlations with self-reported decision outcomes such as bankruptcy and type 2 diabetes (Bruine de Bruin et al. 2007; Parker et al. 2015). As Figure 2.1 suggests, some decision tasks reveal age-related declines in performance, while others indicate no change or even improve-ments with age.

This chapter suggests that age differences in decision making compe-tence depend on the demands of the tasks presented. It highlights four main skills relevant to decision making competence and shows differential

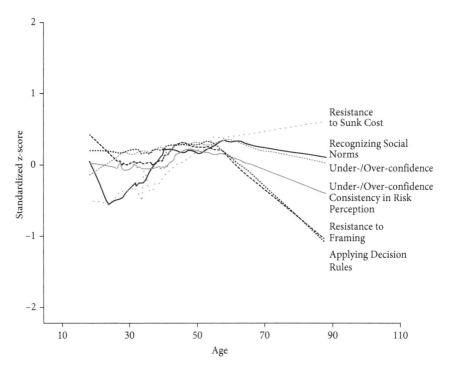

Figure 2.1. Age differences in judgment and decision tasks

Note: Age-spectrum trends in performance on judgment and decision tasks, LOESS fit-line estimation. Resistance to Sunk Costs refers to willingness to discontinue failing commitments with irrecoverable losses; Recognizing Social Norms refers to accurately judging the percentage of peers approving socially undesirable behaviors (e.g., stealing) as compared to actual peer endorsements; Under-/Over-confidence refers to expressing confidence in true/false statements of general knowledge that correspond to knowledge scores across statements; Consistency in Risk Perception refers to judging probabilities for specific events (e.g., surviving or dying in terrorist attack) while adhering to the rules of probability theory; Resistance to Framing refers to making consistent choices between options independent of whether they are negatively or positively described; Applying Decision Rules refers to accurately applying decision rules to choose between presented products (e.g., choose option with highest average product rating across features).

Source: Strough et al. (2015).

changes with age (Figure 2.2). These skills are cognitive deliberation, experience, emotion regulation, and focused motivation. Having discussed these skills, we examine potential interventions for improving decision making competence across the lifespan, and a final section focuses on limitations and next steps. This review expands on previous ones with various colleagues (Bruine de Bruin et al. 2014a, 2016a; Peters and Bruine de Bruin 2012; Strough et al. 2015).

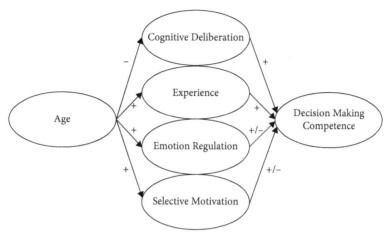

Figure 2.2. Overview of skills relevant to understanding age differences in decision making competence

Note: + reflects positive relationship; − reflects negative relationship; +/− reflects mixed findings.

Source: Author's elaboration.

Cognitive Deliberation and Decision Making

Making decisions involves deliberation about the features of the available options and selecting the one that is most likely to produce desired outcomes. Such deliberation requires fluid cognitive abilities such as processing speed, working memory, executive functions, and numeracy. For example, Table 2.1 shows one item from a decision task referred to as 'Applying Decision Rules'. The presented item asks participants to apply the 'averaging rule' so as to choose between five DVD players. Specifically, the goal is to choose the DVD player that has the highest rating across the dimensions of picture quality, programming options, and reliability of brand. Computing, remembering, and comparing the average ratings for all DVD players create considerable cognitive demands. People with better fluid cognitive abilities tend to perform better on such cognitively demanding decision tasks (Bruine de Bruin et al. 2007).

Age Differences in Cognitive Deliberation

Age-related declines in fluid cognitive abilities are well documented and emerge after people reach their 20s (Salthouse 2004). Indeed, older adults' relatively lower fluid cognitive abilities explain why they tend to perform less well than younger adults on cognitively demanding decision tasks (Bruine

TABLE 2.1 Applying decision rules: an experimental presentation

		Features of the DUD				
		Picture quality	Sound quality	Programming options	Reliability of brand	Price
DVD	A	3	1	5	2	$369
	B	1	2	1	2	$369
	C	5	4	3	1	$369
	D	4	2	3	3	$369
	E	4	4	2	4	$369

Lisa wants the DVD player with the highest average rating across features. Which *one* of the presented DVD players would Lisa prefer?

Source: Bruine de Bruin et al. (2007).

de Bruin et al. 2012, 2015; Del Missier et al. 2013; Finucane et al. 2005; Peters and Bruine de Bruin 2012). Older adults make more mistakes when they are asked to apply decision rules to choose between products (Bruine de Bruin et al. 2012; Del Missier et al. 2013). As the number of options increases and decisions become more difficult, older adults are especially less likely to select the optimal option (Besedeš et al. 2012).

Nevertheless, it should be noted that cognitive deliberation may not be relevant to all decisions; that is, performance on some decision tasks relies relatively little on decision makers' cognitive deliberation. It has even been argued that too much cognitive deliberation may be harmful when making some decisions (Wilson and Schooler 1991). For example, students who are explicitly asked to deliberate while choosing dorm room posters are less satisfied with their choices two weeks later, compared to controls receiving no such instructions (Wilson et al. 1993). While such decisions have not been studied with age-diverse samples, it is possible that they require other skills such as those learned with age-related life experience.

Experience and Decision Making

After years of working in a specific domain, people may develop experience-based knowledge or crystallized cognitive ability. Experience-based knowledge may be gained through deliberate practice and training, and, if so, people with experience-based knowledge may make better decisions.

For example, consider the decision task outlined in Table 2.2. It involves 'sunk costs' or a prior investment that is no longer recoverable. Because sunk costs are lost independent of how the decision maker proceeds, the

TABLE 2.2 Resistance to sunk costs: an experimental presentation

You are buying a gold ring on layaway for someone special. It costs $200 and you have already paid $100 on it, so you owe another $100. One day, you see in the paper that a new jewelry store is selling the same ring for only $90 as a special sale, and you can pay for it using layaway. The new store is across the street from the old one. If you decide to get the ring from the new store, you will not be able to get your money back from the old store, but you would save $10 overall.

Would you be more likely to continue paying at the old store or buy from the new store?

1	2	3	4	5	6
Most likely to continue paying at the old store				Most likely to buy from the new store	

Source: Bruine de Bruin et al. (2007).

economic sunk cost rule posits that these should not be taken into account. The normatively correct decision is to discontinue prior investments if they no longer represent the best available course of action. Correlational evidence suggests that students who have taken economics classes are more likely to accurately follow economic rules when making decisions (Larrick et al. 1993). By contrast, individuals without training in economics often find it difficult to decide to discontinue because they feel bad about having 'wasted' their prior investments (Arkes and Blumer 1985).

Experienced decision makers may not have to think very hard about their decisions, because they already know what to do. When deciding if a hypothetical couple should open an Individual Retirement Account (IRA), financial experts need less time to make a decision, compared to non-experts (Hershey et al. 1990). When making decisions, therefore, experience-based knowledge is thought to decrease reliance on fluid cognitive ability.

Age Differences in Experience

Experience-based knowledge or crystallized cognitive ability accumulates with age. For instance, adults have more vocabulary knowledge than younger adults (Salthouse 2004), presumably because they have had more experience using their language. It has similarly been argued that older adults' accumulated life experience may explain why they perform better when making judgments and decisions in social contexts, as opposed to abstract contexts (Hess 2005).

Older adults' experience-based financial knowledge can also help them to make better decisions about personal finances. For example, age-related improvements in crystallized cognitive abilities explain why older adults perform better in hypothetical financial decisions (Li et al. 2013, 2015).

Table 2.3 presents one example of a hypothetical decision in which participants are asked to pay off credit cards. Older adults are more likely than younger ones to pay off high-interest credit cards, as financial experts would

TABLE 2.3 Credit card repayment decision: an experimental presentation

Imagine you have two credit card accounts: a MasterCard account with a $100 balance and a 10 percent annual percentage rate (APR) and a Visa account with a $1,000 balance and a 15 percent APR. You just received a $1,000 government stimulus rebate and you decided to use the entire rebate to repay debt.

Please indicate how much you would repay:

___ on the MasterCard account

___ on the Visa account

Source: Li et al. (2013).

recommend. Older adults also perform better in actual credit card decisions (Agarwal et al. 2009) and have better credit scores (Li et al. 2015). Across these studies, older adults' experience-based knowledge counteracted age-related declines in fluid cognitive abilities. As a result, it has been argued that peak performance for financial decisions occurs when people are in their 50s (Agarwal et al. 2009).

Older adults are also better able than younger adults to discontinue commitments that are no longer beneficial, even in the face of larger sunk costs (Bruine de Bruin et al. 2014b; Strough et al. 2008). As noted earlier, Table 2.2 shows an example of a decision that involved sunk cost. In part, older adults' ability to make better decisions about sunk costs is due to age-related changes in semantic memory, which may store knowledge about economic rules (Del Missier et al. 2013). In other words, older adults may have learned about the sunk cost rule from their prior experience.

Of course, what older adults take away from their experiences may not always be beneficial to their decision making. Learning from experience requires repeated judgments with immediate feedback, something that occurs in weather forecasting, but is rare in most other domains (for a review, see Keren 1991). Repeated exposure to misinformation can actually increase misguided confidence in its accuracy, especially among older adults (Skurnik et al. 2005). Thus the usefulness of previous experiences depends on the accuracy of the acquired knowledge.

Emotion Regulation and Decision Making

People's judgments and decisions are also influenced by their emotions, and these often emerge before cognitive deliberation has started (Zajonc 1980). Some emotions are integral to the decision at hand, such as when the perceived risks associated with a new technology are higher if people feel more negative about it (for a review, see Slovic et al. 2002). Incidental emotions can also influence decisions despite being unrelated to the task at hand, such as when investors' positive emotional responses to the weather lead to more optimistic trading decisions (Hirshleifer and Shumway 2003). Although emotions have originally been seen as distracting people from cognitive deliberation and threatening the quality of their decisions, it has been posited that emotions can also improve the quality of decisions, by focusing attention and improving information processing (for a review, see Peters 2006).

Age Differences in Emotion Regulation

As people age, they develop a deeper understanding of emotional states (Labouvie-Vief et al. 1989). Older adults also have better emotion regulation in the face of adversity, focusing on the positive, while younger adults keep dwelling on the negative (Sütterlin et al. 2012; Torges et al. 2008). Perhaps as a result, emotional well-being tends to increase with age through the 60s, and older people generally report experiencing more positive than negative emotions (Carstensen et al. 2000; Charles et al. 2001). This finding may be explained by older adults' increased realization that they should make the best of the limited time they have left to live (Carstensen 1995).

Older adults' focus on the positive may also affect their decision making. Older adults ruminate less about past losses, which contributes to their better ability to apply the sunk cost rule (Bruine de Bruin et al. 2014b). They also spend more time looking at positive-emotional information than at negative-emotional information (Mather and Carstensen 2005). Perhaps as a result, older adults are just as likely as younger adults to remember positive information, but they remember negative information less well (Mikels et al. 2005). Older adults' better memory for positive information also increases their feelings of post-choice satisfaction (Kim et al. 2008). Of course, a selective focus on positive information may not be beneficial for every decision task.

Selective Motivation and Decision Making

Performance on difficult tasks is thought to be partly influenced by motivation. For example, Table 2.4 shows an example of an item from a test of

TABLE 2.4 Numeracy: an experimental presentation

In the BIG BUCKS LOTTERY, the chances of winning a £10 prize are 1 percent. What is your best guess about how many people would win a £10 prize if 1,000 people each buy a single ticket from BIG BUCKS? _____

Source: Schwartz et al. (1997).

'numeracy' or number ability, which experimental participants often find frustrating. Individuals who self-report higher motivation to think hard about complex problems do tend to perform better on such numeracy items (Bruine de Bruin et al. 2015).

Motivation is also relevant to decision making. Some decision makers may be motivated to 'maximize' and systematically compare all available options to identify the very best. Others may prefer 'satisficing' by selecting an option that is 'good enough' on key attributes. Although maximizing should typically lead to better decision outcomes, satisficing may lead to choices that are just as good, especially when time is limited or options are too difficult to distinguish (Payne et al. 1993). Moreover, maximizers' tendency to engage in counterfactual comparisons with alternatives they could have selected instead puts them at risk for regret, dissatisfaction, and clinical depression (Bruine de Bruin et al. 2016a; Iyengar et al. 2006; Schwartz et al. 2002). Hence, motivated decision makers do not necessarily experience better outcomes.

Age Differences in Selective Motivation

As people get older, they become more selective about how to spend their cognitive effort. For instance, they may no longer be as motivated to work hard on cognitively demanding tasks such as the numeracy item presented in Table 2.4. Older adults also perform less well on numeracy items, which has been statistically explained by their lower self-reported motivation to think hard about complex problems (Bruine de Bruin et al. 2015). They also report being less motivated to use effortful choice strategies such as maximizing (Bruine de Bruin et al. 2016b). In studies of actual choice behavior, older adults reduce their cognitive effort by considering less information and comparing fewer options (Chen and Sun 2003; Johnson 1990).

Older adults do invest more effort in decisions when they perceive the context as personally relevant (Hess et al. 2013) or when they are explicitly asked to try harder (Kim et al. 2005). Cognitive effort can be measured via relative increases in systolic blood pressure as compared to a state of rest (Hess and Ennis 2012). The correlation between self-reported motivation and this objective measure of cognitive effort is higher in older adults than in younger adults (Ennis et al. 2013). This finding suggests that older adults think relatively harder when they are more motivated.

Suggestions for Interventions

If people experience difficulties in making their decisions, interventions may be needed. Ideally, such interventions should build on decision makers' strengths while addressing their weaknesses. It might therefore be useful to take into account age-related changes in cognitive deliberation, experience-based knowledge, emotions, and motivation. Here, I offer a few suggestions for potential useful interventions which of course would still need to be tested for their effectiveness.

Interventions Targeting Cognitive Deliberation

According to the 'use it or lose it' hypothesis, deliberate exercise is needed to prevent the decline of cognitive deliberative skills (for a review, see Park et al. 2007). Cognitive skills training for older adults tends to focus on teaching strategies for counteracting age-related declines in memory, reasoning, and speed of processing (Ball et al. 2002). Due to brain plasticity persisting even in older age, stroke patients of all ages can show dramatic improvement after extensive training and practice (Hallett 2001).

Yet it is also possible that older adults are averse to deliberate cognitive training. Perhaps due to concerns about age-related cognitive declines, older adults often do not feel confident about their performance on cognitively demanding decision tasks (Bruine de Bruin et al. 2012). They also feel less motivated to think hard about complex problems (Bruine de Bruin et al. 2015). Interventions that encourage older adults to use their cognitive deliberative skills in enjoyable leisure activities have been proposed as potentially being more effective (Park et al. 2007).

In addition to training, external aids may be developed to support cognitive deliberation. The provision of organizational charts and medication organizers has been useful for helping older adults with medication adherence (Park et al. 1992). Visual icon arrays make risk information easier to understand for adults of all ages (Galesic et al. 2009). Icon arrays show icons for individuals with negative outcomes as part of a larger set of icons representing the overall at-risk population. Yet research shows that visual displays should focus on a simple take-home message and avoid complex animations (Zikmund-Fisher et al. 2012). Indeed, 'less is more' when presenting information to aid decisions, especially for individuals who have limited ability to deliberate about numbers (Peters et al. 2007).

Another strategy for addressing problems with cognitive deliberation is to reduce the complexity of decisions, for example through reducing the number of options. Adults of all ages benefit from smaller choice sets, which have been associated with better decisions and higher post-choice satisfaction (Besedeš et al. 2012; Botti and Iyengar 2006; Hanoch et al. 2011; Tanius et al. 2009). A 'tournament' strategy for introducing subsets of options may also improve older adults' decisions (Besedeš et al. 2015). Thus various intervention strategies may be useful for confronting low motivation among decision makers.

Interventions Targeting Experience-Based Knowledge

A review of the literature suggests that deliberate practice from an early age is needed to build expertise (Ericsson et al. 2007). For instance, decision making competence has successfully been included in the high-school curriculum. High-school students who are randomly assigned to history classes that discuss the potential decision errors of historical figures improve their decision making competence, as compared to controls taking standard history classes (Jacobson et al. 2012). Youth development accounts, practical financial interventions, and financial education bring promise for promoting better financial decisions (Lusardi and Mitchell 2014; Shobe and Sturm 2007). Teaching simple rules may be more effective than teaching complex rules which can create cognitive overload and choice avoidance. Indeed, people who apply simple rules to retirement planning tend to save as much as those who engage in complex planning, and more than those who have no plan (Binswanger and Carman 2012). Teaching financial rules of thumb is even more effective than standard accounting training for teaching small entrepreneurs (Drexler et al. 2014).

It has been proposed that older adults may benefit from interventions that help them to rely on their experience-based knowledge (Park et al. 2007). Correlational evidence does indeed suggest that, by relying on knowledge acquired with age, older adults may be able to counteract age-related declines in their ability to deliberate (Agarwal et al. 2009; Li et al. 2013, 2015).

Interventions Targeting Emotions

There is also evidence that individuals who receive short-term boosts to their mood use more efficient decision strategies (Isen and Means 1983). Positive mood inductions may increase the flexibility and effort with which decision makers complete interesting tasks (for a review, see Carpenter et al. 2013). Although negative mood inductions increase efforts devoted to less interesting tasks (Forgas 2013), invoking rumination about negative mood may actually undermine people's ability to execute academic tasks (Lyubomirsky et al. 2003). Age differences in responses to mood inductions have not yet been studied, but positive-mood inductions have been found to lead older adults age 63–85 to increase cognitive deliberation and performance on choices between risky prospects (Carpenter et al. 2013).

Longer-term emotion-focused interventions may also be possible. Cognitive behavioral therapy, physical exercise, and social activities may distract depressed individuals from disruptive rumination, and thus they could improve their performance on cognitive tasks (for a review, see Nolen-Hoeksema et al. 2008). Although few studies have examined effects of emotion-focused interventions on decision making in non-clinical populations, there is initial evidence with student samples that the encouragement of positive action-focused coping skills can help to overcome dysfunctional decision avoidance (Van Putten et al. 2009). As noted earlier, correlational evidence has suggested that better emotion regulation in terms of coping with irrecoverable losses helps decision makers overcome the sunk-cost bias (Bruine de Bruin et al. 2014b). Thus, promoting positive mood among older adults may potentially improve their decision making competence.

Interventions Targeting Selective Motivation

Interventions may be ineffective if people lack the motivation to put in the effort. Providing financial incentives for better performance improves intelligence test performance among young people (Duckworth et al. 2011). Yet a meta-analysis conducted across multiple studies has suggested that financial incentives can also undermine intrinsic motivation to engage with the task (Deci et al. 1999). To date, there have been no studies of age differences in responsiveness to financial incentives, in the context of improving decisions.

To motivate older adults to put effort into their decisions, information should be made more personally relevant. As noted, older adults will work harder on tasks they perceive as personally relevant (Hess et al. 2013). Adding the personal narratives of others may compel people of all ages to engage with presented information, though it may distract from decision-relevant statistical facts (for reviews, see Bekker et al. 2013; Winterbottom et al. 2008). Especially low-numerate individuals pay more attention to concrete narratives than to abstract statistics (Dieckmann et al. 2009).

The instructions provided as part of a decision aid can also influence people's motivation to complete specific goals. Younger adults are more likely to implement an action if they have been asked to imagine when and how they would perform it (Gollwitzer and Sheeran 2006). Older adults also benefit from such goal-focused instructions, for example for remembering glucose monitoring (Liu and Park 2004). Older adults may further be motivated by instructions that encourage emotional rather than cognitive processing when making their decisions, perhaps because it motivates them to focus on their strengths rather than their weaknesses (Mikels et al. 2010). Older adults may also perform better when they are instructed to give reasons for their choices (Kim et al. 2005).

If motivation is especially low, this could provide a rationale to delegate decisions to others. Although older adults value their autonomy as decision makers (Delaney et al. 2015), they are more likely than younger adults to seek financial advisors (Milner and Rosenstreich 2013). Advice may also be sought from friends and family members (Loibl and Hira 2006), which may especially be favored by older adults as they increasingly value select close relationships (Fung et al. 1999). Additionally, people of all ages who feel unmotivated to make a specific decision may welcome 'nudge' interventions that promote a recommended default (Johnson and Goldstein 2003). A well-known example of default setting pertains to auto-enrolment retirement savings plans (Thaler and Bernartzi 2004). Yet not everyone will welcome the liberal paternalism of 'nudge' interventions.

Limitations and Next Steps

A main limitation of emerging research on age differences in decision making competence is that studies to date have mainly been conducted on cross-sectional rather than on longitudinal samples. This leaves the possibility open that differences between age groups reflect generational effects and not aging (for example, see Schaie 1965). Indeed, it is possible that current generations will prefer more autonomy and choice than previous generations as they age. Fortunately, measures of decision making competence are increasingly being added to longitudinal studies and national lifespan samples (for example, see Del Missier et al. 2013). Such studies are also needed to better understand how age-related developments in fluid and crystallized cognitive abilities, motivation, and emotions interact to support the quality of people's decisions across the lifespan.

Another limitation is that decision making competence has mostly been measured with hypothetical decision tasks. While performance on hypothetical decision making tasks has slowly been linked with better real-world decision outcomes (Bruine de Bruin et al. 2007), it is important to expand measurement to include real-world decisions. Additionally, a better understanding is needed of the skills that support decision making competence in older age, as well as their interactions. Age-related cognitive declines are well documented, through a battery of validated measures of fluid cognitive ability, working memory, and executive functioning. By comparison, understanding and measurement are less developed for the skills that may potentially improve with age to benefit older adults' decisions. The measures currently used to assess decision-relevant experience, emotions, and motivation are mostly based on self-reports rather than actual performance (for a review, see Appelt et al. 2011). Because self-perceptions change with age, self-reported performance may show age differences that do not translate into actual performance (Bruine de Bruin et al. 2012).

A key next step is to develop and test interventions for improving decisions across the lifespan. High-priority foci would address age-related changes in cognitive deliberation, experience, emotions, and motivation. Interventions should focus on the needs of specific audiences, and they must also be tested for effectiveness before they are disseminated (for a review, see Bruine de Bruin and Bostrom 2013). Ultimately, research on age differences in decision making competence will help people of all ages make better decisions, thus producing better life outcomes and overall well-being.

References

Agarwal, S., J. C. Driscoll, X. Gabaix, and D. Laibson (2009). 'The Age of Reason: Financial Decisions over the Life-Cycle with Implications for Regulation'. *Brookings Papers on Economic Activity* 2(1): 51–117.

Appelt, K. C., M. F. Milch, M. J. Handgraaf, and E. U. Weber (2011). 'The Decision Making Individual Differences Inventory and Guidelines for the Study of Individual Differences in Judgment and Decision-Making Research'. *Judgment and Decision Making* 6(3): 252–62.

Arkes, H. R. and C. Blumer (1985). 'The Psychology of Sunk Cost'. *Organizational Behavior and Human Decision Processes* 35(1): 124–40.

Ball, K., D. B. Berch, K. F. Helmers, J. B. Jobe, M. D. Leveck, M. Marsiske, J. N. Morris, G. W. Rebok, D. M. Smith, S. L. Tennstedt, F. W. Unverzagt, and S. L. Willis (2002). 'Effects of Cognitive Training Interventions with Older Adults'. *Journal of the American Medical Association* 288(18): 2271–81.

Bekker, H. L., A. E. Winterbottom, P. Butow, A. J. Dillard, D. Feldman-Stewart, F. J. Fowler, M. Jibaja-Weiss, V. A. Shaffer, and R. J. Volk (2013). 'Do Personal Stories Make Patient Decision Aids More Effective?' *BMC Medical Informatics and Decision Making* 13(2): 1–9.

Besedeš, T., C. Deck, S. Sarangi, and M. Shor (2012). 'Age Effects and Heuristics in Decision Making'. *Review of Economics and Statistics* 94(2): 580–95.

Besedeš, T., C. Deck, S. Sarangi, and M. Shor (2015). 'Reducing Choice Overload Without Reducing Choices'. *Review of Economics and Statistics* 97(4): 793–802.

Binswanger, J. and K. G. Carman (2012). 'How Real People Make Long-Term Decisions: The Case of Retirement Preparation'. *Journal of Economic Behavior and Organization* 81(1): 39–60.

Botti, S. and S. S. Iyengar (2006). 'The Dark Side of Choice: When Choice Impairs Social Welfare'. *Journal of Public Policy & Marketing* 25(1): 24–38.

Bruine de Bruin, W. and A. Bostrom (2013). 'Assessing What to Address in Science Communication'. *Proceedings of the National Academy of Sciences* 110(3): 14062–8.

Bruine de Bruin, W., A. Y. Dombrovski, A. M. Parker, and K. Szanto (2016a). 'Late Life Depression, Suicidal Ideation, and Attempted Suicide: The Role of Individual Differences in Maximizing, Regret, and Negative Decision Outcomes'. *Journal of Behavioral Decision Making* 29(4): 363–71.

Bruine de Bruin, W., S. McNair, A. L. Taylor, B. Summers, and J. Strough (2015). 'Thinking about Numbers Is Not My Idea of Fun: Need for Cognition Mediates Age Differences in Numeracy Performance'. *Medical Decision Making* 35(1): 22–6.

Bruine de Bruin, W., A. M. Parker, and B. Fischhoff (2007). 'Individual Differences in Adult Decision-Making Competence'. *Journal of Personality and Social Psychology* 92(5): 938–56.

Bruine de Bruin, W., A. M. Parker, and B. Fischhoff (2012). 'Explaining Adult Age Differences in Decision-Making Competence'. *Journal of Behavioral Decision Making* 25(4): 352–60.

Bruine de Bruin, W., A. M. Parker, and B. Fischhoff (2014a). 'Individual Differences in Decision-Making Competence Across the Lifespan'. In E. A. Wilhelms and V. F. Reyna (eds.), *Neuroeconomics, Judgment, and Decision Making*. New York: Psychology Press, pp. 219–29.

Bruine de Bruin, W., A. M. Parker, and J. Strough (2014b). 'Getting Older Isn't All That Bad: Better Decisions and Coping when Facing Sunk Costs'. *Psychology and Aging* 29(3): 642–7.

Bruine de Bruin, W., A. M. Parker, and J. Strough (2016b). 'Choosing to Be Happy? Age Differences in "Maximizing" Decision Strategies and Experienced Emotional Well-Being'. *Psychology and Aging* 31(3): 295–300.

Carpenter, S. M., E. Peters, D. Västfjäll, and A. M. Isen (2013). 'Positive Feelings Facilitate Working Memory and Complex Decision Making Among Older Adults'. *Cognition and Emotion* 27(1): 184–92.

Carstensen L. L. (1995). 'Evidence for a Life-Span Theory of Socio-Emotional Selectivity Theory'. *Current Directions in Psychological Science* 4(5): 151–6.

Carstensen, L. L., M. Pasupathi, U. Mayr, and J. R. Nesselroade (2000). 'Emotional Experience in Everyday Life Across the Adult Life Span'. *Journal of Personality and Social Psychology* 79(4): 644–55.

Charles, S. T., C. A. Reynolds, and M. Gatz (2001). 'Age-Related Differences and Change in Positive and Negative Affect Over 23 Years'. *Journal of Personality and Social Psychology* 80(1): 136–51.

Chen, Y. and Y. Sun (2003). 'Age Differences in Financial Decision Making: Using Simple Heuristics'. *Educational Gerontology* 29(7): 627–35.

Deci, E. L., R. Koestner, and R. M. Ryan (1999). 'A Meta-Analytic Review of Experiments Examining the Effects of Extrinsic Rewards on Intrinsic Motivation'. *Psychological Bulletin* 125(6): 627–68.

Delaney, R., J. Strough, W. Bruine de Bruin, and A. Parker (2015). 'Variations in Decision-Making Profiles by Age and Gender: A Cluster-Analytic Approach'. *Personality and Individual Differences* 85(1): 19–24.

Del Missier, F., T. Mäntylä, P. Hansson, W. Bruine de Bruin, A. M. Parker, and L. G. Nilsson (2013). 'The Multifold Relationship Between Memory and Decision Making: An Individual Differences Study'. *Journal of Experimental Psychology: Learning, Memory, and Cognition* 39(5): 1344–64.

Dieckmann, N. F., P. Slovic, and E. Peters (2009). 'The Use of Narrative Evidence and Explicit Likelihood by Decision Makers Varying in Numeracy'. *Risk Analysis* 29(10): 1473–88.

Drexler, A., G. Fischer, and A. Schoar (2014). 'Keeping It Simple: Financial Literacy and Rules of Thumb'. *American Economic Journal: Applied Economics* 6(2): 1–32.

Duckworth, A. L., P. D. Quinn, D. R. Lynam, R. Loeber, and D. R. Stouthamer-Loeber (2011). 'Role of Test Motivation in Intelligence Testing'. *Proceedings of the National Academy of Sciences* 108(19): 7716–20.

Ennis, G. E., T. M. Hess, and B. T. Smith (2013). 'The Impact of Age and Motivation on Cognitive Effort: Implications for Cognitive Engagement in Older Adulthood'. *Psychology and Aging* 28(2): 495–504.

Ericsson, K. A., M. J. Prietula, and E. T. Cokely (2007). 'The Making of an Expert'. *Harvard Business Review* 85(7): 114–22.

Finucane, M. L., C. K. Mertz, P. Slovic, and E. S. Schmidt (2005). 'Task Complexity and Older Adults' Decision-Making Competence'. *Psychology and Aging* 20(1): 71–84.

Forgas, J. P. (2013). 'Don't Worry, Be Sad! On the Cognitive, Motivational, and Interpersonal Benefits of Negative Mood'. *Current Directions in Psychological Science* 22(3): 225–32.

Fung, H. H., L. L. Carstensen, and A. M. Lutz (1999). 'Influence of Time on Social Preferences: Implications for Life-Span Development'. *Psychology and Aging* 14(4): 595–604.

Galesic, M., R. Garcia-Retamero, and G. Gigerenzer (2009). 'Using Icon Arrays to Communicate Medical Risks: Overcoming Low Numeracy'. *Health Psychology* 28(2): 210–16.

Gollwitzer, P. M. and P. Sheeran (2006). 'Implementation Intentions and Goal Achievement: A Meta-Analysis of Effects and Processes'. *Advances in Experimental Social Psychology* 38(6): 69–119.

Hallett, M. (2001). 'Plasticity of the Human Motor Cortex and Recovery from Stroke'. *Brain Research Reviews* 36(2–3): 169–74.

Hanoch, Y., S. Wood, A. Barnes, P. J. Liu, and T. Rice (2011). 'Choosing the Right Medicare Prescription Drug Plan: The Effect of Age, Strategy Selection, and Choice Set Size'. *Health Psychology* 30(6): 719–27.

Hershey, D. A., D. A. Walsh, S. J. Read, and A. S. Chulef (1990). 'The Effects of Expertise on Financial Problem Solving: Evidence for Goal Directed Problem-Solving Scripts'. *Organizational Behavior and Human Decision Processes* 46(1): 77–101.

Hess, T. M. (2005). 'Memory and Aging in Context'. *Psychological Bulletin* 131(3): 383–406.

Hess, T. M. and G. E. Ennis (2012). 'Age Differences in the Effort and Costs Associated with Cognitive Activity'. *Journals of Gerontology, Series B: Psychological Sciences and Social Sciences* 67(4): 447–55.

Hess, T. M., T. L. Queen, and G. E. Ennis (2013). 'Age and Self-Relevance Effects on Information Search During Decision Making'. *Journals of Gerontology, Series B: Psychological Sciences and Social Sciences* 68(5): 703–11.

Hirshleifer, D. and T. Shumway (2003). 'Good Day Sunshine: Stock Returns and the Weather'. *Journal of Finance* 58(3): 1009–32.

Isen, A. M. and B. Means (1983). 'The Influence of Positive Affect on Decision-Making Strategy'. *Social Cognition* 2(1): 18–31.

Iyengar, S. S., R. E. Wells, and B. Schwartz (2006). 'Doing Better but Feeling Worse: Looking for the "Best" Job Undermines Satisfaction'. *Psychological Science* 17(2): 143–50.

Jacobson, D., A. Parker, C. Spetzler, W. Bruine de Bruin, K. Hollenbeck, D. Heckerman, and B. Fischhoff (2012). 'Improved Learning in US History and Decision Competence with Decision-Focused Curriculum'. *PLOS One* 7(9): 1–3.

Johnson, E. J. and D. Goldstein (2003). 'Do Defaults Save Lives?' *Science* 302(5649): 1338–9.

Johnson, M. M. S. (1990). 'Age Differences in Decision Making: A Process Methodology for Examining Strategic Information Processing'. *Journal of Gerontology* 45(2): 75–8.

Keren, G. (1991). 'Calibration and Probability Judgments: Conceptual and Methodological Issues'. *Acta Psychologica* 77(3): 217–73.

Kim, S., D. Goldstein, L. Hasher, and R. T. Zacks (2005). 'Framing Effects in Younger and Older Adults'. *Journals of Gerontology, Series B: Psychological Science and Social Science* 60(4): 215–18.

Kim, S., M. K. Healey, D. Goldstein, L. Hasher, and U. J. Wiprzycka (2008). 'Age Differences in Choice Satisfaction: A Positivity Effect in Decision Making'. *Psychology and Aging* 23(1): 33–8.

Labouvie-Vief, G., M. DeVoe, and D. Bulka, D. (1989). 'Speaking About Feelings: Conceptions of Emotion Across the Life Span'. *Psychology and Aging* 4(4): 425–37.

Larrick, R. P., R. E. Nisbett, and J. N. Morgan (1993). 'Who Uses the Cost–Benefit Rules of Choice? Implications for the Normative Status of Microeconomic Theory'. *Organizational Behavior and Human Decision Processes* 56(3): 331–47.

Li, Y., M. Baldassi, E. J. Johnson, and E. U. Weber (2013). 'Complementary Cognitive Abilities: Economic Decision Making and Aging'. *Psychology and Aging* 28(3): 595–613.

Li, Y., J. Gao, A. Z. Enkavi, L. Zaval, E. U. Weber, and E. J. Johnson (2015). 'Sound Credit Scores and Financial Decisions Despite Cognitive Aging'. *Proceedings of the National Academy of Sciences* 112(1): 65–9.

Liu, L. L. and D. C. Park (2004). 'Aging and Medial Adherence: The Use of Automatic Processes to Achieve Effortful Things'. *Psychology and Aging* 19(2): 318–25.

Loibl, C. and T. Hira (2006). 'A Workplace and Gender-Related Perspective on Financial Planning Information Sources and Knowledge Outcomes'. *Financial Services Review* 15(1): 21–42.

Lusardi, A. and O. S. Mitchell (2014). 'The Economic Importance of Financial Literacy: Theory and Evidence'. *Journal of Economic Literature* 52(1): 5–44.

Lyubomirsky, S., F. Kasri, and K. Zehm (2003). 'Dysphoric Rumination Impairs Concentration on Academic Tasks'. *Cognitive Therapy and Research* 27(3): 309–30.

Mather, M. and L. L. Carstensen (2005). 'Aging and Motivated Cognition: The Positivity Effect in Attention and Memory'. *Trends in Cognitive Sciences* 9(10): 496–502.

Mikels, J. A., G. R. Larkin, P. A. Reuter-Lorenz, and L. L. Carstensen (2005). 'Divergent Trajectories in the Aging Mind: Changes in Working Memory for Affective versus Visual Information with Age'. *Psychology and Aging* 20(4): 542–53.

Mikels, J. A., C. E. Löckenhoff, S. A. Maglio, L. A. Carstensen, M. K. Goldstein, and A. Garber (2010). 'Following Your Heart or Your Head: Focusing on Emotions versus Information Differentially Influences the Decisions of Younger and Older Adults'. *Journal of Experimental Psychology: Applied* 16(1): 87–95.

Milner, T. and D. Rosenstreich (2013). 'Insights into Mature Consumers of Financial Services'. *Journal of Consumer Marketing* 30(3): 248–57.

Nolen-Hoeksema, S., B. E. Wisco, and S. Lyubomirsky (2008). 'Rethinking Rumination'. *Perspectives on Psychological Science* 3(5): 400–24.

Park, D. C., A. H. Gutchess, M. L. Meade, and E. A. L. Stine-Morrow (2007). 'Improving Cognitive Function in Older Adults: Nontraditional Approaches'. *Journals of Gerontology, Series B: Psychological Sciences and Social Sciences* 62(1): 45–52.

Park, D. C., R. W. Morell, D. Frieske, and D. Kincaid (1992). 'Medication Adherence Behaviors in Older Adults: Effects of External Cognitive Supports'. *Psychology and Aging* 7(2): 252–6.

Parker, A. M., W. Bruine de Bruin, and B. Fischhoff (2015). 'Negative Decision Outcomes Are More Common Among People with Lower Decision-Making Competence: An Item-Level Analysis of the Decision Outcome Inventory (DOI)'. *Frontiers in Psychology* 363(1): 1–7.

Payne, J. W., J. R. Bettman, and E. J. Johnson (1993). *The Adaptive Decision Maker.* New York: Cambridge University Press.

Peters, E. (2006). 'The Functions of Affect in the Construction of Preferences'. In S. Lichtenstein and P. Slovic (eds.), *The Construction of Preference.* New York: Cambridge University Press, pp. 454–63.

Peters, E. and W. Bruine de Bruin (2012). 'Aging and Decision Skills'. In M. K. Dhami, A. Schlottmann, and M. Waldmann (eds.), *Judgment and Decision Making as a Skill: Learning, Development, and Evolution.* New York: Cambridge University Press, pp. 113–39.

Peters, E., N. Dieckmann, A. Dixon, J. H. Hibbard, and C. K. Mertz (2007). 'Less is More in Presenting Quality Information to Consumers'. *Medical Care Research and Review* 64(2): 169–90.

Salthouse, T. A. (2004). 'What and When of Cognitive Aging'. *Current Directions in Cognitive Science* 13(4): 140–4.

Schaie, K. W. (1965). 'A General Model for the Study of Developmental Problems'. *Psychological Bulletin* 64(2): 92–107.

Schwartz, B., A. Ward, J. Monterosso, S. Lyubomirsky, K. White, and D. R. Lehman (2002). 'Maximizing versus Satisficing: Happiness is a Matter of Choice'. *Journal of Personality and Social Psychology* 83(5): 1178–97.

Schwartz, L. M., S. Woloshin, W. C. Black, and H. G. Welch (1997). 'The Role of Numeracy in Understanding the Benefit of Screening Mammography'. *Annals of Internal Medicine* 127(11): 966–72.

Shobe, M. A. and S. L. Sturm (2007). 'Youth Individual Development Accounts: Retirement Planning Initiatives'. *Children and Schools* 29(3): 172–81.

Skurnik, I., C. Yoon, D. C. Park, and N. Schwarz (2005). 'How Warnings about False Claims Become Recommendations'. *Journal of Consumer Research* 31(4): 713–24.

Slovic, P., M. Finucane, E. Peters, and D. G. MacGregor (2002). 'Rational Actors or Rational Fools: Implications of the Affect Heuristic for Behavioral Economics'. *Journal of Socio-Economics* 31(4): 329–42.

Strough, J., C. M. Mehta, J. P. McFall, and K. L. Schuller (2008). 'Are Older Adults Less Subject to the Sunk-Cost Fallacy than Younger Adults?' *Psychological Science* 19(7): 650–2.

Strough, J., A. M. Parker, and W. Bruine de Bruin (2015). 'Understanding Life-Span Developmental Changes in Decision-Making Competence'. In T. Hess, J. Strough, and C. Löckenhoff (eds.), *Aging and Decision Making: Empirical and Applied Perspectives*. London: Elsevier Academic Press, pp. 235–57.

Sütterlin, S., M. C. S. Paap, S. Babic, A. Kübler, and C. Vögele (2012). 'Rumination and Age: Some Things Get Better'. *Journal of Aging Research* 2012: Article 267327.

Tanius, B. E., S. Wood, Y. Hanoch, and T. Rice (2009). 'Aging and Choice: Applications to Medicare Part D'. *Judgment and Decision Making* 4(1): 92–101.

Thaler, R. H. and S. Bernartzi (2004). 'Save More Tomorrow™: Using Behavioral Economics to Increase Employee Saving'. *Journal of Political Economy* 112(1): S164–S187.

Torges, T. M., A. J. Stewart, and S. Nolen-Hoeksema (2008). 'Regret Resolution, Aging, and Adapting to Loss'. *Psychology and Aging* 23(1): 169–80.

Van Putten, M., M. Zeelenberg, and E. Van Dijk (2009). 'Dealing with Missed Opportunities: Action vs. State Orientation Moderates Inaction Inertia'. *Journal of Experimental Social Psychology* 45(4): 808–15.

Wilson, T. D., D. J. Lisle, J. W. Schooler, S. D. Hodges, K. J. Klaaren, and S. J. LaFleur (1993). 'Introspection about Reasons Can Reduce Post-Choice Satisfaction'. *Personality and Social Psychology Bulletin* 19(3): 331–9.

Wilson, T. D. and J. W. Schooler (1991). 'Thinking Too Much: Introspection can Reduce the Quality of Preferences and Decisions'. *Journal of Personality and Social Psychology* 60(2): 181–92.

Winterbottom, A., H. L. Bekker, M. Conner, and A. Mooney (2008). 'Does Narrative Information Bias Individuals' Decision Making?' *Social Science and Medicine* 67(12): 2079–88.

Zajonc, R. B. (1980). 'Feeling and Thinking: Preferences Need No Inferences'. *American Psychologist* 35(2): 151–75.

Zikmund-Fisher, B. J., H. O. Witteman, M. A. Fuhrel-Forbis, N. L. Exe, V. C. Kahn, and M. Dickson (2012). 'Animated Graphics for Comparing Two Risks: A Cautionary Tale'. *Journal of Medical Internet Research* 14(4): 1–13.

Chapter 3

Challenges for Financial Decision Making at Older Ages

Keith Jacks Gamble

Recent research studies reveal that seniors exhibit worse financial decision making. For example, in an analysis of transaction records from a discount brokerage, Korniotis and Kumar (2011) showed that older investors' investment selections were less skillful. Similarly, Agarwal et al. (2009) found that the prevalence of suboptimal credit decisions increased past age 53, and Pottow (2012) revealed that bankruptcy filings among those age 65 and older constituted the fastest-growing demographic group. Each of these existing studies indirectly examined the effects of cognitive aging on financial ability by comparing across individuals of different ages. Such comparisons confound the effect of cognitive decline with other differences among people of different ages. For example, Malmendier and Nagel (2011) found the cohort effect of early-life economic conditions on risk-taking decisions made decades later. Direct measures of cognition collected repeatedly from the same individuals are needed to identify the effect of a decrease in cognition on financial capabilities.

This chapter describes research results from analyses of longitudinal data developed at the Rush University Alzheimer's Disease Center's Memory and Aging Project (MAP), a large cohort study of aging (Bennett et al. 2012). The fact that participants in the project are tested yearly provides the data needed to identify, within individuals, the impact of decreases in cognition on financial literacy, financial confidence, and financial decisions. Here I focus on analyses restricted to participants in the project without dementia, as determined by detailed clinical evaluations. These individuals may experience declines in cognitive ability considered part of normal aging and have at most what are considered to be mild cognitive impairments. Even these mild declines in cognitive performance reveal evidence of diminished financial capabilities.

In what follows, I first provide an overview of research results made possible by the Rush Memory and Aging Project. The following section provides more detailed descriptions of the data collected and the methods used. A final section concludes.

Overview of Research Findings

Overall my research shows that a decrease in cognition is a significant predictor of a decrease in financial literacy among seniors. Drops in cognition are associated with decreases in each of the components of financial literacy measured, both numeracy and financial knowledge. Moreover, analysis finds that a decrease in cognition predicts a drop in self-confidence in general, but importantly, it does not predict a decrease in confidence in managing one's own finances. Participants may not recognize or may be reluctant to admit to this decline in their financial capability. The detrimental effects of cognitive aging on the financial choices of older people can potentially be mitigated with help for financial decisions provided within or outside of the household. Our analysis finds that individuals who experience a decrease in cognition are more likely to stop managing their own finances and pass on this responsibility to a spouse, and they are more likely to get financial help from outside their household. Yet there are still many participants who experience cognitive decreases who do not get help with their financial decisions. Even among the participants experiencing statistically significant decreases in cognition, about half get no help with their financial decisions. While these participants are likely to benefit from trustworthy, knowledgeable advice, knowing whom to trust regarding financial matters can be problematic for seniors.

Trusting untrustworthy solicitors with financial matters is a growing problem, as illustrated by recent surveys. Anderson (2013) noted that fraud complaints have increased fivefold in the past decade in the United States according to the Federal Trade Commission; over a million complaints were filed in 2010. The FINRA Foundation conducted a fraud survey in 2012 using a representative sample of Americans age 40+, and the results showed that people age 65+ were targeted more often and were more likely to lose money when targeted, compared to respondents in their 40s (FINRA Investor Education Foundation 2013). The types of financial fraud revealed in that study included '419' frauds (Nigerian email fraud), lottery scams, penny stock scams, boiler room calls, pyramid schemes, and free lunch seminars that were actually sales pitches. In addition, the 2012 Senior Financial Exploitation Study found that 56 percent of Certified Financial Planner (CFP) professionals had an older client who had been financially exploited, with an average estimated loss of about $50,000 per victim (CFP Board of Standards 2012).

Little is known about why many seniors are susceptible to financial fraud and what factors contribute to this vulnerability. One reason is a lack of data that include the required information about fraud victimization along with personal characteristics of victims and those not victimized. The MAP provides a notable exception: it includes yearly self-reports of fraud victimization along with demographic characteristics and measures of cognition, financial literacy, and decision making. A little more than one in ten participants reported being recently victimized by financial fraud.

We use this rich dataset to test two hypotheses concerning the causes of fraud victimization and one concerning the consequences. We hypothesize that decreases in cognition predict an increased likelihood of being victimized by fraud. Results show that a one standard deviation decrease in cognitive slope is estimated to increase the odds of fraud victimization by one-third. This increase in the likelihood of fraud victimization could be due to scammers targeting those with larger decreases in cognition more often, and it could also be due to those people with greater decreases in cognition becoming more vulnerable to financial scams. While we cannot address the former explanation with our data, we can address the latter one. For this test we use a 'susceptibility to scam' score, which employs a set of six survey questions designed to capture actions and beliefs consistent with providing an opportunity for scammers. For example, participants are asked if they have difficulty ending a phone call and if they believe persons over the age of 65 are often targeted by con artists. We do find that a decrease in cognitive slope predicts a higher scam susceptibility score.

Our second fraud-related hypothesis is that over-confidence in one's financial knowledge is a significant predictor of the odds of becoming a victim of financial fraud. Over-confidence is known to be a significant factor in explaining the poor investment decision making of households. For example, Barber and Odean (2000) showed that households lost money by frequently trading stocks, and Barber and Odean (2001) explained this behavior by investor over-confidence. Goetzmann and Kumar (2008) found that investors who were over-confident diversified their investment portfolio less, thus taking on more risk than was necessary to achieve the same level of expected return. Our measure of over-confidence in the Rush data combines participants' answers to a set of standard financial literacy questions with their confidence in each answer. Over-confidence is defined as getting the literacy questions wrong while thinking that they are right. We find that over-confidence is a significant risk factor for becoming a victim of financial fraud. A one standard deviation increase in over-confidence increases the odds of falling victim to fraud by 26 percent. Financial knowledge, not just general knowledge, protects against fraud: years of education is not a significant predictor of the likelihood of being victimized by fraud.

Our third fraud-related hypothesis concerns the impact of financial fraud on victims' willingness to take on financial risk. Thaler and Johnson (1990) demonstrated that, after taking losses, many decision makers showed an increased willingness to take on risk in an effort to break even. We also find that financial fraud victims exhibit an increased willingness to take risk relative to those not victimized.

Data Description and Methods

We employ two measures of willingness to take financial risk. First, fraud victims report an increased assessment of their lifetime willingness to take on financial risk, relative to the decline in non-victims' assessment of their lifetime willingness. Second, fraud victims become increasingly willing to accept a gamble with an equally likely chance of doubling their annual incomes as cutting them by one-tenth. Taken at face value, this gamble is highly attractive due to the large potential gain and limited loss. Yet, such promises of large gains with ostensibly limited downside risk are character- istic of sales pitches by those peddling fraudulent investments. Thus we interpret this result that fraud victims become more attracted to such a gamble as particularly concerning for the risk of repeated fraud victimiza- tion. Both results regarding the increased willingness of fraud victims to take on risk are robust to comparisons of fraud victims to otherwise similar non- victims (see Gamble et al. 2014, 2015).

Data Collection and Construction of Measures

The dataset we use is collected by the Rush MAP. Since beginning in 1997, the survey has enrolled older participants from the Chicago metropolitan area. Participants undergo yearly interviews and detailed clinical evaluation, includ- ing medical history, as well as neurological and neuropsychological examin- ations. The MAP data include demographic information for all participants including sex and education. Participants are mostly female (only one-quarter are male), well-educated older Americans; the average age is a little over 80 years old. The participants average three years of higher education. In 2010, a financial decision making assessment was added to MAP.

In our analysis we exclude data from participants diagnosed with demen- tia at the time of their financial decision making assessment. Dementia was diagnosed in accordance with the standards set by the National Institute of Neurologic and Communicative Disorders and Stroke and the Alzheimer's Disease and Related Disorders Association (Bennett et al. 2005). At the time of these analyses, over 500 participants without dementia at the initial decision making assessment had completed at least two decision making assessments, needed to observe changes in decision making measures over time. To analyze the risk factors for financial fraud victimization, we also examined over 700 participants without dementia who had completed at least one decision making assessment.

Yearly cognitive test scores for each participant are measured with nine- teen tests divided into five cognitive domains: episodic memory, perceptual speed, semantic memory, visuo-spatial ability, and working memory. Episodic memory captures the memory of specific events, whereas semantic memory captures the knowledge of concepts. Working memory captures the ability to store and process transitory information. Perceptual speed involves the ability to process information quickly and make mental comparisons. Visuo-spatial ability involves understanding visual representations and the spatial relationships among objects. Raw scores of each of the nineteen cognitive tests are converted to z-scores using the baseline mean and standard deviation of the entire MAP cohort on that test. These nineteen z-scores are averaged to compute the global cognitive function score, and the z-scores within each domain are averaged to compute each cognitive domain score. About two-thirds of participants experienced a decrease in their global cognition z-score from their first decision making assessment to their most recent.

The decision making questionnaire also included eighteen standard financial literacy questions, half to test numeracy and half to test financial knowledge. We measure financial literacy, numeracy, and knowledge by adding the number of correct answers in each category of questions. Participants were made aware that they could respond that they did not know the answer, and they could refuse to answer any question. These responses are treated as incorrect answers in this analysis. The first two financial knowledge questions concerned the Federal Deposit Insurance Corporation and its role in the financial system. Then participants were asked what investments mutual funds hold and how bond prices react to interest rates. The final five financial knowledge questions were in true–false format. The first two asked about the benefits of diversification and whether an older person should hold riskier investments compared to a younger person. The final three asked about paying off credit card debt, the value of frequent stock trading, and the average historical return of stocks relative to bonds.

Each financial knowledge question also included a follow-up question asking for the participant's confidence in her answer to the previous knowledge question. Confidence may be assessed on a four-point scale from 'extremely confident' to 'not at all confident'. We measure financial knowledge by counting the number of correct answers given to the nine financial literacy questions. Confidence in financial knowledge is measured by summing the scores to each confidence question (extremely confident scored as a three, fairly confident as a two, a little confident as a one, and not at all confident as a zero). Overall participants indicate they were fairly confident for each question. We measure over-confidence in financial knowledge by summing the scores to the confidence questions for which the participant got the associated financial knowledge question wrong. Thus, over-confidence is measured as a combination of poor financial knowledge plus a lack of awareness of poor knowledge. A participant who scored low on financial knowledge would not be counted over-confident if she reported being not at all confident in her answers.

Two additional measures of confidence are also included. We assess self-confidence using a single question that asked participants to report their general level of confidence on a ten-point scale, with 1 indicating that they were not at all confident, and 10 indicating that they were completely confident. Participants displayed a high level of self-confidence, as their self-confidence score averaged just over 7 on the ten-point scale. We assess financial confidence with a single question that asked participants to report to what extent they agreed with the statement: 'I am good at managing day-to-day financial matters such as keeping up with checking accounts, credit cards, payments, and budgeting.' Responses are reported on a seven-point scale from 'strongly agree' indicating the highest level of financial confidence (6), to 'strongly disagree' indicating the lowest level of financial confidence (0). Participant confidence in managing their own finances was similarly high on average (about five out of six), meaning that most participants agreed with the statement that they were good at managing their day-to-day financial matters.

Participants were also asked who was primarily responsible for making their financial decisions. They were asked explicitly if they, their spouse, their child, or someone else was responsible, and they were asked to specify the relationship for a response that included someone else. Accordingly, we can identify participants who made their own financial decisions, households who made their own financial decisions (participant or spouse), participants that got help with financial decisions (spouse or other person specified, possibly in addition to self), and participants that got help from outside (someone other than the participant or spouse was included as primarily responsible). Consistent with their high confidence in their ability to manage finances and their high confidence in their financial knowledge, the vast majority of participants were primarily or jointly responsible for their financial decisions at the time of their first decision making assessment. Just under one-half got help with financial decisions, including from a spouse, child, or outside advisor. Just one-quarter got help with financial decisions from someone other than a spouse. Over time, fewer participants made their own financial decisions and more got help.

The decision making questionnaire included a question asking participants if, in the past year, they have been a victim of financial fraud or had been told they were a victim of financial fraud. We use this self-report to identify those participants who answered this question affirmatively during any of their yearly evaluations as fraud victims. We use the data from each participant's first decision making questionnaire to predict which participants would report being recently victimized by financial fraud at the first or any subsequent yearly evaluation.

The decision making questionnaire included six questions to measure each participant's susceptibility to scams. The first five questions asked participants to what extent they agreed with five statements on a seven-point scale from 'strongly agree' to 'strongly disagree'. Three statements concerned the participant's vulnerability to phone calls from a scammer. One stated that if 'something sounds too good to be true, then it probably is'. Another stated that persons over the age of 65 'are often targeted by con-artists'. The sixth and final item in the susceptibility to scams measure asked whether the participant was enrolled in the national do-not-call registry. The first five responses are each scored from one to seven, to match the strength of the response to the question. For example, a response of 'strongly agree' to a statement indicating vulnerability scores a seven, while a response of 'strongly disagree' to the statement scores a one. Not being enrolled in the do-not-call registry scores a seven, while being enrolled scores a one. The susceptibility to scams measure is calculated as the sum of scores for the six questions. The average scam susceptibility score is 21 out of a maximum 42.

We use two types of questions for assessing participant inclination to take on financial risk. The first asked participants to report their lifetime willing-ness to take financial risks on a ten-point scale, from not at all willing (1) to completely willing (10). The second assessment of risk preferences asked participants if they would be willing to take on an investment opportunity that would double their annual income with a 50 percent probability, and cut it by 10 percent with a 50 percent probability.

Cognitive Changes

We use linear regression analysis to identify the effect of a change in cognition on several financial decision making variables. Since the focus of this chapter is on understanding the impact of decreases in cognition on finan-cial decision making, we also conduct robustness checks to ensure that the results provided hold true when applied to only the subset of participants who experienced a decrease in cognition. Changes in cognition are associ-ated with changes in financial literacy and its components. We find that a one-unit change in cognition is associated with a literacy score change of about one, which comes from a 0.65 change in numeracy and a 0.44 change in financial knowledge. The size of these effects of cognitive changes on financial literacy is modest, but it is important to consider that the changes in cognition measured occurred over just two to three years. Individuals experiencing cognitive decreases will also likely experience further decreases over time. Accordingly, the impact of decreases in cogni-tion on financial literacy is expected to accumulate with age.

We next examine how changes in global cognition are linked to a variety of confidence measures. First, we examine the effect of a decrease in cognition on general self-confidence, and we find that a one-unit decrease in cognition is associated with about a one-point decrease in self-confidence.

Yet, we find a very different result for the effect of a decrease in cognition on one's confidence for managing financial matters, as these are not statistically associated with changes in confidence in managing one's finances. Participants do not appear to recognize fully the detrimental effect of decreased cognition on their financial ability, despite their decrease in self-confidence in general.

We now examine to what extent those participants who experienced a decrease in their cognitive score got help with their financial decision making. A one-unit decrease in cognition results in triple the odds that a participant stopped making her own financial decisions. Participants who experienced a decrease in their cognition were more likely to obtain help with making financial decisions. A one-unit decrease in measured cognition resulted in more than double the odds that a participant obtained help with her financial decisions. This result includes obtaining help from a spouse as well as anyone outside the household. Typically, help from outside the household was provided by a son, a daughter, or a professional financial advisor.

Despite the strong association between decreases in cognition and seeking help with financial decisions, there were still many participants who experienced significant declines in their cognition who were not getting help. We use each participant's complete history of cognitive scores, including those prior to the start of the decision making assessment, to determine each person's long-term cognitive trajectory. The number of annual cognition scores for participants in our sample ranged from two for the most recent enrollees, to fifteen for long-time participants; on average participants had about seven. For each participant we determined the slope of cognitive ability by running a simple linear regression of cognition scores on age and a constant. There were about 150 participants who experienced both decreased cognition during the decision making assessment and a statistically significant cognitive decline during their entire participation in MAP. Of these participants, only about half got help with their financial decision making.

Financial Fraud

Next we examine whether declining cognition is predictive of fraud incidence. To test this hypothesis, we use the panel of participants who began participating in MAP prior to the decision making sub-study and subsequently completed at least one decision making questionnaire. For each participant with more than one cognition score, we run a linear regression of cognition scores on age at the time of testing, and we use the estimated slope coefficient as our measure of cognitive slope. Data are available on about 400 participants having an average of about six cognition scores (with a minimum of two and a maximum of fifteen scores). There are many participants who have positive cognitive slopes due to the practice effect of taking the same cognitive tests each year. Because our focus is on those participants with decreasing cognitive ability, we conduct further analysis on this subset of participants whom we term the cognitive slope sample.

Results weakly support our hypothesis: a one standard deviation decrease in cognitive slope is estimated to increase odds of fraud victimization by about one-third. The unconditional odds of recent fraud victimization in this cognitive change sample are 11 percent; a one standard deviation increase in over-confidence increases these odds to 15 percent. The result is robust to including age, sex, and education in the regression as control variables. Age is the only demographic control variable of the three found to have a statistically significant effect. Surprisingly, the coefficient on age is negative, indicating that older participants are less likely to report being victimized by fraud. This is surprising since older participants have higher scam susceptibility scores. A potential explanation for these findings is that older participants may be less likely to admit having been a victim of fraud, or they may be less likely to be aware of their victimization.

We also test whether steeper decreases in cognition are predictive of higher susceptibility to scams using a regression of each participant's scam susceptibility score on her cognitive slope measure, again computed using only scores prior to the first decision making questionnaire. The scam susceptibility score used in this test is the one collected in each participant's first decision making questionnaire. We predict a negative coefficient on cognitive slope, and results support this conjecture. A one standard deviation decrease in cognitive slope is estimated to increase scam susceptibility by about 21 percent of a one standard deviation change in scam susceptibility.

We also hypothesize that over-confidence regarding financial knowledge is associated with fraud victimization. To test this, we use data on all participants in the decision making sub-study with at least one survey conducted when the participant was not diagnosed with dementia. There were over 700 such participants, termed the over-confidence sample. We test the hypothesis using a logistic regression of fraud victimization on participant over-confidence scores from their first decision making questionnaires. Our results support the hypothesis: over-confidence in financial knowledge is a significant predictor of being victimized by financial fraud, and a standard deviation increase in over-confidence increases the estimated odds of fraud victimization by about 26 percent. The unconditional odds of recent fraud victimization in this subsample are 13 percent; a one standard deviation increase in over-confidence increases these odds to 17 percent. Among the demographic control variables, only age is statistically significant. This result corresponds with the small, but statistically significant difference in mean ages between fraud victims and those not victimized. Our results also show that the age difference does not drive the significant difference in over-confidence between the two groups. We also test whether either of the two components of over-confidence is, by itself, associated with fraud victimization, but neither one is. Accordingly our prior result for over-confidence is driven by the unique mix of its component parts.

The last fraud-related hypothesis is that being victimized by financial fraud increases people's propensity to take on financial risk. To calculate the before and after change from victimization, the fraud victim must not have reported being victimized at the time of the first decision making survey, a restriction that excluded thirty-one fraud victims from the previous subsample. We compare the changes for fraud victims to those of non-victims, and we calculate changes from their first decision making survey. To test the hypothesis, we compare victims' changes and non-victims' changes, and we also find a fraud propensity-matched non-victim for each victim. This is how we test the difference in changes for significance, to better isolate the impact of fraud victimization from the selection effect of being a fraud victim.

There are fifty-nine fraud victims in this subsample, and they report a lifetime willingness to take financial risk that increases, on average, after the fraud. By comparison, those not victimized exhibit a slight decrease in lifetime willingness to take on financial risk. Correspondingly, the proportion of fraud victims willing to accept the 50–50 gamble with the chance to double annual income or cut it by 10 percent increases from 12 percent before the fraud, to 29 percent afterwards, a seventeen percentage point increase. By contrast, the percentage of non-victims willing to accept the gamble remained unchanged over the same period.

Because being a victim of fraud is not random, this difference includes both the impact of fraud on risk taking, and a selection effect of the difference in characteristics of fraud victims and those not victimized. To better isolate the impact of fraud from the selection effect, we employ propensity matching of fraud victims to non-victims. Fraud propensity scores are calculated for each participant in the after fraud subsample, using the model previously developed with over-confidence and age as statistically significant predictors of fraud victimization. Each fraud victim was matched to the non-victim with the closest fraud propensity score, effectively finding the non-victim most similar in over-confidence and age. Then we compute the propensity-match difference in financial risk-taking changes, by subtracting the change of the propensity-matched non-victim from the change in each fraud victim. The average difference of these propensity-matched changes is statistically significant, and it implies that one impact of fraud is to increase victims' willingness to take on financial risk.

Further evidence of the impact of fraud on victim risk behavior is evident in changes in victim willingness to risk some of their annual income for a chance to double it. About 17 percent more fraud victims are willing to risk

10 percent of their annual incomes afterwards than before being victimized. By contrast, there is virtually no change in the willingness of non-fraud victims to accept this 10 percent income gamble over the same period. We again use propensity matching to better isolate the impact of fraud victimization from the selection effect of being prone to fraud. The propensity-matched difference in fraud victim and matched non-victim changes in willingness to accept the 10 percent income gamble is 22 percent. This result provides further evidence that the impact of fraud victimization is an increased propensity to take on risk.

Conclusion

This chapter identifies challenges for financial decision making at older ages using data collected by the Rush MAP. Seniors are vulnerable to declines in cognitive ability, and diminished cognition coincides with impaired financial decision making. Our analysis reveals that declines in cognition are associated with decreases in financial literacy, yet many participants do not recognize this change. Although participants experiencing declines in their cognitive performance did show significant drops in their general self-confidence, their confidence in their ability to manage their finances as well as their confidence in their financial knowledge did not fall despite drops in measured cognition. Whether help was sought or not, participants who experienced a decrease in their cognitive score were more likely to obtain help with their financial decisions, though perhaps not as many received assistance as needed.

We have also identified two risk factors for senior financial fraud and one consequence for victims' future financial decision making. We find that decreasing cognition is predictive of higher susceptibility to scam and future fraud incidence. Cognitive changes may be evident to those spending time with and caring for affected seniors, and our results show these changes provide a warning sign for fraud vulnerability. In addition, we find that over-confidence in financial knowledge is a significant risk factor for seniors becoming a victim of financial fraud. Increasing the financial knowledge of older adults is likely to help protect them from becoming financial fraud victims. In cases where raising financial knowledge is impossible, increasing awareness of one's limitations may help protect against the harmful effects of over-confidence. Finally, our analysis identifies increased willingness to take financial risk as a consequence of fraud victimization. This increase in risk acceptance may make victims vulnerable to subsequent exploitation.

Protecting finances from abuse should be an important part of seniors' late life planning. Unfortunately, money is often kept out of the conversation with caregivers, as noted. One recent study found that only 2 percent of seniors reported being asked about their ability to manage money by their health care providers (Investor Protection Trust 2010). While 19 percent of adult children of senior parents who were in touch with their parent's health care provider had raised concerns about mental comprehension, only 5 percent had raised concerns about the handling of money.

Additional research is needed to further inform these conversations and enhance planning. Financial victimization of seniors is a large and growing problem, yet the availability of data to study this problem is very limited. New data sources help us understand the factors that predict fraud victimization and its consequences, as well as to design effective solutions to limit the harmful consequences of cognitive decline and the impact of senior financial fraud.

References

Agarwal, S., J. C. Driscoll, X. Gabaix, and D. Laibson (2009). 'The Age of Reason: Financial Decisions over the Life-Cycle and Implications for Regulation'. *Brookings Papers on Economic Activity* 40(2): 51–117.

Anderson, K. (2013). *Consumer Fraud in the United States, 2011: The Third FTC Survey.* Washington, DC: Federal Trade Commission. <https://www.ftc.gov/sites/default/files/documents/reports/consumer-fraud-united-states-2011-third-ftc-survey/130419fraudsurvey_0.pdf>.

Barber, B. M. and T. Odean (2000). 'Trading is Hazardous to our Wealth: The Common Stock Investment Performance of Individual Investors'. *Journal of Finance* 55(2): 773–806.

Barber, B. M. and T. Odean (2001). 'Boys Will Be Boys: Gender, Overconfidence, and Common Stock Investment'. *Quarterly Journal of Economics* 116(1): 261–92.

Bennett, D. A., J. A. Schneider, A. S. Buchman, L. L. Barnes, P. A. Boyle, and R. S. Wilson (2012). 'Overview and Findings from the Rush Memory and Aging Project'. *Current Alzheimer Research* 9(6): 646–63.

Bennett, D. A., J. A. Schneider, A. S. Buchman, C. Mendes de Leon, J. L. Bienais, and R. S. Wilson (2005). 'The Rush Memory and Aging Project: Study Design and Baseline Characteristics of the Study Cohort'. *Neuroepidemiology* 25(4): 163–75.

Certified Financial Planner Board of Standards (2012). *Senior Financial Protection Survey.* Washington, DC: Certified Financial Planner Board of Standards. <https://www.cfp.net/docs/news-events—supporting-documents/senior-americans-financial-exploitation-survey.pdf?sfvrsn=0>.

FINRA Investor Education Foundation (2013). *Financial Fraud and Fraud Susceptibility in the United States.* Washington, DC: FINRA Investor Education Foundation. <http://www.finrafoundation.org/web/groups/sai/@sai/documents/sai_original_content/p337731.pdf>.

Gamble, K. J., P. A. Boyle, L. Yu, and D. A. Bennett (2014). 'Causes and Consequences of Financial Fraud Among Older Americans'. CRR Working Paper No. 2014–13. Chestnut Hill, MA: Center for Retirement Research at Boston College.

Gamble, K. J., P. A. Boyle, L. Yu, and D. A. Bennett (2015). 'Aging and Financial Decision Making'. *Management Science* 61(11): 2603–10.

Goetzmann, W. N. and A. Kumar (2008). 'Equity Portfolio Diversification'. *Review of Finance* 12(3): 433–63.

Investor Protection Trust (2010). *Elder Investment Fraud and Financial Exploitation.* Washington, DC: Investor Protection Trust. <http://www.investorprotection.org/downloads/EIFFE_Survey_Report.pdf>.

Korniotis, G. M. and A. Kumar (2011). 'Do Older Investors Make Better Investment Decisions?' *Review of Economics and Statistics* 93(1): 244–65.

Malmendier, U. and S. Nagel (2011). 'Depression Babies: Do Macroeconomic Experiences Affect Risk Taking?' *Quarterly Journal of Economics* 126(1): 373–416.

Pottow, J. (2012). 'The Rise in Elder Bankruptcy Filings and Failure of US Bankruptcy Law'. *The Elder Law Journal* 19(1): 220–57.

Thaler, R. H. and E. J. Johnson (1990). 'Gambling with the House Money and Trying to Break Even: The Effects of Prior Outcomes on Risky Choice'. *Management Science* 36(6): 643–60.

Chapter 4

Retirement and Cognitive Functioning: International Evidence

Raquel Fonseca, Arie Kapteyn, and Gema Zamarro

The topic of how retirement affects cognitive function has attracted much interest over the last decade. The subject is of interest for at least two key reasons. First is the desire for a better understanding of the effect of prolonging working life at older ages on well-being. Second is interest in the policy implications of these effects on how countries deal with under-funded retirement plans and aging populations. Encouraging individuals to delay retirement could have significant financial and non-financial (e.g., health and well-being) implications for individuals and societies. Given the importance of this topic, this chapter surveys the recent literature on the effects of retirement on cognitive functioning at older ages, and assesses the robustness of estimates of the effect of retirement on cognitive capability.

It is fair to say that there is no clear consensus in the literature on the effect of retirement on cognitive functioning. Some studies find that being retired leads to a decline in cognition, but richer specifications (i.e., including fixed effects, dynamic specifications, or alternative specifications of instrumental variables) often lead to large changes in the size and significance of the estimated effects. Other papers find a negative effect of retirement on cognition (e.g., Rohwedder and Willis 2010; Bonsang et al. 2012; Mazzonna and Peracchi 2012, 2014), while still other studies find small or even positive effects, especially when these are disaggregated by different types of occupations (e.g., Coe et al. 2012; Bianchini and Borella 2014). Other papers find significant effects only for women (Coe and Zamarro 2011).

The present study uses datasets across several countries—namely the US Health and Retirement Study (HRS), the English Longitudinal Study of Ageing (ELSA), and the Survey of Health, Ageing and Retirement in Europe (SHARE)—to replicate several of these analyses. Our goal is to get a better understanding of the sources of the different effects found in the literature. We show that results are very sensitive to differences in econometric specifications. In particular, the use of country fixed effects to control for unobserved country differences tends to reduce the estimated effect of retirement on cognition dramatically, suggesting that unobserved differences across countries affect both retirement ages and cognitive decline. This remains true for different subgroups including blue-collar/white-collar jobs; physically demanding jobs; or high-skilled jobs.

In what follows, we first survey the empirical literature on aging and cognitive functioning. Second, we summarize results found in prior empirical literature on the effect of retirement on episodic memory. We focus on studies using similar datasets (HRS, SHARE, and ELSA), definitions of cognition, and instrumental variables to capture causal effects. Third, we replicate several of these results using the same datasets. We discuss the factors that appear to explain differences found across papers that use different specifications, including the endogeneity of right-hand side variables, and heterogeneity across gender, occupation, or skill levels. Finally, we conclude.

Measuring Cognitive Function and its Determinants

Our goal is to understand whether being retired affects cognitive functioning. In this section, we first briefly describe the different measures of cognitive functioning used in the literature we survey. Second, we summarize the main findings in the literature on aging and cognition, as well as the main factors affecting cognitive ability and its decline.

Cognitive Functioning

Following the psychological theory on cognition (Cattell–Horn–Carroll theory),[1] we identify two types of cognitive functioning: fluid intelligence and crystallized intelligence. Fluid intelligence involves processes related to recall, in particular, episodic memory, i.e., working memory, including long-term memory and how fast we process information (perceptual speed).[2] Crystallized intelligence relates to our knowledge and verbal learning, primarily affected by education. Crystallized intelligence seems to be rather stable over time and can even improve with age (Hertzog et al. 2008; Dixon et al. 2004; Park et al. 2002; Schaie 1994), while fluid intelligence is more likely to decline with age (Anderson and Craik 2000; Prull et al. 2000). The environment can also affect memory at older ages, as well as the intellectual stimulus individuals face routinely (Salthouse 2006, 2009; Small 2002; van Praag et al. 2000). Most economic studies on cognitive function focus on fluid abilities likely to affect dementing illnesses such as memory or attention (Morris et al. 2001; Adam et al. 2007b). The decline in fluid cognition may affect individual decision making and adversely affect well-being. The papers discussed in the following all use similar measures of cognitive functioning, namely on immediate and delayed recall.

Prior Evidence on Cognitive Functioning, Aging, and Factors other than Retirement

To better understand how the process of aging can affect cognitive functioning, we describe findings across several disciplines including psychology, epidemiology, gerontology, neuroscience, and economics. Schaie (1989), who reviewed findings from the Seattle Longitudinal Study on adult cognitive development, found an important decline in cognitive functioning at later ages. This decline in cognitive abilities with age was also documented by Hertzog et al. (2008), Bäckman et al. (2005), Dixon et al. (2004), Peterson et al. (2002), Anderson and Craik (2000), Prull et al. (2000), and Schaie (1994), among others. Demographic variables such as gender may correlate with cognitive functioning as well, although results in the literature are mixed. Lei et al. (2012) found lower cognitive functioning for women than for men; Johnson and Bouchard (2007) reported better memory among women than among men; and Halpern (2012) showed small or no evidence of cognitive functioning differences by gender.

Cognitive reserve refers to the phenomenon that people whose brains show extensive Alzheimer's pathology may have manifested very little clinical cognitive impairment when alive. Evidence suggests that education, activities, and occupation can affect people's cognitive reserve (e.g., Stern 2002, 2003). The role of education in cognition has been studied by Banks and Mazzonna (2012), Maurer (2010), McFadden (2008), and Evans et al. (1993), among others. Other factors, such as leisure activities, lifestyle, behavior, and social networks, may also affect cognitive functioning and have also been studied in the literature.[3]

Does Retirement Affect Cognitive Functioning?

A main reason economists seek to evaluate whether retirement affects cognitive functioning is that they try to understand how retirement might affect well-being at older ages and possibly to extend employees' working lives. During recent decades, many countries have increased retirement eligibility ages for public pensions and/or are switching from defined benefit to defined contribution pension systems. These reforms can have different effects upon countries and individuals, including people's employment decisions. If employment status were to have an effect on individuals' cognitive functioning, the implications for policymaking would differ depending on the direction of the effect. For instance, if staying longer in the labor market were thought to be protective of memory capacity, encouraging workers to work longer would support pension system financial sustainability (Dave et al. 2008; Bonsang et al. 2012). It could also potentially reduce health care and long-term care expenditures, assuming that implied memory loss is related to increased risk of dementia and increases in disability (Albert et al. 2002; Lyketsos et al. 2002; Tabert et al. 2002). It would further aid autonomy and the capacity for sound financial decisions, including saving decisions (Christelis et al. 2010; Banks et al. 2010; Brown et al. 2012), and more generally it would enhance well-being and quality of life at later ages (OECD 2013).

Prior studies reach conflicting conclusions on the effects of retirement on memory, both with respect to the sign and size of the effect. The studies we review here use comparable measures of cognitive abilities, although they differ in their definitions of retirement. Commonly used datasets are (1) the Health and Retirement Study (HRS) for the US; (2) the English Longitudinal Study of Ageing (ELSA) for England; and (3) the Survey of Health, Ageing and Retirement (SHARE) for Europe.[4]

One of the first studies of the effect of retirement on cognitive function was by Adam et al. (2007a). Using HRS, SHARE, and ELSA data for the year 2004, they reported a negative effect of retirement on a word recall test. They used the sum of the number of correct answers on an immediate ten-item word recall test and the number of correct answers to the same list of items, about 10 minutes later. They considered both individual retirement status and how long the person had been retired. Their analysis did not provide a causal interpretation of the impact of retirement on cognitive abilities.

Table 4.1 summarizes nine recent studies on the same topic. As one can see, the studies differ with respect to the number of countries used in the analysis; whether the analysis was solely based on a cross-section of countries, or whether longitudinal data were used; the age range considered; and whether men and women were analyzed separately. Some studies differentiated between blue- and white-collar jobs before retirement (i.e., Mazzonna and Peracchi 2014; Bianchini and Borella 2014).

All the studies in the table defined cognitive functioning with the measure used by Adam et al. (2007a), i.e., the sum of immediate and delayed recalled words from a list of ten words. We denote this variable simply as 'word recall' from now on, and it ranges from 0 to 20.[5, 6]

Three main definitions of retirement can be identified. The first focuses on self-reported labor force status. Sometimes this definition also takes into account whether individuals are receiving old age pension benefits. 'Retired' is generally defined as a (0, 1) dummy variable. A second definition follows Lazear (1986) by equating being retired as not working for pay. The third definition is a continuous variable related to retirement duration.[7] Most authors measure retirement duration as the elapsed time between the individual's retirement date and interview date (Coe et al. 2012) and/or the elapsed time since the last job ended (Bonsang et al. 2012).

TABLE 4.1 Dataset, samples, dependent and independent variables in the reviewed papers

Authors	Countries	Dataset	Year	Sample	Cognitive abilities	Retirement	Explanatory variables
Rohwedder and Willis (2010)	United States, England, and 11 European countries	HRS, SHARE, and ELSA	2004	Men and women together (60–64 years)	Memory test scores (recall summary score 20)	Retired (dummy)	Different age forms
Coe and Zamarro (2011)	Europe 11 countries	SHARE	2004	Men (50–69 years old)	1. Memory test scores (recall summary score 20) 2. Verbal fluency	Retired (dummy) (cond. working age 50)	Demographic; SES; health and country dummies
Coe et al. (2012)	US	HRS	1996–2008	1. Blue- and white-collar workers 2. 50–70 years old 3. Men and women together	1. Self-rated memory 2. Immediate, delayed, and total word recall 3. Working memory 4. Numeracy	Retirement duration (years in retirement) continuous variable	Demographic; education; wave dummies
Bonsang et al. (2012)	US	HRS	1998–2008	Men and women together (51–75 years old) working at 50	Memory test scores (recall summary score 20)	Retirement duration (non-parametric specification) after one year of retirement	Different age forms
Mazzonna and Peracchi (2012)	Europe 11 countries	SHARE	2004–2006	1. 50–70 years old 2. Men and women separately	1. Immediate memory 2. Delay memory 3. Orientation in time 4. Verbal fluency 5. Numeracy	Retirement duration (years in retirement) continuous variable	Demographic; SES; country, cohort, and regional dummies

Study	Region	Data source	Years	Sample	Cognition measures	Retirement variable	Controls
Mazzonna and Peracchi (2014)	Europe 10 countries	SHARE	2004–2006	Men and women separately. Occupations: physical demanding job	1. Memory test scores (recall summary score 20) 2. Verbal fluency 3. Numeracy 4. Cognitivity Index (PCA)	Retired (dummy) and retirement duration (years in retirement) continuous variable	Demographic; SES; health
Celidoni et al. (2013)	Europe	SHARE	2004–2010	Men and women separately and all together	Memory test scores (recall summary score 20)	Lag of retired dummy + retirement duration	Demographic; SES; health
Bingley and Martinello (2013)	US, England, and 11 European countries	HRS, SHARE, and ELSA	2004	Men and women separately and all together	Memory test scores (recall summary score 20)	Retired (dummy)	Different age forms and years of schooling
Bianchini and Borella (2014)	Europe	SHARE	2004–2010	Men and women together, 50–70 working at age 50. Blue-/white-collar workers	Memory test scores (recall summary score 20)	Retired (dummy) and retirement duration	Demographic; SES; health; behavior; learning and contextual factor

Source: Authors' computations.

All studies control for age in some form. While Rohwedder and Willis (2010) and Bonsang et al. (2012) did control for age, they did not explore the effects of other covariates. By contrast, as Table 4.1 shows, other studies included a large number of other covariates including years of schooling, demographic, socio-economic status (SES hereafter), health, country dummies, wave dummies, cohort, and regional dummies.

Some authors allow for what is called a 'honeymoon phase' (Atchley 1976, 1982), which refers to the fact that, when people first retire, they often spend more time engaging in activities that they lacked time for when working. These activities could have a positive effect on their cognitive abilities or delay their decline. Though this phase does not last long (Ekerdt et al. 1983; Gall et al. 1997; Mein et al. 2003; Mojon-Azzi et al. 2007; Westerlund et al. 2010), it must be taken into account when analyzing the relationship between retirement and cognition (Bonsang et al. 2012; Mazzonna and Peracchi 2012, 2014; Bianchini and Borella 2014). Occupational characteristics such as being a blue-collar worker or having a physically demanding job can also affect cognitive functioning differently from those associated with being a white-collar worker or having an intellectually engaging job (Jorm et al. 1998; Potter et al. 2008). Several studies (Coe et al. 2012; Mazzonna and Peracchi 2014; Bianchini and Borella 2014) have evaluated how occupation can mediate the effect of retirement on cognitive functioning.

Retirement and Cognitive Function: Causal or Not?

Most authors begin with a descriptive analysis showing correlations of retirement and cognition. For instance, Rohwedder and Willis (2010) and Adam et al. (2007a) documented a positive relationship between working and cognitive functioning. Both studies compared the employment rates of men age 60–64 and 50–54, and they noted a fall in the number of words recalled by men age 60–64 relative to men age 50–54 across a number of SHARE countries, England, and the US. When Adam et al. (2007a) controlled for occupational activities, they found that not working was negatively and significantly correlated with recall. Rohwedder and Willis (2010), using working for pay versus not working as their retirement variable, found that retired individuals' memory scores decreased by an average of 4.9 words (on a 0–20 scale) with retirement.

Coe and Zamarro (2011) used a broad retirement definition, including as retirees: retired, homemakers, and disabled and sick individuals out of the labor force. This variable was conditioned on having been working for pay at age 50. Their study confirmed a significant but small negative association between retirement and cognition when demographics, SES, and health controls were included (the estimated coefficient implied a 0.28 reduction in the number of words recalled out of twenty, significant at 5 percent). Effects of retirement on verbal fluency were found to be insignificant. The cross-country analyses undertaken in these three papers were based exclusively on data from 2004.

Coe et al. (2012) and Bonsang et al. (2012) focus only on US HRS panel data, and they used a continuous retirement duration variable as an explanatory variable instead of the retirement dummy. Coe et al. (2012) found no significant correlation of word recall and retirement for blue-collar workers, but they did find a highly significant small negative correlation for white-collar workers (–0.04 fewer words recalled on a 0–20 scale). They also explored other cognitive function indicators such as numeracy and self-rated memory, and found similar results. Mazzonna and Peracchi (2012) separately examined immediate and delayed recall as well as an 'orientation in time' variable, and verbal fluency and numeracy. They found a significant but small negative correlation of retirement duration on both immediate recall and delayed recall (–0.010* to –0.018*** fewer words on a 0–10 scale).

These results are interesting but cannot be interpreted as causal because cognitive endowments could affect both cognitive functioning outcomes and retirement decisions. For instance, less educated individuals or people with more physically demanding jobs might retire earlier than highly educated individuals or individuals with more intellectually challenging jobs (Glymour et al. 2008; Evans et al. 1993; Jorm et al. 1998; Potter et al. 2008). Additionally, common factors like preferences, behavior, or health could affect both retirement and cognitive abilities (Frederick 2005; Benjamin et al. 2006; Dohmen et al. 2007). To address these issues, some authors also analyzed the effect of retirement on cognition using instrumental variable (IV) approaches. Eligibility ages for both early and full pension benefits were typically used as instruments, derived from the institutional information in *Pensions at a Glance* (OECD 2011) and/or provided by the US Social Security Administration (2014). The instruments used capture the timing of eligibility for public pensions, and most of the studies used these policy variables in relation to the interview date and the respondent's age. An exception is Coe et al. (2012) who used as an instrument the early retirement windows offered by employers as reported in the HRS.

To be suitable instruments, these variables must be correlated with retirement but affect cognition only through their effect on retirement, and not vice versa. Earlier studies on the effect of retirement on health have shown that these proposed instruments are very strong predictors of retirement behavior (Charles 2004; Coe and Lindeboom 2008; Neuman 2008; Bound and Waidmann 2007).

The studies reviewed in Table 4.2 offer a less clear-cut conclusion. We summarize the various approaches in Table 4.2.

Table 4.2 Instrument and different instrumental approaches: results

Authors	Countries	Year	Dependent variable	Instruments	Empirical strategy	Results
Rohwedder and Willis (2010)	US, England, and 11 European countries	2004	Words recalled out of 20	Eligible age for early and for full pension benefits	IV	Ret. Dum. −4.666***
Coe and Zamarro (2011)	Europe 11 countries	2004	Words recalled out of 20	Eligible age for early and for full pension benefits	IV	Ret. Dum. −0.0390
Coe et al. (2012)	US	1996–2008	Words recalled out of 20	The offering of an early retirement window	IV	Ret. Dur. 0.37845*** (blue-collar) 0.00521 (white-collar)
Bonsang et al. (2012)	US	1998–2008	Words recalled out of 20	Eligible age for early and for full pension benefits	IV–FE	Ret. Dur. −1.021***
Mazzonna and Peracchi (2012)	Europe 11 countries	2004–2006	1. Im. 2. Delay	Eligible age for early and for full pension benefits	IV	Ret. Dur. M. −0.025*** (im.) 0.009 (del.) W. −0.055*** (im.) −0.029*** (del.)
Mazzonna and Peracchi (2014)	Europe 10 countries	2004–2006	Cognitivity index (PCA)	Eligible age for early and for full pension benefits	IV–FE	Ret. Dur. −0.06*** M. −0.069*** W. −0.057***
Celidoni et al. (2013)	Europe	2004–2010	Words recalled out of 20	Eligible age for early and for full pension benefits	IV–FE	Ret. Dur. −0.2***
Bingley and Martinello (2013)	US, England, and 11 European countries	2004	Words recalled out of 20	Eligible age for early and for full pension benefits. Controlled for years of schooling	IV	Ret. Dum. −3.014*** M. −5.485*** W. −1.607**
Bianchini and Borella (2014)	Europe	2004–2010	Words recalled out of 20	Eligible age for early and for full pension benefits	IV–FE	Ret. Dur. 0.3919***

Source: Authors' computations.

To overview the instrumental variable results, Rohwedder and Willis (2010) found a significant reduction of 4.67 words on a scale of 0 to 20 with retirement (significant at the 1 percent level). However, this effect disappeared when Coe and Zamarro (2011) controlled for country dummies. Coe et al. (2012) showed a significant and positive effect for US blue-collar workers, with a coefficient of about 0.38 additional words. Bingley and Martinello (2013) showed that the effect of retirement on cognition declined when they controlled for years of schooling (–3.0 versus –5.6 reduction in words recalled). When estimating the model for men and women separately, they found a lower effect of retirement on word recall for women than for men. Mazzonna and Peracchi (2012) accounted for attrition, cohort effects, and learning effects, and they found a small significant negative effect of retirement duration on cognitive abilities (–0.025 words per year in retirement in immediate memory recall for men, and –0.055 words per year in retirement for women in immediate recall).

To deal with unobserved heterogeneity across individuals, some authors have adopted a fixed effect (FE) approach in the instrumental variable setting. For instance, Bonsang et al. (2012) reported a significant and negative retirement coefficient of –1.01 words in a baseline model using fixed-effect methods. After controlling for different age specifications and retirement durations, they found less robust results. Using principal components analysis, Mazzonna and Peracchi (2014) constructed a cognitive capability index based on various cognition measures. They analyzed a dummy for retirement similar to that in Rohwedder and Willis (2010), and they also analyzed the effect of retirement duration as in Mazzonna and Peracchi (2012). They found a small negative effect of retirement duration with their cognitive index, so that more time in retirement implied a larger decrease in cognitive functioning. They also found a positive effect of immediate retirement on cognition for white-collar jobs, and no significant effect for blue-collar jobs, as well as a negative effect of retirement duration for both groups. When only using fixed effects and controlling for age and time dummies, Celidoni et al. (2013) found a positive but small effect on the retirement dummy (–0.4) and a small negative and significant coefficient for retirement duration (–0.10). People recalled –0.13 fewer words per year in retirement (on a 0–20 scale), depending on the specification of age. The authors also found a small negative effect of –0.2 words per year in retirement on cognition with a combined IV–FE approach and excluding the retirement dummy from the regressions. Bianchini and Borella (2014) interacted the number of years in retirement with the retirement dummy for individuals who actually retired during the sample period, so that they were observed both when working and retired. Interestingly, using a similar approach to Celidoni et al. (2013), they found the opposite result: a significant small positive effect of retirement duration on cognition (with an estimated increase in words recalled on a 0–20 scale equal to 0.39 per year in retirement).

In summary, most studies reported small and sometimes insignificant effects of retirement on cognition. The exceptions were Rohwedder and Willis (2010), Bonsang et al. (2012), and Bingley and Martinello (2013) who found significant negative effects of retirement on words recalled (about –3 and –5 words on a scale of 0 to 20 words for Rohwedder and Willis (2010) and Bingley and Martinello (2013), respectively, and about –1 word per year in retirement for Bonsang et al. (2012).

Disaggregating Cognitive Abilities and Reconciling Results

To better understand the sources of differential effects of retirement on cognition documented in the prior literature, we also use the HRS, ELSA, and SHARE surveys from 2004 to 2012. We also focus on countries with at least three waves (thirteen countries).[8] (Descriptive statistics for the baseline samples appear in Appendix A and Appendix Tables 4A.1 and 4A.2.)

Our goal is to reconcile the divergent results in the literature by evaluating different econometric specifications and operationalizations of retirement. In particular we estimate effects of retirement on cognitive ability using Ordinary Least Squares (OLS), Instrumental Variable Methods, Fixed Effects and Instrumental Variable Fixed Effect (IV–FE) methods, for all surveys combined.[9]

We also present specifications using a variety of control variables. A first specification includes none at all, while a second specification adds age, cohort, and gender. Note that by controlling for age, we account for the natural decline of memory with age. Therefore, our estimates of the effect of retirement capture changes in the age trajectory due to retirement. The third specification adds country fixed effects to the set of controls. The final two specifications include as controls demographic information (marital status and level of education), and health outcomes (self-reported health, number of limitations with activities, and medical conditions). We are aware that the last two specifications could raise endogeneity issues. For instance, in the former specification, marital status could affect cognitive abilities via social activities as part of the family network. In the latter specification, one might be concerned that health is affected by cognition, while health could also be affected by retirement. We have conducted various robustness checks including incorporating income, wealth, and other social network control variables. Since the results do not differ much, they are reported in Appendix A.

Our first retirement definition is based on self-reports of current job status (SR_Ret). The second definition includes homemakers with those who say they are sick or disabled in the set of retirees, but we condition on working at the age of 50 (NW1_Ret), as in Coe and Zamarro (2011). Our third definition of retirement is the most inclusive and defines as retired all those not working now (NW2_Ret), as in Rohwedder and Willis (2010).

To address the potential endogeneity of retirement (i.e., that cognitive decline may affect when someone retires), we instrument using two variables that indicate whether the respondent was eligible for full or early retirement public pensions using the country- and gender-specific pension-eligibility ages described in Appendix B.[10]

Pooled Results

Table 4.3 presents the estimates for all surveys pooled together. Overall, the Ordinary Least Square (OLS) estimates reveal a significant negative correlation between retirement and cognition scores (on a 0–20 scale) ranging from –1.28 words for specifications without controls, to –0.28 words with more detailed controls. The more controls we add, the lower the estimated coefficient. The size of the effect does vary depending on the definition of retirement used: for instance, the definition based on the respondent reporting not working (NW2_Ret) generates the highest estimated negative effects, followed by NW1_Ret and self-reported retirement status (SR_Ret) (similar results appear in Appendix Tables 4A.3–4A.8).

The IV estimates are mostly larger than the OLS results,[11] but results change dramatically when country fixed effects are included. Excluding country controls means that our estimates are based on variation within and across countries. Hence cognition levels of those above retirement age are compared with cognition levels of those below. Including country fixed effects changes the sources of identification and interpretation of the estimated retirement effects. Specifically, with country effects, retirement impacts are estimated by comparing individuals in the same country above and below retirement eligibility age (Coe and Zamarro 2011). In most cases, combining country fixed effects with IV restores the estimated negative effect of retirement on cognition, but the effects become mostly small and often insignificant.

Heterogeneity across Individuals

If the causal effect of retirement on cognition is heterogeneous across respondents, then the estimated effect recovered by IV will be a weighted average of the effects for those individuals induced to change their decisions

TABLE 4.3 Effects of retirement on cognition for all countries

	SR_Ret				NW1_Ret				NW2_Ret			
	OLS	IV	FE	IV–FE	OLS	IV	FE	IV–FE	OLS	IV	FE	IV–FE
1. No controls	-1.19***	-2.18***	0.05	-0.23*	-1.18***	-2.28***	0.02	-0.34***	-1.27***	-2.74***	-0.08**	-0.41**
	(0.02)	(0.02)	(0.03)	(0.09)	(0.02)	(0.03)	(0.02)	(0.09)	(0.02)	(0.03)	(0.02)	(0.13)
2. Years, cohorts, gender	-0.83***	-5.68***	0.006	-0.78	-0.97***	-6.19***	-0.007	-0.78	-1.12***	-8.77***	-0.09***	-1.19
	(0.02)	(0.20)	(0.03)	(0.52)	(0.02)	(0.23)	(0.03)	(0.46)	(0.02)	(0.39)	(0.02)	(1.02)
3. 2 + Country fixed effects	-0.60***	-0.70**	0.006	-0.78	-0.69***	-0.61**	-0.007	-0.09***	-0.88***	-0.70	-0.78	-1.19
	(0.02)	(0.26)	(0.03)	(0.52)	(0.02)	(0.26)	(0.03)	(0.02)	(0.02)	(0.44)	(0.46)	(1.02)
4. 3 + Demographics	-0.44***	-0.70**	0.007	-0.80	-0.46***	-0.48	-0.005	-0.77	-0.61***	-0.61	-0.09**	-1.09
	(0.02)	(0.25)	(0.03)	(0.52)	(0.02)	(0.26)	(0.03)	(0.46)	(0.02)	(0.42)	(0.03)	(0.99)
5. 4 + Health controls	-0.28***	-0.75**	0.007	-0.65	-0.28***	-0.57*	-0.008	-0.08**	-0.41***	-0.81*	-0.65	-0.90
	(0.02)	(0.23)	(0.03)	(0.47)	(0.02)	(0.24)	(0.03)	(0.02)	(0.02)	(0.36)	(0.43)	(0.86)

Notes: Ordinary Least Squares (OLS); Instrumental Variable Methods (IV); Fixed Effects (FE); Instrumental Variable Fixed Effect Methods (IV–FE). Retirement definitions: SR_Ret is based on self-reports of current job status; NW1_Ret includes homemakers along with those who say they are sick or disabled into the set of retirees, but conditions on working at the age of 50; NW2_Ret defines as retired all those who are not working now.

Source: Authors' computations.

because of the instrument. In our case, the instruments are based on retirement eligibility, so the issue is which labor force participants are induced to retire once they reach the eligibility age. This is what is known as the local average treatment effect (LATE; Imbens and Angrist 1994; Angrist and Pischke 2015). Accordingly, studies that estimate the same model with different IVs or use samples from different populations may obtain very different estimates of the causal effects.

Average cognitive scores differ between men and women. Men recall 9.58 words on average while women recall 10.39 words. These numbers are quite stable over the period studied. Figure 4.1 shows that the averages vary across countries, but women always score better than men. Moreover, Table 4.4 shows results of OLS estimates by gender, which are seen to be similar. In the IV specifications, results for women mostly retain significant and negative coefficients even controlling for all covariates, while for men the coefficients of interest lose significance once we control for country fixed effects. The IV–FE estimates for men are statistically insignificant, while for women,

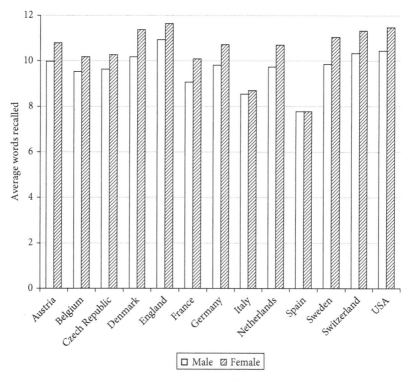

Figure 4.1. Cognitive functioning and gender differences
Source: Authors' computation.

TABLE 4.4 Effect of retirement on cognition for all countries by gender

Men

	SR_Ret				NW1_Ret				NW2_Ret			
	OLS	IV	FE	IV-FE	OLS	IV	FE	IV-FE	OLS	IV	FE	IV-FE
1. No controls	-1.28***	-2.18***	0.03	0.04	-1.21***	-2.09***	-0.001	-0.19	-1.34***	-2.58***	-0.10**	-0.19
	(0.03)	(0.04)	(0.04)	(0.13)	(0.03)	(0.04)	(0.04)	(0.13)	(0.03)	(0.05)	(0.04)	(0.18)
2. Years, cohorts, gender	-0.89***	-4.86***	-0.04	0.24	-0.89***	-4.76***	-0.04	-0.20	-1.07***	-6.87***	-0.13**	-0.17
	(0.04)	(0.25)	(0.05)	(0.65)	(0.04)	(0.26)	(0.05)	(0.59)	(0.03)	(0.42)	(0.04)	(1.12)
3. 2 + Country fixed effects	-0.65***	0.05			-0.69***	0.11			-0.92***	0.49		
	(0.04)	(0.33)			(0.04)	(0.32)			(0.03)	(0.48)		
4. 3 + Demographics	-0.48***	0.01	-0.01	0.28	-0.49***	0.11	-0.03	-0.15	-0.66***	0.38	-0.10*	-0.05
	(0.04)	(0.32)	(0.05)	(0.64)	(0.04)	(0.32)	(0.05)	(0.59)	(0.03)	(0.46)	(0.04)	(1.09)
5. 4 + Health controls	-0.32***	0.04	-0.02	0.34	-0.28***	0.10	-0.01	-0.08	-0.43***	0.29	-0.09*	0.17
	(0.04)	(0.31)	(0.05)	(0.59)	(0.04)	(0.31)	(0.05)	(0.55)	(0.03)	(0.43)	(0.04)	(1.01)

Women

	SR_Ret				NW1_Ret				NW2_Ret			
	OLS	IV	FE	IV-FE	OLS	IV	FE	IV-FE	OLS	IV	FE	IV-FE
1. No controls	-1.16***	-2.18***	0.08	-0.51***	-1.29***	-2.44***	0.05	-0.49***	-1.40***	-2.89***	-0.06	-0.61**
	(0.03)	(0.04)	(0.04)	(0.15)	(0.03)	(0.05)	(0.04)	(0.14)	(0.03)	(0.05)	(0.04)	(0.19)
2. Years, cohorts, gender	-0.77***	-6.60***	0.05	-2.13*	-1.04***	-7.79***	0.01	-1.46*	-1.17***	-10.02***	-0.07*	-3.05
	(0.04)	(0.35)	(0.05)	(0.83)	(0.04)	(0.41)	(0.04)	(0.71)	(0.03)	(0.65)	(0.04)	(1.88)
3. 2 + Country fixed effects	-0.56***	-1.62***			-0.66***	-1.52***			-0.85***	-2.51**		
	(0.04)	(0.44)			(0.03)	(0.47)			(0.03)	(0.88)		
4. 3 + Demographics	-0.4***	-1.57***	0.04	-2.24**	-0.42***	-1.27***	0.01	-1.54*	-0.57***	-2.13**	-0.08*	-2.89
	(0.04)	(0.41)	(0.05)	(0.84)	(0.03)	(0.45)	(0.04)	(0.72)	(0.03)	(0.79)	(0.04)	(1.81)
5. 4 + Health controls	-0.25***	-1.58***	0.03	-1.83*	-0.26***	-1.39***	-0.005	-1.29	-0.38***	-2.17***	-0.08	-2.38
	(0.04)	(0.37)	(0.05)	(0.73)	(0.03)	(0.42)	(0.04)	(0.66)	(0.03)	(0.64)	(0.04)	(1.44)

Notes: Ordinary Least Squares (OLS); Instrumental Variable Methods (IV); Fixed Effects (FE); Instrumental Variable Fixed Effect Methods (IV-FE). Retirement definitions: SR_Ret is based on self-reports of current job status; NW1_Ret includes homemakers along with those who say they are sick or disabled into the set of retirees, but conditions on working at the age of 50; NW2_Ret defines as retired all those who are not working now.

Source: Authors' computations.

the estimated effects of retirement on cognition remain negative and mostly statistically significant even when country fixed effects and covariates are included.

As Bingley and Martinello (2013) argued, the differences in eligibility ages across gender could be correlated with education level. Table 4.5 provides a breakdown of results for two different education levels. Here, the OLS and IV estimates are similar across the two groups, although the coefficients are smaller for better-educated than lower-educated individuals. The IV–FE models generate generally insignificant results for both groups.

It is also of interest to differentiate results by occupation. One variable we use measures physical effort in the current job directly, while a second variable is constructed by matching people's reported occupations to administrative classifications (ISCO coding for continental Europe, SOC2010 for England, Census coding for the US) to distinguish between blue-collar and white-collar jobs. (More details about the variables can be found in Appendix A.) We find that people working in physically demanding jobs recall about 10 words, while those in less physically demanding jobs recall about 11. Similar differences arise when comparing blue-collar jobs and white-collar jobs. Table 4.6 summarizes results according to the physically demanding job definition.

To sum up the results, our analysis shows that the estimated effects of retirement on cognition are quite sensitive to model specification. In particular, results are especially sensitive to the inclusion of country fixed effects used to control for unobserved country differences. When these are controlled for, estimated effects of retirement on cognition are small and mostly insignificant.

Conclusions

In this chapter we have reviewed the empirical literature estimating the effects of retirement on cognitive function. We use several internationally comparable datasets and show there is wide variation in outcomes. In particular, estimates are very sensitive to econometric specifications, and the use of country fixed effects in particular dramatically reduces the estimated effect of retirement on cognition. This is also true for population subgroups distinguished by blue-collar/white-collar, physical demands, and job skill level. The upshot of our work is therefore that previous studies' findings must be considered quite fragile. It should be pointed out that our IV strategy aims to identify a sharp immediate effect of retirement on cognition, rather than considering the effect of retirement duration on

TABLE 4.5 Effect of retirement on cognition for all countries by skill education

Middle and low-skilled workers

	SR_Ret				NW1_Ret				NW2_Ret			
	OLS	IV	FE	IV–FE	OLS	IV	FE	IV–FE	OLS	IV	FE	IV–FE
1. No controls	-1.07***	-1.91***	0.07	0.05	-1.05***	-2.07***	0.06	-0.04	-1.09***	-2.45***	-0.05	-0.01
	(0.03)	(0.04)	(0.04)	(0.13)	(0.03)	(0.04)	(0.04)	(0.13)	(0.03)	(0.05)	(.03)	(0.18)
2. Years, cohorts, gender	-0.73***	-2.5***	0.03	-0.09	-0.86***	-2.64***	-0.01	-0.03	-0.95***	-3.01***	-0.03	-0.26
	(0.03)	(0.60)	(0.05)	(0.51)	(0.03)	(0.13)	(0.04)	(0.49)	(0.03)	(0.15)	(0.49)	(1.13)
3. 2 + Country fixed effects	-0.52***	-0.62*			-0.61***	-0.39			-0.73***	-0.45		
	(0.03)	(0.28)			(0.03)	(0.30)			(0.03)	(0.51)		
4. 3 + Demographics	-0.04	-0.21	-0.04	-0.21	-0.01	-0.16	-0.01	-0.16	-0.09**	-0.43	-0.09**	-0.43
	(0.05)	(0.53)	(0.05)	(0.53)	(0.04)	(0.50)	(0.04)	(0.50)	(0.04)	(1.13)	(0.03)	(1.13)
5. 4 + Health controls	-0.04	-0.16	-0.04	-0.16	-0.35***	0.08	-0.35***	0.08	-0.56***	0.37	-0.56***	0.37
	(0.05)	(0.49)	(0.05)	(0.49)	(0.04)	(0.62)	(0.04)	(0.62)	(0.04)	(1.14)	(0.04)	(1.14)

Higher-skilled workers

	SR_Ret				NW1_Ret				NW2_Ret			
	OLS	IV	FE	IV–FE	OLS	IV	FE	IV–FE	OLS	IV	FE	IV–FE
1. No controls	-0.70***	-1.54***	0.04	-0.66***	-0.60***	-1.51***	-0.02	-0.74***	-0.68***	-1.92***	-0.11*	-0.95***
	(0.04)	(0.05)	(0.05)	(0.16)	(0.03)	(0.05)	(0.04)	(0.15)	(0.04)	(0.07)	(0.04)	(0.19)
2. Years, cohorts, gender	-0.39***	-1.55***	0.08	-2.27	-0.36***	-1.69***	0.03	-1.6	-0.55***	-2.09***	-0.07	-2.19
	(0.05)	(0.16)	(0.05)	(1.56)	(0.04)	(0.17)	(0.05)	(1.05)	(0.04)	(0.24)	(0.05)	(2.30)
3. 2 + Country fixed effects	-0.39***	-0.03			-0.35***	0.08			-0.56***	0.37		
	(0.05)	(0.75)			(0.04)	(0.62)			(0.04)	(1.14)		
4. 3 + Demographics	-0.39***	-0.06	0.07	-2.27	-0.35***	0.03	0.01	-1.63	-0.55***	0.24	-0.08	-2.02
	(0.05)	(0.75)	(0.05)	(1.57)	(0.04)	(0.61)	(0.05)	(1.05)	(0.04)	(1.11)	(0.05)	(2.21)
5. 4 + Health controls	-0.26***	-0.34	0.07	-2.04	-0.19***	-0.24	0.01	-1.7	-0.39***	-0.34	-0.06	-2.19
	(0.05)	(0.64)	(0.06)	(1.32)	(0.04)	(0.56)	(0.05)	(0.97)	(0.04)	(0.88)	(0.05)	(1.93)

Notes: Ordinary Least Squares (OLS); Instrumental Variable Methods (IV); Fixed Effects (FE); Instrumental Variable Fixed Effect Methods (IV–FE). Retirement definitions: SR_Ret is based on self-reports of current job status; NW1_Ret includes homemakers along with those who say they are sick or disabled into the set of retirees, but conditions on working at the age of 50; NW2_Ret defines as retired all those who are not working now.

Source: Authors' computations.

TABLE 4.6 Effect of retirement on cognition for all countries by physically demanding job

Physically demanding job

	SR_Ret				NW1_Ret				NW2_Ret			
	OLS	IV	FE	IV-FE	OLS	IV	FE	IV-FE	OLS	IV	FE	IV-FE
1. No controls	-0.33*** (0.09)	-1.81*** (0.18)	-0.19* (0.08)	-0.32 (0.17)	-0.24** (0.08)	-1.61*** (0.16)	-0.18** (0.07)	-0.44** (0.16)	-0.30*** (0.08)	-2.84*** (0.29)	-0.15* (0.07)	-0.55** (0.19)
2. Years, cohorts, gender	-0.47*** (0.10)	-2.86*** (0.35)	-0.18 (0.10)	0.13 (1.30)	-0.31*** (0.57)	-2.81*** (0.34)	-0.13 (0.09)	-0.37 (1.14)	-0.48*** (0.10)	-4.77*** (0.25)	-0.09 (0.09)	1.28 (2.92)
3. 2 + Country fixed effects	-0.17 (0.11)	2.28 (1.93)			-0.07 (0.09)	1.87 (1.50)			-0.34*** (0.10)	3.61 (4.32)		
4. 3 + Demographics	-0.14 (0.11)	2.69 (2.17)	0.13 (1.30)	-0.19 (0.10)	-0.05 (0.09)	-0.23* (0.10)	-0.37 (1.14)	-0.13 (0.09)	2.11 (1.59)	3.21 (3.16)	1.28 (2.92)	-0.09 (0.09)
5. 4 + Health controls	-0.03 (0.11)	1.39 (1.79)	-0.17 (0.11)	-0.35 (1.33)	0.05 (0.09)	-0.10 (0.10)	-0.11 (0.10)	-0.75 (1.14)	1.04 (1.43)	4.95 (4.10)	-0.05 (0.09)	-0.07 (2.46)

Not physically demanding job

	SR_Ret				NW1_Ret				NW2_Ret			
	OLS	IV	FE	IV-FE	OLS	IV	FE	IV-FE	OLS	IV	FE	IV-FE
1. No controls	-0.37*** (0.04)	-1.87*** (0.09)	0.10* (0.04)	-0.08 (0.08)	-0.29*** (0.04)	-1.61*** (0.08)	0.07* (0.03)	-0.20* (0.08)	-0.25*** (0.05)	-3.01*** (0.16)	-0.02 (0.04)	-0.26** (0.10)
2. Years, cohorts, gender	-0.56*** (0.05)	-3.33 (0.18)	0.14** (0.05)	0.35 (1.05)	-0.42*** (0.23)	-3.28*** (0.17)	0.12** (0.04)	0.29 (0.69)	-0.47*** (0.07)	-5.52*** (0.34)	0.02 (0.04)	2.23 (2.94)
3. 2 + Country fixed effects	-0.20*** (0.05)	-0.39 (0.90)			-0.15** (0.05)	0.12 (0.71)			-0.36*** (0.05)	7.07 (6.27)		
4. 3 + Demographics	-0.19*** (0.05)	-0.51 (0.93)	0.13* (0.05)	0.45 (1.12)	-0.12** (0.04)	0.33 (0.71)	0.12** (0.04)	0.32 (0.70)	-0.28*** (0.05)	6.65 (9.11)	0.03 (0.04)	2.36 (2.85)
5. 4 + Health controls	-0.14** (0.05)	-0.75 (0.78)	0.12* (0.05)	0.32 (0.90)	-0.07 (0.04)	-0.10 (0.66)	0.11* (0.04)	0.22 (0.62)	-0.21*** (0.05)	3.05 (3.18)	0.02 (0.05)	3.70 (3.49)

Notes: Ordinary Least Squares (OLS); Instrumental Variable Methods (IV); Fixed Effects (FE); Instrumental Variable Fixed Effect Methods (IV-FE). Retirement definitions: SR_Ret is based on self-reports of current job status; NW1_Ret includes homemakers along with those who say they are sick or disabled into the set of retirees, but conditions on working at the age of 50; NW2_Ret defines as retired all those who are not working now.

Source: Authors' computations.

cognitive decline. Our review of the literature suggests that the effects of those estimates are equally fragile.

Appendix

Appendix A: Data Description

We use data from several longitudinal surveys of the over-50 population: the Health and Retirement Study (HRS) for the US, the English Longitudinal Study of Ageing (ELSA) for England, and the Study of Health, Ageing and Retirement in Europe (SHARE). Since SHARE was introduced in 2004, we focus our analysis on the year 2004 and subsequent waves of all surveys through 2012. We analyze five waves for HRS and ELSA, and four waves for SHARE (wave 3 of SHARE collects life histories and does not contain cognitive abilities variables). HRS, ELSA, and SHARE all cover a wide range of topics including demographics (age, gender, and education), labor supply, income, pension benefits, wealth, health, and cognitive function. They contain identical question wordings whenever possible.

Cognitive Functioning Variables

All three surveys ask several questions about cognitive functioning. Their measures of cognitive abilities are comparable and follow similar interview procedures. Here we describe the construction of the word recall variable for each survey.

HRS: The interviewer read a list of ten nouns (e.g., lake, car, army, etc.) to the respondent. Immediate word recall: After reading the list, individuals were asked to recall as many words as possible. The list could be given in any order. Between waves, the list of nouns may have changed. Delayed word recall: After approximately five minutes of being asked other survey questions (e.g., about other cognition items), individuals were asked to recall the list again in any order. The sum of the outcomes of both Immediate Word Recall (10 words) and Delayed Word Recall (10 words) is used to build a recall summary score. Values range from 0 to 20.

ELSA: A list of ten nouns could be read from a computer screen or by the interviewer if there were technical issues. Respondents were given the following instructions:

> The computer will now read a set of 10 words. I would like you to recall as many as you can. We have purposely made the list long so it will be difficult for anyone to recall all the words. Please listen carefully to the set of words as they

cannot be repeated. When it has finished, I will ask you to recall aloud as many of the words as you can, in any order. Is this clear?

After several other questions were asked, the respondent was asked to recall the words again. The summary test recall score is the sum of both immediate and delayed word recall for a maximum of 20. Values range from 0 to 20.

SHARE: As in ELSA, a list of ten nouns could be read from a computer screen. At the beginning of the immediate word recall exercise, the interviewer read this message:

Please listen carefully, as the set of words cannot be repeated. When I have finished, I will ask you to recall aloud as many of the words as you can, in any order. Is this clear?

As in the HRS, for the delayed word recall the respondent was asked to recall the words again after several questions were asked about other cognitive abilities. The summary test recall score is again the sum of both the immediate and delayed word recall for a maximum of 20. A drawback of SHARE is that all respondents in the household in waves 1 and 2 could receive the exact same test each time. The survey corrected this issue in waves 4 and 5.

Retirement

All three surveys ask similar questions about current work status and retirement status.

HRS measures self-reported work status by asking: (1) working now, (2) unemployed and looking for work, (3) temporarily laid off, on sick or other leave, (4) disabled, (5) retired, (6) homemaker, (7) other (specify). For the salaried workers, there is a follow-up question whether individuals are currently working for pay.

ELSA measures self-reported work status by asking: (1) retired, (2) employed, (3) self-employed, (4) unemployed, (5) permanently sick or disabled, (6) looking after home or family, (7) other, and (8) spontaneous: semi-retired.

SHARE measures self-reported work status by asking: (1) retired, (2) employed or self-employed (including working for family business), (3) unemployed and looking for work, (4) permanently sick or disabled, (5) homemaker, (6) other (renter, living off own property, student, doing voluntary work).

We define three binary measures of retirement: SR_Ret is based on self-reported current work status; NW1_Ret also includes as retired homemakers, sick or disabled, and those non-temporarily away from the labor force (if respondents declared they worked at age 50); NW2_Ret includes all those who are not working now.

Other Covariates

Demographic variables include age, age-squared, female, being married or in a couple, and interactions with being female. Other controls include as cohort, years and country dummies, and three education levels (tertiary, secondary, and primary).

Several health variables are used. A binary indicator is included for having at least one major chronic condition from a list including cancer, lung disease, heart attack, and stroke. A second indicates having at least one minor chronic condition from a list including hypertension, diabetes, and arthritis. Self-reported health is also included (= 1 if the individual reports bad or poor health and 0 otherwise). Impairment indicators (ADLA and iADLA) for limitations with daily activities are also considered. Similar questions are asked in all surveys about difficulties in five basic activities: bathing, dressing, eating, getting in and out of bed, and walking across a room. Individuals are classified as having any ADL limitation if they reported limitations with one or more of the five activities. Those who reported having some difficulty with preparing meals, shopping, making phone calls, taking medications, and managing money are classified as having an iADL limitation.

Physically demanding jobs are coded as follows. ELSA distinguishes four categories: sedentary occupation, standing occupation, physical work, and heavy manual work. We set the variable 'physically demanding job' equal to 1 for the last two categories, and 0 otherwise. HRS asks directly if the current job requires physical effort 'whether all/almost all the time', 'most of the time', 'some of the time', and 'none/almost none of the time'. We set a 'physically demanding job' variable equal to 1 for 'all/almost all the time', and 0 otherwise. In SHARE, individuals are asked: 'My job is physically demanding. Would you say you "strongly agree", "agree", "disagree" or "strongly disagree"?' In our analyses the 'physically demanding job' variable is set to 1 for 'strongly agree', and 0 otherwise. Our blue-collar and white-collar definitions are based on SHARE's ISCO coding and the HRS 1980 and 2000 census coding. For ELSA we use the categories in the SOC2010 volume 3: the National Statistics Socio-Economic classification (NS-SEC rebased on SOC2010). Blue-collar jobs are defined as those that involve routine or manual work; white-collar jobs are defined as managerial and professional occupations or intermediate occupations.

TABLE 4A.1 Descriptive statistics

Variable	ALL COUNTRIES					SHARE				
	Obs.	Mean	Std. dev.	Min.	Max.	Obs.	Mean	Std. dev.	Min.	Max.
Words recalled (0–20 scale)	169,487	10.36	3.38	0	20	91,485	9.86	3.41	0	20
SR_Ret	142,545	0.47	0.50	0	1	75,733	0.51	0.50	0	1
NW1_Ret	157,945	0.52	0.50	0	1	84,831	0.56	0.50	0	1
NW2_Ret	173,559	0.49	0.50	0	1	92,422	0.52	0.50	0	1
Age	174,395	60.51	5.70	50	70	93,061	60.29	5.73	50	70
Female	174,395	0.55	0.50	0	1	93,061	0.54	0.50	0	1
Married	171,965	0.79	0.41	0	1	90,653	0.82	0.39	0	1
Education	167,031	1.84	0.72	1	3	89,422	1.91	0.63	1	3
Skill: 1 Unskilled	167,031	0.64	0.48	0	1	89,422	0.75	0.43	0	1
Bad health	168,452	0.24	0.43	0	1	93,061	0.26	0.44	0	1
ADLAs	173,896	0.08	0.28	0	1	92,679	0.06	0.23	0	1
IADLAs	173,888	0.03	0.17	0	1	92,679	0.02	0.13	0	1
Minor conditions	173,884	0.56	0.50	0	1	92,623	0.46	0.50	0	1
Major conditions	173,836	0.22	0.41	0	1	92,623	0.17	0.37	0	1
Physically demanding job	54,202	0.22	0.41	0	1	19,141	0.20	0.40	0	1
Occupation: 1 Blue-collar	62,516	0.39	0.49	0	1	18,115	0.47	0.50	0	1

Variable	ELSA					HRS				
	Obs.	Mean	Std. dev.	Min.	Max.	Obs.	Mean	Std. dev.	Min.	Max.
Words recalled (0–20 scale)	30,567	11.33	3.30	0	20	47,435	10.70	3.18	0	20
SR_Ret	26,900	0.44	0.50	0	1	39,912	0.42	0.49	0	1
NW1_Ret	29,965	0.49	0.50	0	1	43,149	0.47	0.50	0	1
NW2_Ret	31,609	0.48	0.50	0	1	49,528	0.44	0.50	0	1
Age	31,630	60.57	5.42	50	70	49,704	60.89	5.77	50	70

(continued)

TABLE 4A.1 Continued

Variable	ELSA					HRS				
	Obs.	Mean	Std. dev.	Min.	Max.	Obs.	Mean	Std. dev.	Min.	Max.
Female	31,630	0.54	0.50	0	1	49,704	0.57	0.50	0	1
Married	31,622	0.78	0.41	0	1	49,690	0.74	0.44	0	1
Education	27,917	1.96	0.89	1	3	49,692	1.64	0.73	1	3
Skill: 1 Unskilled	27,917	0.58	0.49	0	1	49,692	0.49	0.50	0	1
Bad health	25,687	0.21	0.41	0	1	49,704	0.23	0.42	0	1
ADLAs	31,612	0.12	0.33	0	1	49,605	0.11	0.31	0	1
IADLAs	31,612	0.03	0.16	0	1	49,597	0.05	0.22	0	1
Minor conditions	31,621	0.55	0.50	0	1	49,640	0.74	0.44	0	1
Major conditions	31,621	0.23	0.42	0	1	49,592	0.31	0.46	0	1
Physically demanding job	11,612	0.28	0.45	0	1	23,449	0.20	0.40	0	1
Occupation: 1 Blue-collar	19,851	0.39	0.49	0	1	24,550	0.33	0.47	0	1

Notes: The following are the variables listed in the above table: Survey of Health, Ageing and Retirement in Europe (SHARE), English Longitudinal Study of Ageing (ELSA), and US Health and Retirement Study (HRS).

Source: Authors' computations.

Appendix B: Early and Full Retirement Ages

TABLE 4A.2 Early and full retirement ages across the OECD nations

Early and full retirement ages (full retirement ages in parentheses)

Country	2004		2006		2008		2010		2012	
	Males	Females	Males	Females	Males	Females	Males	Females	Males	Females
Austria	65(65)	60(60)	65(65)	65(65)	65(65)	65(65)	62(65)	60(65)	62(65)	62(65)
Belgium	60(65)	60(65)	60(65)	60(65)	60(65)	60(65)	60(65)	60(65)	62(65)	62(65)
Czech Republic	60(65)	58(63)	60(65)	58(63)	60(65)	60(64)	60(65)	60(64)	64(69)	64(69)
Denmark	65(65)	65(65)	65(65)	65(65)	65(65)	65(65)	67(67)	67(67)	67(67)	67(67)
France	60(60)	60(60)	60(60)	60(60)	61(61)	61(61)	56–60(65)	56–60(65)	60(67)	60(67)
Germany	63(65)	63(65)	63(65)	63(65)	63(67)	63(67)	63(67)	63(67)	63(67)	63(67)
Italy	60(65)	60(65)	60(65)	60(60)	60(65)	60(60)	61(65)	60(60)	62(67)	62(67)
Netherlands	60(65)	60(65)	60(65)	60(65)	60(65)	60(65)	65(65)	65(65)	67(67)	67(67)
Spain	60(65)	60(65)	60(65)	60(65)	60(65)	60(65)	61(65)	61(65)	65(67)	65(67)
Sweden	61(65)	61(65)	61(65)	61(65)	61(65)	61(65)	61(65)	61(65)	61(65)	61(65)
Switzerland	63(65)	62(64)	63(65)	62(64)	63(65)	62(64)	63(65)	62(64)	63(65)	62(64)
England	65(65)	65(65)	68(68)	68(68)	68(68)	68(68)	68(68)	68(68)	68(68)	68(68)
United States*	62(65+)	62(65+)	62(65+)	62(65+)	62(65+)	62(65+)	62(65+)	62(65+)	62(65+)	62(65+)

*Full retirement age depends on birth year.

Sources: OECD *Pensions at a Glance* several years.

Appendix C: First State Estimations

TABLE 4A.3 First-stage results, pooled data

Dependent variables		SR_Ret	NW1_Ret	NW2_Ret
			First stage	
1. No controls	*Above full retirement age*	0.25***	0.22***	0.20***
		(0.003)	(0.003)	(0.003)
	Above early retirement age	0.42***	0.38***	0.29***
		(0.003)	(0.003)	(0.003)
2. Years, cohorts, gender	*Above full retirement age*	0.48***	0.04***	0.04***
		(0.004)	(0.004)	(0.004)
	Above early retirement age	0.14***	0.12***	0.08***
		(0.003)	(0.003)	(0.003)
3. 2 + Country fixed effects	*Above full retirement age*	0.031***	0.025***	0.022***
		(0.004)	(0.004)	(0.004)
	Above early retirement age	0.10***	0.10***	0.05***
		(0.003)	(0.003)	(0.003)
4. 3 + Demographics	*Above full retirement age*	0.035***	0.025***	0.024***
		(0.004)	(0.004)	(0.004)
	Above early retirement age	0.10***	0.10***	0.05***
		(0.003)	(0.003)	(0.003)
5. 4 + Health controls	*Above full retirement age*	0.05***	0.04***	0.08***
		(0.004)	(0.004)	(0.19)
	Above early retirement age	0.12***	0.11***	0.03
		(0.003)	(0.003)	(0.02)

Notes: The following are the variables listed in the above table: self-reports of current job status (SR_Ret), homemakers with those who say they are sick or disabled (NW1_Ret), and all those who are not working now (NW2_Ret).

Source: Authors' computations.

TABLE 4A.4 First-stage results by skill group, pooled data

Dependent variables		First stage: unskilled workers			First stage: middle and skilled workers		
		SR_Ret	NW1_Ret	NW2_Ret	SR_Ret	NW1_Ret	NW2_Ret
1. No controls	Above full retirement age	0.22***	0.19***	0.18***	0.30***	0.27***	0.23***
		(0.00)	(0.00)	(0.00)	(0.00)	(0.00)	(0.00)
	Above early retirement age	0.45***	0.39***	0.29***	0.34***	0.35***	0.25***
		(0.00)	(0.00)	(0.00)	(0.00)	(0.00)	(0.00)
2. Years, cohorts, gender	Above full retirement age	0.04***	0.04***	0.04***	0.03***	0.03***	0.02*
		(0.00)	(0.00)	(0.00)	(0.00)	(0.00)	(0.00)
	Above early retirement age	0.16***	0.13***	0.08***	0.06***	0.07***	0.03***
		(0.00)	(0.00)	(0.00)	(0.00)	(0.00)	(0.00)
3. 2 + Country fixed effects	Above full retirement age	0.03***	0.03***	0.02***	0.03***	0.02**	0.02**
		(0.00)	(0.00)	(0.00)	(0.00)	(0.00)	(0.00)
	Above early retirement age	0.12***	0.11***	0.06***	0.05***	0.07***	0.03***
		(0.00)	(0.00)	(0.00)	(0.00)	(0.00)	(0.00)
4. 3 + Demographics	Above full retirement age	0.03***	0.02***	0.02***	0.03***	0.01**	0.02*
		(0.00)	(0.00)	(0.00)	(0.00)	(0.00)	(0.00)
	Above early retirement age	012***	011***	0.06***	0.06***	0.07***	0.03***
		(0.00)	(0.00)	(0.00)	(0.00)	(0.00)	(0.00)
5. 4 + Health controls	Above full retirement age	0.04***	0.03***	0.03***	0.04***	0.03***	0.03***
		(0.00)	(0.00)	(0.00)	(0.00)	(0.00)	(0.00)
	Above early retirement age	0.13***	0.11***	0.06***	0.06***	0.08***	0.05***
		(0.00)	(0.00)	(0.00)	(0.00)	(0.00)	(0.00)

Notes: The following are the variables listed in the above table: self-reports of current job status (SR_Ret), homemakers with those who say they are sick or disabled (NW1_Ret), and all those who are not working now (NW2_Ret).

Source: Authors' computations.

TABLE 4A.5 First-stage results by physically demanding jobs groups, pooled data

	Dependent variables	SR_Ret	NW1_Ret	NW2_Ret	SR_Ret	NW1_Ret	NW2_Ret
		First stage: physically demanding job			First stage: more intellectual job		
1. No controls	Above full retirement age	0.25***	0.23***	0.13***	0.28***	0.27***	0.14***
		(0.014)	(0.01)	(0.01)	(0.007)	(0.007)	(0.006)
	Above early retirement age	0.24***	0.26***	0.14***	0.20***	0.25***	0.13***
		(0.011)	(0.01)	(0.01)	(0.005)	(0.005)	(0.005)
2. Years, cohorts, gender	Above full retirement age	0.024***	−0.03**	0.01	0.08***	0.05***	−0.01
		(0.017)	(0.02)	(0.02)	(0.008)	(0.006)	(0.08)
	Above early retirement age	0.07***	0.01	0.09***	0.03***	0.06***	−0.001
		(0.011)	(0.01)	(0.01)	(0.005)	(0.006)	(0.005)
3. 2 + Country fixed effects	Above full retirement age	0.01***	0.00	−0.03	0.06***	0.04***	−0.007
		(0.016)	(0.004)	(0.02)	(0.008)	(0.009)	(0.008)
	Above early retirement age	0.05***	0.07***	0.01	0.03***	0.06***	0.01
		(0.013)	(0.01)	(0.01)	(0.006)	(0.007)	(0.006)
4. 3 + Demographics	Above full retirement age	−0.006	0.014	0.05***	0.06***	0.04***	−0.009
		(0.01)	(0.02)	(0.02)	(0.009)	(0.009)	(0.008)
	Above early retirement age	0.06***	0.07***	0.01	0.03***	0.06***	0.01
		(0.01)	(0.014)	(0.01)	(0.006)	(0.007)	(0.006)
5. 4 + Health controls	Above full retirement age	0.01***	−0.00	−0.03	0.07***	0.05***	0.002
		(0.02)	(0.02)	(0.02)	(0.009)	(0.009)	(0.008)
	Above early retirement age	0.06***	0.07***	0.02*	0.04***	0.07***	0.02***
		(0.01)	(0.01)	(0.01)	(0.006)	(0.007)	(0.006)

Notes: The following are the variables listed in the above table: self-reports of current job status (SR_Ret), homemakers with those who say they are sick or disabled (NW1_Ret), and all those who are not working now (NW2_Ret).

Source: Authors' computations.

TABLE 4A.6 First-stage results by blue-collar jobs and white-collar jobs, pooled data

Dependent variables	SR_Ret	NW1_Ret	NW2_Ret	SR_Ret	NW1_Ret	NW2_Ret
	First stage: blue-collar jobs			First stage: white-collar jobs		
1. No controls						
Above full retirement age	0.27***	0.26***	0.13***	0.27***	0.26***	0.14***
	(0.01)	(0.01)	(0.009)	(0.008)	(0.008)	(0.007)
Above early retirement age	0.25***	0.28***	0.16***	0.18***	0.23***	0.11***
	(0.008)	(0.008)	(0.007)	(0.006)	(0.006)	(0.005)
2. Years, cohorts, gender						
Above full retirement age	0.05***	0.03**	−0.04***	−0.26***	0.05***	−0.003
	(0.012)	(0.013)	(0.012)	(0.012)	(0.01)	(0.009)
Above early retirement age	0.08***	0.10***	0.02***	0.002***	0.04***	−0.02***
	(0.008)	(0.008)	(0.008)	(0.000)	(0.007)	(0.006)
3. 2 + Country fixed effects						
Above full retirement age	0.03***	0.02	−0.04***	0.06***	0.04***	0.001
	(0.012)	(0.013)	(0.012)	(0.01)	(0.01)	(0.009)
Above early retirement age	0.06***	0.08***	0.03***	0.02***	0.05***	−0.02
	(0.009)	(0.01)	(0.009)	(0.007)	(0.008)	(0.007)
4. 3 + Demographics						
Above full retirement age	0.016	0.009	−0.05***	0.06***	0.03***	−0.003
	(0.01)	(0.01)	(0.012)	(0.01)	(0.01)	(0.009)
Above early retirement age	0.06***	0.08***	0.03***	0.02*	0.05***	−0.03
	(0.009)	(0.01)	(0.009)	(0.007)	(0.008)	(0.007)
5. 4 + Health controls						
Above full retirement age	0.02*	0.02	−0.03**	0.07***	0.05***	0.008
	(0.013)	(0.013)	(0.012)	(0.01)	(0.01)	(0.009)
Above early retirement age	0.06***	0.09***	0.03***	0.03***	0.06***	0.005
	(0.009)	(0.01)	(0.009)	(0.008)	(0.008)	(0.007)

Notes: The following are the variables listed in the above table: self-reports of current job status (SR_Ret), homemakers with those who say they are sick or disabled (NW1_Ret), and all those who are not working now (NW2_Ret).

Source: Authors' computations.

Appendix D: Disaggregate Estimates for Each of the Three Surveys: HRS, ELSA, and SHARE

TABLE 4A.7 Effect of retirement on cognition by survey

HRS

	SR_Ret				NW1_Ret				NW2_Ret			
	OLS	IV	FE	IV–FE	OLS	IV	FE	IV–FE	OLS	IV	FE	IV–FE
1. No controls	-1.05***	-1.56***	-0.46***	-1.81***	-0.89***	-1.39***	-0.38***	-1.76***	-1.01***	-1.95***	-0.35***	-2.34***
	(0.04)	(0.06)	(0.06)	(0.16)	(0.04)	(0.06)	(0.05)	(0.13)	(0.04)	(0.08)	(0.04)	(0.17)
2. Years, cohorts, gender	-0.89***	-0.30	-0.12	0.20	-0.73***	-0.12	-0.08	-0.08	-0.98***	0.25	-0.13**	0.35
	(0.05)	(0.45)	(0.06)	(0.5)	(0.05)	(0.43)	(0.05)	(0.43)	(0.04)	(0.73)	(0.05)	(0.70)
3. 2 + Demographics	-0.65***	0.23	-0.12	0.19	-0.53***	0.48	-0.08	-0.09	-0.66***	1.18	-0.13**	0.35
	(0.05)	(0.45)	(0.06)	(0.49)	(0.04)	(0.42)	(0.05)	(0.43)	(0.04)	(0.76)	(0.05)	(0.70)
4. 3 + Health controls	-0.37***	0.14	-0.10	0.18	-0.28***	0.29	-0.06	-0.08	-0.40***	0.77	-0.11*	0.29
	(0.05)	(0.43)	(0.06)	(0.49)	(0.04)	(0.40)	(0.05)	(0.43)	(0.04)	(0.67)	(0.05)	(0.69)

ELSA

	SR_Ret				NW1_Ret				NW2_Ret			
	OLS	IV	FE	IV–FE	OLS	IV	FE	IV–FE	OLS	IV	FE	IV–FE
1. No controls	-0.74	-2.54***	0.03	-1.14*	-0.79***	-2.75***	0.04	-1.64***	-0.90***	-2.94***	0.0002	-1.43**
	(0.05)	(0.1)	(0.06)	(0.48)	(0.05)	(0.11)	(0.05)	(0.50)	(0.05)	(0.12)	(0.05)	(0.46)
2. Years, cohorts, gender	-0.83***	-5.68***	0.04	0.03	-0.98***	-6.19***	0.06	0.42	-1.13***	-8.77***	0.01	0.34
	(0.02)	(0.20)	(0.07)	(0.66)	(0.02)	(0.23)	(0.06)	(0.71)	(0.03)	(0.34)	(0.06)	(0.86)
3. 2 + Demographics	0.07	-1.62*	0.07	-0.18	-0.19**	-1.80	0.08	0.16	-0.34***	-2.29*	0.03	0.11
	(0.07)	(0.76)	(0.07)	(0.70)	(0.06)	(0.94)	(0.06)	(0.75)	(0.06)	(1.14)	(0.06)	(0.90)
4. 3 + Health controls	0.15*	-1.97	0.06	-0.33	-0.28***	-2.49	0.06	-0.15	-0.41***	-3.24	0.05	-0.30
	(0.07)	(1.20)	(0.08)	(0.83)	(0.02)	(1.50)	(0.07)	(0.87)	(0.02)	(1.85)	(0.07)	(1.10)

SHARE	SR_Ret				NW1_Ret				NW2_Ret			
	OLS	IV	FE	IV–FE	OLS	IV	FE	IV–FE	OLS	IV	FE	IV–FE
1. No controls	-1.29***	-1.84***	0.38***	0.91***	-1.33***	-2.02***	0.32***	0.99***	-1.43***	-2.31**	0.13**	1.93***
	(0.03)	(0.04)	(0.05)	(0.12)	(0.03)	(0.04)	(0.04)	(0.13)	(0.03)	(0.04)	(0.04)	(0.22)
2. Years, cohorts, gender	-0.75***	-2.13***	-0.04	-0.189	-1.04***	-2.38***	-0.02	0.12	-1.15***	-2.49***	-0.07	0.39
	(0.04)	(0.19)	(0.05)	(0.38)	(0.03)	(0.25)	(0.05)	(0.43)	(0.03)	(0.26)	(0.05)	(0.89)
3. 2 + Country fixed effects	-0.52***	-0.84***			-0.75***	-0.57			-0.83***	-0.65		
	(0.04)	(0.24)			(0.03)	(0.30)			(0.03)	(0.37)		
4. 3 + Demographics	-0.31***	-0.65***	-0.04	-0.19	-1.03***	-2.38***	-0.01	0.12	-1.15***	-2.49***	-0.07	0.39
	(0.04)	(0.24)	(0.05)	(0.38)	(0.03)	(0.25)	(0.05)	(0.43)	(0.03)	(0.26)	(0.04)	(0.88)
5. 4 + Health controls	-0.21***	-0.66**	-0.04	-0.28	-0.75***	-0.56	-0.01	-0.03	-0.83***	-0.65	-0.06	0.09
	(0.04)	(0.23)	(0.056)	(0.40)	(0.03)	(0.30)	(0.05)	(0.45)	(0.03)	(0.37)	(0.04)	(0.89)

Notes: The following are the variables listed in the above table: self-reports of current job status (SR_Ret), homemakers with those who say they are sick or disabled (NW1_Ret), and all those who are not working now (NW2_Ret).

Source: Authors' computations.

Appendix E: Comparing Blue-Collar and White-Collar Jobs

TABLE 4A.8 Effect of retirement on cognition, pooled data by occupation

Blue-collar workers

	SR_Ret				NW1_Ret				NW2_Ret			
	OLS	IV	FE	IV–FE	OLS	IV	FE	IV–FE	OLS	IV	FE	IV–FE
1. No controls	-0.27***	-1.46***	0.02	-0.003	-0.23***	-1.37***	0.03	-0.13	-0.20**	-2.40***	0.02	-0.16
	(0.06)	(0.12)	(0.06)	(0.11)	(0.06)	(0.11)	(0.05)	(0.11)	(0.06)	(0.20)	(0.05)	(0.13)
2. Years, cohorts, gender	-0.35***	-2.51***	-0.04	0.06	-0.21***	-2.29***	0.03	-0.33	-0.35***	-5.48***	0.03	0.56
	(0.07)	(0.37)	(0.07)	(0.84)	(0.06)	(0.32)	(0.06)	(0.68)	(0.07)	(1.01)	(0.06)	(1.59)
3. 2 + Country fixed effects	-0.18*	0.034			-0.08	0.90			-0.27***	0.65		
	(0.07)	(0.38)			(0.06)	(0.32)			(0.07)	(0.74)		
4. 3 + Demographics	-0.16*	0.10	-0.003	-0.25	-0.08	0.25	0.06	-0.62	-0.17*	1.80	0.05	-0.07
	(0.07)	(1.28)	(0.07)	(0.89)	(0.07)	(0.89)	(0.06)	(0.70)	(0.07)	(1.91)	(0.06)	(1.54)
5. 4 + Health controls	-0.10	-0.04	0.002	0.13	-0.04	0.06	0.04	-0.32	-0.09	1.59	0.06	-0.26
	(0.07)	(1.12)	(0.08)	(0.84)	(0.07)	(0.85)	(0.07)	(0.67)	(0.07)	(1.96)	(0.07)	(1.56)

White-collar workers

	SR_Ret				NW1_Ret				NW2_Ret			
	OLS	IV	FE	IV–FE	OLS	IV	FE	IV–FE	OLS	IV	FE	IV–FE
1. No controls	-0.35***	-2.16***	0.03	-0.26*	-0.27***	-1.76***	-0.01	-0.37***	-0.28***	-3.42***	-0.12**	-0.49***
	(0.05)	(0.11)	(0.05)	(0.10)	(0.05)	(0.09)	(0.04)	(0.10)	(0.05)	(0.19)	(0.04)	(0.12)
2. Years, cohorts, gender	-0.48***	-3.45***	0.13*	0.96	-0.33**	-3.35***	0.09	0.85	-0.50***	-5.44***	-0.05	-1.37
	(0.06)	(0.21)	(0.06)	(1.79)	(0.05)	(0.19)	(0.05)	(1.05)	(0.06)	(0.39)	(0.05)	(4.81)
3. 2 + Country fixed effects	-0.15*	0.23			-0.09	1.02			-0.30***	-4.29		
	(0.06)	(1.19)			(0.05)	(0.98)			(0.06)	(0.48)		
4. 3 + Demographics	-0.16*	-0.25	0.10	0.75	-0.08	1.03	0.06	0.97	-0.32***	-12.51	-0.04	0.44
	(0.06)	(1.28)	(0.06)	(1.96)	(0.05)	(1.01)	(0.05)	(1.09)	(0.06)	(24.73)	(0.05)	(5.16)
5. 4 + Health controls	-0.09	-0.76	0.10	-0.20	-0.02	0.06	0.07	0.29	-0.23***	-2.47	-0.04	21.33
	(0.06)	(1.02)	(0.06)	(1.35)	(0.05)	(0.90)	(0.05)	(0.91)	(0.06)	(7.75)	(0.05)	(56.33)

Notes: The following are the variables listed in the above table: self-reports of current job status (SR_Ret), homemakers with those who say they are sick or disabled (NW1_Ret), and all those who are not working now (NW2_Ret).

Source: Authors' computations.

Notes

1. See Cattell (1941), Horn (1965), Horn and Cattell (1967), and Carroll (1993) for details.
2. We need to keep in mind possible measurement errors in using these variables and the context in which cognitive tests are conducted (Morris et al. 1999). These include retesting effects: performance tends to improve when individuals repeat cognitive tests (Ferrer et al. 2004; Rabbitt et al. 2001; Schaie 1996; McArdle and Woodcock 1997).
3. Leisure activities, lifestyle, and social networks are thought to affect cognitive functioning. The idea behind this is that engaging in activities that stimulate an individual's brain may maintain or repair cognitive functioning. Some evidence for the importance of social contacts at older ages can be found in Hertzog et al. (2008), Salthouse (2006), Scarmeas and Stern (2003), Fratiglioni et al. (2004), and Börsch-Supan and Schuth (2013) among others. Some studies relate personality traits like patience and risk aversion to cognition (e.g., Frederick 2005; Benjamin et al. 2006; Dohmen et al. 2007; Midanik et al. 1995).
4. More details about the datasets and variables can be found in Appendix A.
5. See Appendix A for details.
6. Adam et al. (2007a) exclude from the analysis the respondents that cannot recall any words.
7. Adam et al. (2007a) use five dummy variables to define the retirement status in order to capture the retirement duration. The category of working variables was their reference variable and the other variables were ranges as < 5 years retired, [5–9], [10–15], more than 15 years retired and having never worked.
8. The thirteen countries are: Austria, Belgium, Czech Republic, Denmark, France, Germany, Italy, the Netherlands, Spain, Sweden, Switzerland, US, and UK.
9. We also run the models separately for each of the three surveys HRS, ELSA, and SHARE. Results can be found in Appendix D. The OLS estimates confirm the same results through the different surveys. The IV and IV–FE results vary somewhat across surveys but generally retirement is only found to have a significant negative effect on cognition in the models without country fixed effects.
10. The ages for the US refer to Social Security-claiming ages rather than retirement ages; 62 is the earliest age at which one can claim Social Security. For comparison purposes we treat the US early-claiming age and full retirement age similar to the treatment of early and full retirement ages in the European countries.
11. First-stage estimates are presented in Appendix C and show that the instruments are positively related to the retirement variables. These estimates show that the instruments in general continue to be good predictors of retirement despite the multiple definitions of retirement and the alternative specifications. Their coefficients decrease when controls are introduced but they remain significant at 1 percent in almost all cases.

References

Adam, S., E. Bonsang, S. Germain, and S. Perelman (2007a). 'Retirement and Cognitive Reserve: A Stochastic Frontier Approach Applied to Survey Data'. HECULg, CREPP Working Papers No. 4.

Adam, S., M. Van der Linden, A. Ivanoiu, A. C. Juillerat, S. Béchet, and E. Salmon (2007b). 'Optimization of Encoding Specificity for the Diagnosis of Early AD: The RI-48 Task'. *Journal of Clinical and Experimental Neuropsychology* 29(5): 477–87.

Albert, S. M., S. Glied, H. Andrews, Y. Stern, and R. Mayeux (2002). 'Primary Care Expenditures Before the Onset of Alzheimer's Disease'. *Neurology* 59(4): 573–8.

Anderson, N. D. and F. I. M. Craik (2000). 'Memory in the Aging Brain'. In E. Tulving and F. I. M. Craik (eds.), *The Oxford Handbook of Memory*. Oxford: Oxford University Press, pp. 411–25.

Angrist, J. D. and J.-S. Pischke (2015). *Mastering 'Metrics: The Path from Cause to Effect*. Princeton, NJ: Princeton University Press.

Atchley, R. C. (1976). *The Sociology of Retirement*. New York: Halsted Press.

Atchley, R. C. (1982). 'Retirement as a Sociological Institution'. *Annual Review of Sociology* 8(1): 263–87.

Bäckman, L., S. Jones, A. K. Berger, E. J. Laukka, and B. J. Small (2005). 'Cognitive Impairment in Preclinical Alzheimer's Disease: A Meta-Analysis'. *Neuropsychology* 19(4): 520–31.

Banks, J. and F. Mazzonna (2012). 'The Effect of Education on Old Age Cognitive Abilities: Evidence from a Regression Discontinuity Design'. *The Economic Journal* 122(560): 418–48.

Banks, J., C. O'Dea, and Z. Oldfield (2010). 'Cognitive Function, Numeracy and Retirement Saving Trajectories'. *The Economic Journal* 120(548): F381–F410.

Benjamin, D., S. Brown, and J. Shapiro (2006). 'Who is "Behavioral"? Cognitive Ability and Anomalous Preferences'. *Journal of the European Economic Association* 11(6): 1231–55.

Bianchini, L. and M. Borella (2014). 'Cognitive Functioning and Retirement in Europe'. CeRP Working Paper No. 139. Turin: Center for Research on Pensions and Welfare Policies.

Bingley, P. and A. Martinello (2013). 'Mental Retirement and Schooling'. *European Economic Review* 63(c): 292–8.

Bonsang, E., S. Adam, and S. Perelman (2012). 'Does Retirement Affect Cognitive Functioning?' *Journal of Health Economics* 31(13): 490–501.

Börsch-Supan, A. and M. Schuth (2013). 'Early Retirement, Mental Health and Social Networks'. In D. A. Wise (ed.), *Discoveries in the Economics of Aging*. Chicago, IL: University of Chicago Press, pp. 225–54.

Bound, J. and T. Waidmann (2007). 'Estimating the Health Effects of Retirement'. MRRC Working Paper No. 168. Ann Arbor, MI: Michigan Retirement Research Center.

Brown, J. R., A. Kapteyn, E. F. P. Luttmer, and O. S. Mitchell (2012). 'Cognitive Constraints on Valuing Annuities'. NBER Working Paper No. 19168. Cambridge, MA: National Bureau of Economic of Research.

Carroll, J. B. (1993). *Human Cognitive Abilities: A Survey of Factor-Analytic Studies*. Cambridge: Cambridge University Press.

Cattell, R. B. (1941). 'Some Theoretical Issues in Adult Intelligence Testing'. *Psychological Bulletin* 38(7): 592–3.

Celidoni, M., C. Dal Bianco, and G. Weber (2013). 'Early Retirement and Cognitive Decline: A Longitudinal Analysis using SHARE Data'. 'Marco Fanno' Working Paper No. 174. Padua: Department of Economics and Management, University of Padua.

Charles, K. K. (2004). 'Is Retirement Depressing? Labor Force Inactivity and Psychological Well-Being in Later Life'. *Research in Labor Economics* 23: 269–99.

Christelis, D., T. Jappelli, and M. Padula (2010). 'Cognitive Abilities and Portfolio Choice'. *European Economic Review* 54 (1): 18–38.

Coe, N. B. and M. Lindeboom (2008). 'Does Retirement Kill You? Evidence from Early Retirement Windows'. CentER Discussion Paper Series No. 93. Chestnut Hill, MA: Center for Retirement Research.

Coe N. B., H. M. von Gaudecker, M. Lindeboom, and J. Maurer (2012). 'The Effect of Retirement on Cognitive Functioning'. *Health Economics* 21(8): 913–27.

Coe, N. B. and G. Zamarro (2011). 'Retirement Effects on Health in Europe'. *Journal of Health Economics* 30(1): 77–86.

Dave, D., I. Rashad, and J. Spasojevic (2008). 'The Effects of Retirement on Physical and Mental Health Outcomes'. *Southern Economic Journal* 75(2): 497–523.

Dixon, R., L. Backman, and L. G. Nilsson (2004). *New Frontiers in Cognitive Aging*. Oxford: Oxford University Press.

Dohmen, T., A. Falk, D. Huffman, and U. Sunde (2007). 'Are Risk Aversion and Impatience Related to Cognitive Ability?' *American Economic Review* 100(3): 1238–60.

Ekerdt, D. J., R. Bosse, and J. S. Locastro (1983). 'Claims that Retirement Improves Health'. *Journal of Gerontology* 38(2): 231–6.

Evans D. A., L. A. Beckett, M. S. Albert, L. E. Hebert, P. A. Scherr, H. H. Funkenstein, and J. O. Taylor (1993). 'Level of Education and Change in Cognitive Function in a Community Population of Older Persons'. *Annals of Epidemiology* 3(1): 71–7.

Ferrer, E., T. A. Salthouse, W. F. Stewart, and B. S. Schwartz (2004). 'Modeling Age and Retest Processes in Longitudinal Studies of Cognitive Abilities'. *Psychology and Aging* 19(2): 243–59.

Fratiglioni, L., S. Paillard-Borg, and B. Winblad (2004). 'An Active and Socially Integrated Lifestyle in Late Life Might Protect Against Dementia'. *The Lancet, Neurology* 3(6): 343–53.

Frederick, S. (2005). 'Cognitive Reflection and Decision Making'. *Journal of Economic Perspectives* 19(4): 25–42.

Gall, L. T., D. R. Evans, and J. Howard (1997). 'The Retirement Adjustment Process: Changes in the Well-Being of Male Retirees Across Time'. *Journal of Gerontology Series B: Psychological Sciences and Social Sciences* 52(3) 110–17.

Glymour, M. M., I. Kawachi, C. S. Jencks, and L. F. Berkman (2008). 'Does Childhood Schooling Affect Old Age Memory or Mental Status? Using State Schooling Laws as Natural Experiments'. *Journal of Epidemiology and Community Health* 62(6): 532–7.

Halpern, D. F. (2012). *Sex Differences in Cognitive Abilities*. New York: Psychology Press.

Hertzog, C., A. F. Kramer, R. Wilson, and U. Lindenberg (2008). 'Enrichment Effects on Adult Cognitive Development: Can the Functional Capacity of Older Adults be Preserved and Enhanced?' *Psychological Science in the Public Interest* 9(1): 1–65.

Horn, J. L. (1965). 'Fluid and Crystallized Intelligence: A Factor Analytic and Developmental Study of the Structure among Primary Mental Abilities'. Unpublished doctoral dissertation, University of Illinois, Champaign.

Horn, J. L. and R. B. Cattell (1967). 'Age Differences in Fluid and Crystallized Intelligence'. *Acta Psychologica* 26(2): 107–29.

Imbens, G. W. and J. D. Angrist (1994). 'Identification and Estimation of Local Average Treatment Effects'. *Econometrica* 62(2): 467–75.

Johnson, W. and T. J. Bouchard (2007). 'Sex Differences in Mental Ability: A Proposed Means to Link them to Brain Structure and Function'. *Intelligence* 35(3): 197–209.

Jorm, A. F., B. Rodgers, A. S. Hendersen, A. E. Korten, P. A. Jacomb, H. Christensen, and A. Mackinnon (1998). 'Occupation Type as a Predictor of Cognitive Decline and Dementia in Old Age'. *Age and Ageing* 27(4): 477–83.

Lazear, E. P. (1986). 'Retirement from the Labor Force'. *Handbook of Labor Economics* 1(5): 305–55.

Lei, X., H. Yuqing, J. J. McArdle, J. P. Smith, and Y. Zhao (2012). 'Gender Differences in Cognition among Older Adults in China'. *Journal of Human Resources* 47(4): 951–71.

Lyketsos, C. G., O. Lopez, B. Jones, A. L. Fitzpatrick, J. Breitner, and S. DeKosky (2002). 'Prevalence of Neuropsychiatric Symptoms in Dementia and Mild Cognitive Impairment: Results from the Cardiovascular Health Study'. *Journal of the American Medical Association* 288(12): 1475–83.

McArdle, J. J. and J. R. Woodcock (1997). 'Expanding Test–Retest Designs to Include Developmental Time-Lag Components'. *Psychological Methods* 2(4): 403–35.

McFadden, D. (2008). 'Human Capital Accumulation and Depreciation'. *Applied Economic Perspectives and Policy* 30(3): 379–85.

Maurer, J. (2010). 'Height, Education and Cognitive Function at Older Ages: International Evidence from Latin America and the Caribbean'. *Economics and Human Biology* 8(2): 168–76.

Mazzonna, F. and F. Peracchi (2012). 'Ageing, Cognitive Abilities and Retirement'. *European Economic Review* 56(4): 691–710.

Mazzonna, F. and F. Peracchi (2014). 'Unhealthy Retirement? Evidence of Occupation Heterogeneity'. CEPRA Working Paper 1401. Lugano: Center for Economic and Political Research on Aging.

Mein, G., P. Martikainen, H. Hemingway, S. Stansfeld, and M. Marmot (2003). 'Is Retirement Good or Bad for Mental and Physical Health Functioning? Whitehall II Longitudinal Study of Civil Servants'. *Journal of Epidemiology and Community Health* 57(1): 46–9.

Midanik, L. T., K. Soghikian, L. J. Ransom, and I. S. Tekawa (1995). 'The Effect of Retirement on Mental Health and Health Behaviors: The Kaiser Permanente Retirement Study'. *Journals of Gerontology Series B: Psychological Sciences and Social Sciences* 50(1): S59–S61.

Mojon-Azzi, S., A. Sousa-Poza, and R. Widmer (2007). 'The Effect of Retirement on Health: A Panel Analysis Using Data from the Swiss Household Panel'. *Swiss Medical Weekly* 137(41): 581–5.

Morris, J. C., M. Storandt, J. P. Miller, D. W. McKeel, J. L. Price, E. H. Rubin, and L. Berg (2001). 'Mild Cognitive Impairment Represents Early-Stage Alzheimer Disease'. *Archives of Neurology* 58(3): 397–405.

Morris, M., D. Evans, H. Liesi, and J. Bienias (1999). 'Methodological Issues in the Study of Cognitive Decline'. *American Journal of Epidemiology* 149(9): 789–93.

Neuman, K. (2008). 'Quit Your Job and Get Healthier? The Effect of Retirement on Health'. *Journal of Labor Research* 29(2): 177–201.

OECD (2011). *Pensions at a Glance 2011: Retirement-Income Systems in OECD and G20 Countries.* Paris: Organisation for Economic Co-operation and Development.

OECD (2013). *OECD Guidelines on Measuring Subjective Well-Being.* Paris: Organisation for Economic Co-operation and Development.

Park, D. C., G. Lautenschlager, T. Hedden, N. S. Davidson, A. D. Smith, and P. K. Smith (2002). 'Models of Visuospatial and Verbal Memory across the Adult Life Span'. *Psychology and Aging* 17(2): 299–320.

Peterson, M., A. Kramer, and A. Colcombe (2002). 'Contextual Guidance of Attention in Younger and Older Adults'. *Acta Psychologica* 122(2006): 288–304.

Potter, G. G., M. J. Helms, and B. L. Plassman (2008). 'Associations of Job Demands and Intelligence with Cognitive Performance among Men in Late Life'. *Neurology* 70(19): 1803–8.

Prull, M. W., J. D. E. Gabrieli, and S. A. Bunge (2000). 'Age-Related Changes in Memory: A Cognitive Neuroscience Perspective'. In F. I. M. Craik and A. Timothy (eds.), *Salthouse Handbook of Aging and Cognition II.* Mahwah, NJ: Lawrence Erlbaum Associates, pp. 91–153.

Rabbitt, P., P. Diggle, D. Smith, F. Holland, and L. McInnes (2001). 'Identifying and Separating the Effects of Practice and of Cognitive Ageing during a Large Longitudinal Study of Elderly Community Residents'. *Neuropsychologia* 39(5): 532–43.

Rohwedder, S. and R. J. Willis (2010). 'Mental Retirement'. *Journal of Economic Perspectives* 24(1): 119–38.

Salthouse, T. A. (2006). 'Mental Exercise and Mental Aging'. *Perspectives on Psychological Science* 1(1): 68–87.

Salthouse, T. A. (2009). 'When Does Age-Related Cognitive Decline Begin?' *Neurobiology of Aging* 30(4): 507–14.

Scarmeas, N. and Y. Stern (2003). 'Cognitive Reserve and Lifestyle'. *Journal of Clinical and Experimental Neuropsychology* 25(5): 625–33.

Schaie, T. A. (1994). 'The Course of Adult Intellectual Development'. *American Psychologist* 49(4): 304–13.

Schaie, T. A. (1996). *Intellectual Development in Adulthood: The Seattle Longitudinal Study.* New York: Cambridge University Press.

Schaie, W. (1989). 'The Hazards of Cognitive Aging'. *The Gerontologist* 29(4): 484–93.

Small, G. W. (2002). 'What We Need to Know about Age Related Memory Loss'. *British Medical Journal* 324(7352): 1502–5.

Stern, Y. (2002). 'What is Cognitive Reserve? Theory and Research Application of the Reserve Concept'. *Journal of the International Neuropsychological Society* 8(3): 448–60.

Stern, Y. (2003). 'The Concept of Cognitive Reserve: A Catalyst for Research'. *Journal of Clinical and Experimental Neuropsychology* 25(5): 589–93.

Tabert, M. H., S. M. Albert, L. Borukhova-Milov, Y. Camacho, G. Pelton, X. Liu, Y. Stern, and D. P. Devanand (2002). 'Functional Deficits in Patients with Mild Cognitive Impairment: Prediction of AD'. *Neurology* 58(5): 758–64.

United States Social Security Administration (2014). *Retirement Age Calculator.* Washington, DC: Social Security Administration. <https://www.ssa.gov/planners/retire/ageincrease.html>.

Van Praag, H., G. Kempermann, and F. H. Gage (2000). 'Neural Consequences of Environmental Enrichment'. *Nature Reviews Neuroscience* 1(3): 191–6.

Westerlund, H., J. Vahtera, J. E. Ferrie, A. Singh-Manoux, J. Pentti, M. Melchior, C. Leineweber, M. Jokela, J. Siegrist, M. Goldberg, and M. Kivimaki (2010). 'Effect of Retirement on Major Chronic Conditions and Fatigue: French GAZEL Occupational Cohort Study'. *British Medical Journal* 341(1): c6149.

Part II
Tools for Retirement Planning and Decision Making

Chapter 5

Choosing a Financial Advisor: When and How to Delegate?

Hugh Hoikwang Kim, Raimond Maurer, and Olivia S. Mitchell

We examine how and when delegating one's investment decisions to a financial advisor can enhance consumer well-being, taking into account the fact that workers need to spend time to manage their own portfolios. When workers manage their own money, this reduces their opportunity to undertake on-the-job learning. Therefore, self-management of personal investments reduces future labor market earnings. We first investigate how introducing an investment delegation option at different points in workers' careers can change results. Young investors have few investable assets but they have the longest horizon to benefit from sound financial advice. Thus it is not clear *ex ante* whether younger investors benefit more from having a delegation option. We also compare these outcomes with what would obtain if the worker instead adopted simple rule-based investment portfolios such as conventional Target Date Funds (TDFs) with age-linked investment glide paths. We explore welfare gains of a few portfolio rules with fixed asset allocations. Our goal is to quantify the benefits of having access to personalized financial advice versus portfolios managed according to simple rules, at different stages over the life cycle.

Our baseline model reflects widely observed portfolio management patterns of individual investors, namely *portfolio inertia*. A great deal of empirical research shows that most workers are inactive investors: that is, they tend to 'set and forget' their investment portfolios. For instance, Ameriks and Zeldes (2004) showed that over a twelve-year period, three-quarters of the retirement account holders they examined never altered their retirement asset allocations at all; similarly, Agnew et al. (2003) reported that almost 90 percent of retirement account holders never altered their portfolios. Such inertia also applies to non-retirement accounts, in that a majority of equity owners exhibited portfolio inertia in the Panel Study of Income Dynamics (PSID) data (Bilias et al. 2010). A prominent explanation for why investors display such inertia is the fact that financial management requires people to pay substantial amounts of monetary or non-monetary transaction costs. In this chapter, we build a baseline model of investor inertia based on the time costs that people need to incur when self-managing their portfolios (Kim et al. 2016).

A Life Cycle Model of Rational Investor Inertia

At the outset, we outline a baseline model of rational inertia used for evaluating financial advice over the life cycle (Kim et al. 2016).[1]

Time Cost of Financial Management

We posit individual investors who are not financial experts and who must incur time cost (or mental resources) when managing their financial portfolios. Time costs become particularly important when individuals gain job-specific human capital on their jobs via learning by doing (Arrow 1962; Becker 1964). In such a case, devoting time to investment management comes at the cost of reducing workers' future labor earnings.

Inertia vs. Active Management

We consider portfolio inertia as one investment management method. If an investor chooses *portfolio inertia* in period t, he keeps his current stock balance for the next period, and the next period's stock balance is only influenced by the stock market return. By choosing portfolio inertia, he incurs no time cost for managing his financial assets, sparing him the need to analyze new information to reshuffle this portfolio. By electing *active portfolio management*, he could determine a new mix of equity and bonds, but in turn, this requires him to incur time cost. This latter will be deducted from his available time for working, and he may lose an opportunity to accumulate more job-specific skills. We formulate the lifetime discounted utility for each portfolio management method and allow the investor to optimally choose the portfolio management method with the higher-value function.[2] Thus, central to the rational inertia model are two competing costs: an opportunity cost for human capital accumulation, and suboptimal portfolio allocation for a long time.

Preferences

The consumer has a time-separable power utility function defined over a composite good consisting of current consumption + and time devoted to leisure L_t, which is given by $U_t(C_t, L_t) = \frac{1}{1-\gamma}(C_t L_t^a)^{1-\gamma}$. Here $a > 0$ captures the investor's preference for leisure relative to consumption and the parameter γ measures relative risk aversion.

Labor Earnings

Yearly labor income (E_t) is determined by the individual's job-specific human capital level (H_t), wage shock (Y_t), and labor supply (l_t):

$$E_t = (1 - h_t)(1 - \tau_t)l_t H_t Y_t U_t,$$

where h_t and τ_t represent housing expenditures and labor income tax, respectively. U_t is a temporary idiosyncratic shock in the labor market. After the (exogenous) age-65 retirement age $(t = 45)$, the individual stops working $(l_t = 0)$ and receives a lifelong pension benefit equal to a fraction of his final labor earnings.

We have calibrated this model for the US using information on labor income patterns, mortality, retirement benefits, and capital market parameters (see Kim et al. 2016). Our calibrated parameters appear in the Appendix. Consistent with most prior life cycle models (e.g., Cocco et al. 2005), our baseline model matches well with empirically observed patterns of labor earnings, consumptions, stock balance, and wealth accumulation/decumulation profiles (Figure 5.1).

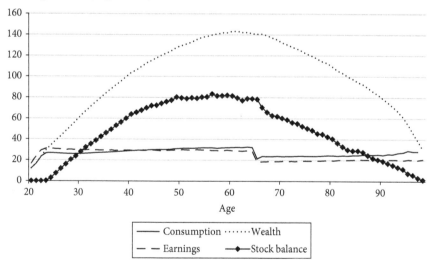

Figure 5.1. Life cycle profiles of key variables from a baseline model

Notes: This figure shows average life cycle profiles of key variables when only active management or inertia are available, generated from 2,000 independent simulations based on the baseline specification. All dollar amounts are in $1,000s deflated to year 2012.

Source: Kim et al. (2016).

When Does Financial Delegation Make Sense?

We model the main benefit of having the option to delegate one's investment decisions to a financial advisor as the time saved for accumulating more job-specific skills or human capital (Kim et al. 2016). When an individual uses an advisor, he must pay a fee for the customized advice. By contrast, if he self-manages his portfolio, this takes time which reduces his opportunity to invest in job-related human capital that can enhance his future earnings. Evidently, the attractiveness of delegating to an advisor will vary over the life cycle in a complex manner. For example, younger workers have longer time horizons over which to reap the benefits of financial advice. But they also have little money to manage, so hiring a financial advisor might add little value.

If a worker handles his own portfolio himself (*self-management*), he incurs time costs which can cut into both leisure and work time. The individual seeking to limit such time costs could simply maintain his current portfolio allocation (*inertia*). Alternatively, he could engage a financial advisor (*delegation*) to do the job in exchange for a fixed plus a variable management fee. To evaluate *when* access to financial advice would be most beneficial, we introduce the delegation option at different points over the life cycle. Prior to the introduction of the advice, investors are assumed to either do nothing (i.e., engage in portfolio inertia), or self-manage the account (and thus incur the time cost), whichever is optimal. After access to the advisor is introduced, this remains an option for the rest of his life.

We assume that financial advisors charge an annual management fee which is a percentage of total assets under management (AUM), along with a minimum fixed fee. According to documents filed by Registered Investment Advisors (RIAs) reporting to the US Securities and Exchange Commission, we have determined that the average annual percentage fee was 1.41 percent of AUM in 2014. The baseline minimum fixed fee was $2,100 for an investor with a minimum balance of $150,000 ($\approx$$2,100/1.41 percent).

Table 5.1 summarizes how making financial advice available at different ages shapes several key outcome variables, including welfare gains (i.e., the certainty equivalent amount of consumptions), wealth, labor earnings, consumption, labor supply, and leisure time. Four introduction dates are considered for the delegation option, namely ages 20, 30, 45, and 60. What we see is, first, that consumers are always better off when given access to a financial advisor (row (a)). Second, these gains decline with the age when the delegation option is made available. That is, workers can expect a 1.07 percent improvement in lifetime welfare when they have an opportunity to delegate their financial decisions to an advisor from the start of their working lives, at age 20. By contrast, a ten-year delay in the introduction of the delegation option cuts the gains by almost half. When the delegation

Choosing a Financial Advisor 89

TABLE 5.1 Impact of introducing a delegation option at alternative ages: investor gains in well-being

	(1) Age = 20	(2) Age = 30	(3) Age = 45	(4) Age = 60
(a) Welfare gain	1.07	0.51	0.19	0.02
(b) Wealth	20.03	14.42	9.05	7.95
(c) Earnings	5.08	2.95	1.25	1.29
(d) Consumption	6.05	3.86	2.10	2.20
(e) Labor supply	7.53	4.62	2.19	2.14
(f) Leisure	7.28	7.18	6.75	6.10

Notes: This table displays the impact of having access to a financial advisor to whom investment decisions can be delegated, at different points in the life cycle. The model with investor inertia in Kim et al. (2016) is the benchmark case. The table describes the worker's welfare gains and average changes in key variables under the delegation option versus the benchmark without a delegation option. All numbers are in percentage points (%).
Source: Authors' calculations.

option is introduced just prior to retirement, at age 60, the lifetime welfare gain is tiny, only 0.02 percent.

Third, we find that early exposure to financial advisors generates substantial additional lifetime wealth (row (b)). If workers have access to investment delegation from age 20 onward, their average wealth is 20 percent higher than in the no-delegation case. If the delegation is available ten years later, wealth accumulation rises by less, just 14 percent. And for even later ages, the impact on wealth is smaller still. And fourth, delegation also changes income and consumption patterns, as reported in rows (c) and (d) of Table 5.1. Delegation allows workers to provide more labor supply by saving their time (row (e)). Again, we see that making advice accessible early in the work career enhances outcomes the most. We also highlight the interesting pattern that emerges when we compare the result from introducing delegation at age 45 versus age 60. When financial advice is made available only from age 60, people enjoy slightly more consumption compared to when it is introduced at age 45 (2.2 percent vs. 2.1 percent) as well as more income (1.29 percent vs. 1.25 percent), but less leisure (6.1 percent vs. 6.75 percent). The smaller leisure levels produce less measured life satisfaction (0.02 percent vs. 0.19 percent in welfare terms) compared to the benchmark case.

In sum, our results indicate that it is better for investors to have an early opportunity to hire financial advisors, since access to financial management early in life can produce important improvements in wealth and well-being. If financial advisory services are only introduced when people are in their 60s, welfare increases by only small amount (0.02 percent).

Comparing Customized Financial Advice vs. Simplified Investment Portfolios

In our benchmark model of investor inertia (Kim et al. 2016), the benefit of hiring a financial advisor is due to the time saved in financial management. In return, an investor will need to pay fees comprised of a minimum fixed and a variable fee based on total assets under management. To judge how sensitive people's welfare gains are to such costs, we next consider varying fee levels. This question is timely because we observe an emerging industry of low-cost financial advice providers based on modern portfolio theory and sophisticated computer programs, sometimes called 'robo-advisors'. These represent a relatively new phenomenon in the financial advice industry, and they involve the provision of online automated investment services with virtually no human contact (Reklaitis 2015). Compared to human advisors, robo-advisors have a cost advantage since their investment suggestions are pre-programmed based on clients' characteristics and conditions (e.g., risk aversion, background risk, current asset mix). In what follows, we model robo-advisors as investment advice providers charging a lower minimum fixed fee (i.e., requiring a lower minimum balance) than do human advisors. In return, they provide recommended asset mixes derived from solving clients' dynamic portfolio choice problems.

To evaluate results conservatively, we assume that robo-advisors charge an annual management fee of 1.41 percent of AUM, just as do the human advisors, but they levy a lower minimum fixed fee.[3] Table 5.2 reports results for workers having access to robo-advisors from age 20. When there is no minimum annual fee, we see that the young worker's lifetime consumption is higher by 1.3 percentage points, or around 19 percent above the levels with customized but more expensive human financial advisors. As the minimum annual fee rises, this decreases client welfare gains. In other

TABLE 5.2 Welfare consequences of financial advice provision for alternative minimum fees

	(1)	(2)	(3)
	No minimum fee	Minimum fee = $700	Minimum fee = $1,400
Welfare gain	1.30	1.11	1.08

Notes: This table displays the impact of having access to a financial advisor charging alternative annual minimum fixed fees. In each case, the annual variable fee is assumed to be an annual 1.41% of AUM. The model with investor inertia in Kim et al. (2016) is the benchmark case. The table describes the worker's welfare under the delegation option alternative, versus the benchmark without a delegation option. All numbers are in percentage points (%).

Source: Authors' calculations.

TABLE 5.3 Impact of introducing plain-vanilla portfolios in lieu of investor inertia: how the change in investor well-being compares to benchmark, for alternative management fees and equity glide paths

Investment glide path	(1) Mgmt fee = 0.84%	(2) Mgmt fee = 0.5%	(3) Mgmt fee = 0.2%	(4) Mgmt fee = 0%
(a) 60%	0.52	0.63	0.88	1.10
(b) 60% → 20%	0.49	0.59	0.84	1.06
(c) 100-age	0.38	0.56	0.81	0.94
(d) 80-age	0.56	0.69	0.98	1.20

Notes: This table displays the impact of having access to alternative equity paths over the life cycle, versus the benchmark model with investor inertia as in Kim et al. (2016). Each column shows results for different management fees for the glide path products. All numbers are in percentage points (%). The row labeled 60% indicates results for the case where 60% of savings are always invested in stocks. The row labeled 60% → 20% indicates results for the case where the investor's equity fraction is 60% prior to retirement, and then falls to 20% thereafter. The row labeled 100-age indicates results for the case where the fraction of savings invested in equity is 100 minus the investor's age. The row labeled 80-age indicates results for the case where the glide path varies with age but the minimum percentage invested in equity is zero.
Source: Authors' calculations.

words, robo-advisors have a substantial advantage when busy investors seek to delegate financial management.

In Table 5.3 we compare investor well-being when 'plain-vanilla' investment portfolios are offered in lieu of customized financial advice. The first row (a) assumes that the investor must hold 60 percent of his assets in equity, while the second (b) assumes the equity fraction is 60 percent prior to retirement, and 20 percent afterwards. The third row (c) assumes that the equity share equals 100 minus the investor's age, while the final row (d) assumes that the glide path has the equity share fall to zero as of age 80. The latter two examples are akin to the prominent portfolio rule of conventional Target Date Funds, which have become extremely popular in the marketplace over the last two decades.[4] None of these plain-vanilla portfolios takes account of differences in investors' background risk or job-specific earnings patterns. Thus these rules ignore the fact that investors' decisions regarding portfolio allocation and the characteristics of their other sources of investable assets are tightly connected. For example, investors whose labor earnings are quite volatile would prefer investment profiles with a lower equity share to hedge against their labor income risk.

The outcomes reported speak to the question of how plain-vanilla portfolios akin to those seen in the marketplace affect lifetime well-being, across different management fee levels. Column (1) assumes an annual management fee of 0.84 percent of AUM, which is the same as the average fee for TDFs (Yang and Lutton 2014). Columns (2)–(4) show results for successively lower AUM fees. Results show that consumers do benefit from these plain-vanilla portfolios, as compared to the baseline model with no access to delegation options. Nevertheless, the gains are only 30–43 percent of the robo-advisor case. In columns (2)–(3), we show how lower fees increase consumers' levels of well-being, and the final column reports results for a zero management fee. Generally speaking, plain-vanilla investment accounts and zero management fees generate similar (though still lower) welfare gains as compared to robo-advisors. TDFs do not perform better because the equity investment rules depend only on the clients' ages, and they ignore clients' particular circumstances such as human capital risk, wealth levels, and the time costs of portfolio management. Overall, Table 5.3 suggests a customized delegation option such as a robo-advisor could be more desirable than a simple rule-based equity share account standardized for all.

Additional Considerations

Thus far we have noted that having a delegation option tends to increase consumer well-being. Nevertheless this can also give rise to a principal–agent problem, due to information asymmetry and possible conflicts of interest between advisors and investors. For example, financial advisors might attempt to maximize their compensation at the expense of investors' gain. In this chapter, our model considers 'ideal' financial advisors without such agency issues. It might be possible that a sophisticated robo-advisor can mitigate this problem, but including this issue in a life cycle model calls for additional research beyond the scope of the present chapter.

Another question is what an optimal default option would be for inactive investors, taking into account additional decisions including how much clients should contribute to and withdraw from their retirement accounts. This consideration can become an important issue in retirement plans, and automatic default options would appropriately explore optimal contribution and withdrawal patterns over the life cycle, in addition to the portfolio management.

We have also assumed here that there are no communications problems between financial advisors and investors. Nevertheless, fee communications are often shrouded (Anagol and Kim 2012) when investors lack knowledge or have limited time to evaluate information presented. Understanding how financial advisor disclosures shape investor behaviors is likely to have rich policy implications for regulating the financial advisory industry.

Conclusions

We have quantitatively analyzed the impact of having a delegation option at different points over the life cycle. We show that having access to a delegation option in one's early career can have a substantially positive impact on the investor's lifetime welfare. Access to advice at age 60 is less beneficial in the context of our model. And finally, although TDFs are widely used, they appear to deliver lower gains compared to having a financial advisor customize portfolios to investors' specific financial and economic circumstances. Clearly, however, these conclusions about investment advice and portfolio management depend on the costs of each, as well as the benefits.

Acknowledgments

The authors are grateful for research support provided by NIH/NIA Grant # P30 AG12836 and NIH/NICHD Population Research Infrastructure Program R24 HD-044964, and the Pension Research Council/Boettner Center for Pensions and Retirement Security at the University of Pennsylvania. The authors also received research funding from the Metzler Exchange Professor program at the Goethe University of Frankfurt and the Special Research Fund at the SKK GSB, SKK University. The Wharton High Performance Computing Platform provided an excellent setting for the numerical analysis. Opinions, findings, interpretations, and conclusions represent the views of the authors and not those of the affiliated institutions.

Appendix

TABLE 5A.1 Summary of calibrated parameters for the baseline model

Parameter	Baseline value
Working periods	45
Retirement periods	35
Time discounting	0.96
Risk aversion	3
Leisure preference	1.0
Std. dev. of permanent wage shock	0.0710
Std. dev. of human capital shock	0.0434
Std. dev. of transitory wage shock (pre-retirement)	0.1726

(*continued*)

TABLE 5A.1 Continued

Parameter	Baseline value
Std. dev. of transitory earnings shock (post-retirement)	0.28
Risk premium	0.04
Std. dev. of stock return	0.205
Risk-free rate	1.01
Delegation annual fee: variable rate	1. 41% per annum
Delegation annual fee: fixed fee (1.41% of min. req'd balance of $150,000)	$2,115

Note: This table summarizes parameter values for the benchmark case in Kim et al. (2016).
Source: Authors' calculations.

Notes

1. This section summarizes a model developed in Kim et al. (2016) to which readers may refer for a discussion of model parameters.
2. There can be behavioral reasons for why investors are inactive in managing their portfolios. For example, investors may have emotional hurdles to actively manage their financial asset. Although this line of reasoning can be informative, here we focus on the rational optimization framework to provide quantitatively more accurate evaluations of having financial advice over the life cycle.
3. In practice, robo-advisors can charge even less; see <https://investorjunkie.com/42668/true-costs-robo-advisors/>.
4. Not all TDFs implement the same gliding path of equity allocation. Some TDFs use a glide path targeted towards the retirement year (called a 'to' glide path), and others lower the equity allocation through retirement (called a 'through' glide path). The latter group of TDFs have more equity exposure in general (Yang and Lutton 2014).

References

Agnew, J., P. Balduzzi, and A. Sunden (2003). 'Portfolio Choice and Trading in a Large 401(k) Plan'. *American Economic Review* 93(1): 193–215.

Ameriks, J. and S. P. Zeldes (2004). 'How Do Household Portfolio Shares Vary With Age?' Working Paper. New York: Columbia University GSB.

Anagol, S. and H. H. Kim (2012). 'The Impact of Shrouded Fees: Evidence from a Natural Experiment in the Indian Mutual Fund Market'. *American Economic Review* 102(1): 576–93.

Arrow, K. J. (1962). 'The Economic Implications of Learning by Doing'. *Review of Economic Studies* 29(3): 155–73.

Becker, G. (1964). *Human Capital.* Chicago, IL: University of Chicago Press.

Bilias, Y., D. Georgarakos, and M. Haliassos (2010). 'Portfolio Inertia and Stock Market Fluctuations'. *Journal of Money, Credit, and Banking* 42(4): 715–42.

Cocco, J. F., F. J. Gomes, and P. J. Maenhout (2005). 'Consumption and Portfolio Choice over the Life Cycle'. *Review of Financial Studies* 18(2): 491–533.

Kim, H. H., R. Maurer, and O. S. Mitchell (2016). 'Time is Money: Rational Life Cycle Inertia and the Delegation of Investment Management'. *Journal of Financial Economics* 121(2): 427–47.

Reklaitis, V. (2015). 'Why Investors Should Approach Robo-Advisors with Caution'. *Marketwatch.com*, November 27. <http://www.marketwatch.com/story/why-investors-should-approach-robo-advisers-with-caution-2015-11-24>.

Yang, J. and L. P. Lutton (2014). 'Target-Date Series Industry Survey 2014'. *Morningstar Research Report.*

Chapter 6

Advice in Defined Contribution Plans

Gordon L. Clark, Maurizio Fiaschetti, and Peter Tufano

Defined contribution (DC) pension plan participants are often encouraged to seek advice so as to fashion saving strategies that take into account their goals and objectives, expected income, and risk tolerance over the short and long terms (North 2015). To the extent that DC plan participants seek advice on these issues, it is widely believed that they begin with friends and relatives, perhaps augmented by the Internet and websites (depending on age and gender; see Clark et al. 2014). These sources may not be as helpful as need be; indeed, what peers say and do can drive participants in different directions (Beshears et al. 2015). In many OECD countries, participants' need for advice is often fulfilled by governments and commercial vendors. For instance, governments can distribute information for retirement planning, maintain interactive websites, and encourage awareness of the issues. Few commentators suggest these efforts have been particularly effective (UK Government 2008).

Whether financial advisors can be trusted to act on behalf of their clients and whether financial advisors are able and/or willing to assume responsibility for their advice are key academic and policy issues (Campbell et al. 2011; Gabaix and Laibson 2006). At the same time, it is apparent that little is known of the nature and scope of the demand for advice by the full range of DC plan participants. In part, this is because many DC plans, especially those in the private sector, have low rates of participation by low-paid employees. Also, in many jurisdictions, DC plan participants tend to search for and select their own advisors. Where advisors are not trusted and/or come at a price, it appears participants are often reluctant to seek advice. In this chapter, we focus on the provision of retirement advice where the provider acts in the interests of participants.

Four issues are of interest. First, we investigate the timing of advice-seeking by DC plan participants as they approach the median age of retirement. Second, we distinguish between advice-seeking in general and advice-seeking relevant to retirement planning, assessing whether participants' advice-seeking on this issue is a distinctive class of advice-seeking. Third, we test whether advice-seeking is responsive to events and macroeconomic trends. Fourth, we assess the patterns of advice-seeking as participants approach the median retirement age by reference to participants' age, gender, account balance, and salary. We rely upon a large database of Australian DC pension plan participants involving approximately 560,000 participants over ten years.[1]

The administrator provides advice without requiring the payment of a fee by the participant in circumstances where the advisor is incentivized to help the participant without regard to the sponsor or other service providers.

This chapter begins with an overview of recent behavioral research that suggests the context in which planning takes place is important (Clark 2014). Thereafter, we introduce the data on advice-seeking, noting the distinctive attributes of the Australian system of mandatory DC pension saving. This is followed by an account of the topics raised by pension plan participants when seeking advice from their multi-employer pension plan administrator. Tests of robustness are used to justify categorical distinctions between advice sought on administrative matters, investment, and retirement planning. We show that advice-seeking on retirement planning comes to dominate other forms of advice-seeking as plan participants approach the Australian median age of retirement. In the concluding section of the chapter, implications are drawn for the design of DC pension schemes and public policy.

Saving for Retirement

Like many cognitive scientists and decision-theorists, we accept that human beings look to the future and/or recognize the virtues of planning for the future; that is, planning for the future is a human trait (Bratman 1987). Whether people are effective planners is more problematic, however. The issue is one of competence in relation to the environment in which they must make decisions and take actions (Clark et al. 2006). For instance, some environments may be benign and/or rewarding when planning for the future, whereas other environments may be so unstable that making plans and acting on behalf of long-term expectations is self-defeating. In a related vein, Simon (1982) has argued that whereas most people are intendedly rational, their best intentions may be confounded by unexpected changes in the environment (Gabaix et al. 2006).

The extent to which people value the future, how they deal with possible losses as opposed to possible gains in welfare, and how they adapt to new information, are just three topics among many that represent the focus of behavioral research (Ainslie 2012; Baron 2008). In the context of risk and uncertainty, it has been shown that, on average, people either discount the long term or discount the immediate future but attribute value in the long term (Laibson 1997). Likewise, it has been shown that, on average, people are more concerned with a possible loss in welfare than they are willing to assume risk to achieve higher well-being. Moreover, many people procrastinate, leaving to the last minute decisions that they must or should take, yet some people more than others overreact to new information and can arbitrarily change their plans for the future (see Kahneman 2011).

Lusardi and Mitchell (2007, 2011) suggested that saving for the future requires more than being an effective decision-maker; it also requires knowledge of the principles underpinning financial planning. They have identified a set of skills relevant to long-term financial decision making and tested respondents at home and abroad in terms of their competence. The results show that financial literacy varies by age, gender, education, and income. Such patterns in financial literacy cut against the plausibility of representing individual retirement planning as simply the expression of well-founded intention and commitment. At issue is whether high levels of financial literacy can reinforce saving for the future *and* reasoned adaptation to changing circumstances, versus whether low levels of financial literacy discourage those concerned from making plans for the future.

Saving for retirement is an especially demanding problem (Zeckhauser 2010). At one level, it involves making forward estimates of one's job tenure, value of human capital, and health and welfare. It also involves making forward estimates of the risk-adjusted rate of return on contributions to a pension saving plan which, in turn, involves making forward estimates of the relative value of plausible long-term investment strategies. For younger workers who face considerable uncertainty as to their long-term job prospects, the rate of return on their education, and longevity, elicit a variety of responses including procrastination and status quo bias (Samuelson and Zeckhauser 1988). Older workers face less uncertainty on these factors and may be more effective at planning for the future because the planning horizon is better defined. Saving for retirement would be more effective if younger workers could imagine themselves as older workers with all the benefits of hindsight. Quite obviously, this is highly problematic.

For these reasons, the average worker may be ill-equipped to make plans for the future. Younger workers may need guidance in framing long-term expectations, and older workers may not have the skills and expertise to take advantage of their accumulated savings and make investments that can generate sustainable incomes. Further, the findings from behavioral research as regards the pervasiveness of decision making biases and anomalies suggest that leaving responsibility for retirement saving to individuals is likely to result in lower social welfare.

Demand for and Supply of Advice

Given their lack of skills and expertise, pension plan participants may, on their own account, reach out for advice. It is widely assumed that the average participant begins with family and friends, work colleagues, and/or third parties who are known to them. It is reasonable to suppose that the advice provided by family and friends may do little more than reinforce expectations. Whether colleagues and the work environment are useful ways through which to learn about saving for the future appears to depend upon factors specific to the workplace, such as the heterogeneity of fellow employees (negative) and the engagement of the employer (positive). In some jurisdictions, trusted third parties can include employers and local bank employees.

Advice-seeking from third parties would seem to be confounded by two intersecting factors. First, just as pension plan participants may lack the skills and expertise to be effective long-term planners, they may also lack the skills and expertise to search for and assess the relative merits of competing advice providers. That is, the cognitive biases and anomalies that discount effective decision making in the context of risk and uncertainty also apply when searching for providers and choosing amongst service providers.[2] Second, those offering advice may do so by proclaiming their independence and trustworthiness while concealing their ties to vendors of financial services and the true cost of their services. In the vernacular of economic theory, asymmetric information confounds the search for and selection of advice providers (Akerlof 1970; Spence 1977; Gabaix et al. 2006).

More generally, little is known about the demand for advice in circumstances where participants trust the advice provider without pressures to take proffered advice and related products. It would also be helpful to know more about the nature and scope of advice sought when the participant does not directly pay either the plan sponsor or the third-party provider of advice. Academics, consultants, and policymakers tend to treat advice relevant to saving for retirement as distinctive, but it is not obvious that pension plan participants carry with them a robust classification system that distinguishes, for example, insurance products from retirement savings products. As such, it is important to understand better the nature and range of topics raised by participants and whether it is reasonable to suppose that seeking advice in this domain is distinctly different from those issues raised when seeking financial advice (in general).

Evidence from behavioral psychology and economics suggests that people are more likely to seek advice when their material circumstances and/or expectations change in unanticipated ways (Harvey 2012). In this respect, uncertainty as regards the future may result in participants being unable to assess the impact of possible future events, or to assign probabilistic estimates of their likelihood in ways that inform savings behavior. This does not necessarily mean that *any* unexpected change in their material circumstances would prompt reconsideration of plans and, possibly, advice-seeking. Such events would have to be significant in relation to competing claims on their attention, since people have limited cognitive resources. This may have two related effects: people could seek advice to compensate for their previous lack of attention, and people could seek advice because changes in their material circumstances trigger attention to the planning process.

On a related issue, Sharpe (2007: 11) has observed that 'investors differ in geographic location, homeownership, profession, and so forth. We term these aspects an individual's *position*. If two people have different positions they may wish to hold different portfolios. Similarly people may have different feelings about risk, present versus future gratification, and so on. We term these an individual's *preferences*.' When the Australian Bureau of Statistics (2011) asked a representative sample of Australians about their retirement incomes, a significant minority of retired women indicated that the main source of funds for meeting living costs came from their partners' incomes. Likewise, when women intending to retire were asked about their sources of expected income, they indicated that they would rely on their partners' incomes, especially when the women were younger. By contrast, male retirees and near-retirees indicated a much lower propensity to rely upon their partners' income.

In essence, an individual's age, gender, household situation, and employment experience can systematically affect advice-seeking relevant to saving for retirement. The timing and volume of advice sought, the topics raised at any point in time and over time, and the relationship between the nature and scope of advice sought and the participants' expectations of retirement income are key issues to building an understanding of the demand for advice. If individual preferences are not constant over time, changing in response to life cycle factors and situational imperatives, including commitments and reliance upon others, then long-term plans may well be discarded and advice sought about how to adapt to new circumstances.

Advice, Retirement, and Events

In this chapter, we focus upon the advice offered by Mercer (Australia), an administrator of more than 120 corporate pension plans. Mercer provides advice via a call center and Internet facility, where those employed to advise participants have no incentive other than to 'help' the participant in a timely manner (Clark et al. 2014).[3] Participants seeking advice about their pension accounts are dealt with immediately and directly. Should they also seek advice about financial planning involving other financial instruments, they are passed to more qualified Mercer financial advisors. Industry super funds are not-for-profit organizations and widely advertise this as a virtue (Association of Superannuation Funds of Australia 2014). In this case, the plan administrator is a commercial entity but it mimics the service ethic of industry superannuation funds. The provision of advice is subject to regulation by the Australian government and its agencies.[4]

Advice Facility

The Mercer database includes information on participants' age, gender, postcodes, account balances, and whether (and when) they sought advice. The call center was established in 2004 and is open five days a week, from 7 a.m. to 8 p.m. (Australian Eastern Standard Time). The web facility was established in 2008 and it is accessible seven days a week. Mercer employs approximately one hundred full-time and part-time advisors who handle calls and web-based inquiries. The variance in advice-seeking is dominated by the day-of-the-week effect, followed by a seasonal effect, and then instances or events that may prompt groups of participants to seek advice. The day-of-the-week effect is centered on Mondays and Tuesdays, and the seasonal effect is centered on the run-up to the end of the financial year (June 30) with a significant fallow period over December and January of each year (Christmas holidays and vacation) (Clark et al. 2014).

Each call and web-based inquiry is logged and, where possible, the topic or topics raised by the participant are identified and recorded. Over the period 2004–13, more than 140 topics were logged in the system. Some calls were single-topic, whereas other calls were multi-topic in nature. The topics raised fell into three broad categories: administrative matters, investment matters, and retirement planning. Over the period 2004–13, administrative matters dominated the call center and web-based facility; calls related to investment matters and retirement planning together accounted for less than 50 percent of all calls. The Mercer system recorded more than 1.5 million calls over the period 2004–13, and approximately 2 million web-based inquiries over the period 2008–13. Early on, the length of calls averaged 3.5 minutes. More recently, calls have averaged 4.5 minutes.

Age of Retirement

Passed in 2004, the federal Age Discrimination Act (ADA) prohibits all forms of direct and indirect discrimination based upon a person's age. In addition to federal legislation, Australian states and territories prohibit age discrimination. Federal legislation covers private employees including those working full-time, part-time, casually, and those employed on contract by agencies and external providers. The ADA does not proscribe compulsory retirement at a certain age, although this is addressed in most states' and territories' statutes. Federal statute treats compulsory retirement at a certain age as an instance of age discrimination rather than an issue significant in its own right. Most public officials and employees are subject to compulsory retirement at a specific age.

Otherwise, there is no official age of retirement in Australia. Through the period 2004–13, 65 years of age was the minimum age for a man or woman to claim the Age Pension. Legislation passed in 2014 provided for a graduated increase in the minimum age from 65 to 67 years of age. The federal government also regulates the 'preservation age', or the age at which individuals can gain access to their superannuation assets. Recent legislation has also provided for a graduated increase in the age to claim access to superannuation assets from 55 to 60 years of age. As in many OECD countries, the Australian government has sought to encourage people to work longer, both full-time and part-time.

Data on the retirement status and retirement intentions of the Australian civilian population were provided by the Australian Bureau of Statistics (ABS 2011). Statistics obtained from the federal government's Multipurpose Household Survey are used by the ABS to provide estimates for Australia taking into account age, gender, and work status, whether in the labor force, unemployed, or not in the workforce. Beginning with the 8.7 million civilian population 45 years and over, it was estimated that 4.9 million were in the labor force, of which 4.7 million were employed and 150,000 were unemployed. Of the 3.8 million not in the labor force, it was estimated that 3.2 million were retired. The ABS provided estimates of those retired by gender and age cohort. Figure 6.1 shows that women had higher rates of retirement in all but the oldest cohort of 70 years or more, being most obvious during their 50s and early 60s. When surveyed, younger women indicated that they would rely on their partners' income for meeting the living costs of retirement at a much higher rate than men who intended to retire at much the same age.

The survey also asked men and women currently in the labor force to estimate their intended age of retirement (Table 6.1). Those not in the labor force included retirees, those not retired and intending to look for either full-time or part-time work, and those who had never worked. Comparing age (cohort) and gender with respect to the intended age of retirement, there was little difference in the average age of intended retirement reported by respondents. Middle-aged cohorts (e.g., 45–9 years and 50–4 years) tended to report a slightly lower average expected age of retirement (61–3 years) than older-age cohorts (e.g., 55–9 years and 60–4 years) (63–5 years). As noted previously, public policy provides incentives to work through to one's 60s. Nonetheless, a large proportion of the population is retired by age 65.

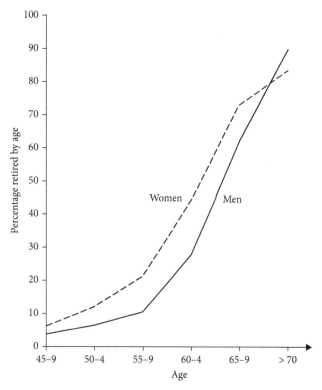

Figure 6.1. Australian rates of retirement by age and sex

Source: Australian Bureau of Statistics (2011).

Global Financial Crisis

Midway through the period 2004–13, the global financial crisis erupted, drastically affecting the financial stability and economic performance of many OECD countries. The US and the UK were particularly adversely affected, prompting high rates of unemployment, high rates of household indebtedness, and a plunge in stock market performance not seen since the Great Depression of the 1930s. Economic recovery thereafter has been protracted and uneven. The response of individuals and households to the crisis has been a significant topic for academics and policymakers (Akerlof et al. 2014).

In the Australian case, the impact of the global financial crisis was 'remarkably mild by the standards of previous Australian recessions' and other OECD countries (Edey 2009; Eslake 2009). Likewise, the downturn in the Australian stock market (2008–9) was short-lived, with a rapid recovery

TABLE 6.1 Relationship between call volume by topics and macroeconomic factors

	Administrative	Investment	Retirement planning
% change stock mkt	1.638	0.416	0.923
	(1.483)	(0.722)	(0.855)
% Δ gdp	−2.275	−1.702	−10.860
	(10.379)	(5.383)	(6.638)
% Δ full_time_employed	35.073	32.688**	27.413*
	(19.100)	(9.386)	(11.366)
% Δ expectation of financial situation next 12 months	−1.194	−0.851	−0.772
	(1.236)	(0.587)	(0.689)
% Δ expectation of economic conditions next 12 months	0.004	1.146	0.970
	(0.816)	(0.621)	(0.763)
% Δ expectation of economic conditions next 5 years	2.087	−0.894	−1.034
	(1.438)	(1.008)	(1.212)
% Δ unemployment expectations	1.753	0.842	0.733
	(1.194)	(0.824)	(0.820)
Year fixed effects	YES	YES	YES
_cons	−0.050	0.239*	0.111
	(0.238)	(0.109)	(0.135)
sigma			
_cons	0.242***	0.123***	0.144***
	(0.040)	(0.020)	(0.026)
N	32	32	32

Notes: 'Sigma_cons' is the regression's estimated standard error. *$p < 0.10$, **$p < 0.05$, ***$p < 0.010$.

Source: Authors' elaboration of Mercer's data and data from the Australian Bureau of Statistics and the Australian Stock Exchange.

to higher levels of performance. It can be hypothesized that the global crisis affected short-term expectations and behavior especially by those who might otherwise have retired. Gerrans (2012) found that the stock market downturn had only a modest effect on the trading activity of superannuation plan participants. Those who did respond were older women with relatively large account balances, rather than men.

Advice-Seeking: Timing and Patterns

Using these data we study patterns of retirement planning over the short term and the long term. A cluster analysis was used to sort the topics identified by call-handlers at the Mercer call center over the period

2004–13 into three categories: administrative, investment, and retirement planning. We were most concerned to discriminate calls related to retirement planning from other categories of calls. Many of the topics used to code calls were related to administrative matters. Calls related to investment matters and retirement planning were dominated by just 15–25 topics each. As such, the clustering routine was more focused on topics at the margins of each category with low counts of inquiry than upon a broad array of topics with high counts of inquiry. Based upon the Calinski-Harabasz (1974) test, it was found that the optimal number of categories was three (thereby justifying the use of the three main categories set out above).

Figure 6.2 displays the proportion of each category on the overall volume of calls over the period 2004–13 on a monthly and yearly basis. As shown by the yearly representation (Figure 6.2, Panel B) the contribution of the administrative matters category to the overall volume of calls dominates those of retirement planning and investments over the whole period. This is partly due to a composition effect, given the higher number of administrative issues potentially affecting participants (e.g., change of contact details, info-kit follow up, magazine not received, etc.) with respect to a relatively smaller number of those regarding the other topics. After the initial setup period of the call center in 2004, both the contribution of administrative and retirement planning calls decreased to surge again in mid-2007 (the former) and in 2006 (the latter), thereafter declining and then again rising, just for the administrative issues, toward the end of the period.

Each category of calls followed much the same path over the entire period, although the volume of calls by category differed. Notable in this regard was a shift after 2008 in the relative level of calls related to retirement planning and to investment matters. The peak in administrative calling frequency in mid-2007 was related to a change in federal government policy in relation to the tax treatment of superannuation (as shown in Figure 6.2, Panel A). The change in policy was announced in May 2006 and implemented on July 1, 2007 (Clark et al. 2014). This caused a peak in participants' interest in June 2007 given the natural tendency to procrastinate until the change was about to be implemented. It is also notable that the increasing importance of calls related to investment matters relative to retirement planning took place at the onset of the global financial crisis, dominating the retirement planning issues for the rest of the sample period.

A test for the existence of co-integration over the period 2004–13 indicated that the hypothesis that the categories of advice-calling were co-determined could not be accepted. We also sought to determine whether the categories of calling were co-determined by the path of the Australian

Panel A. Monthly trend

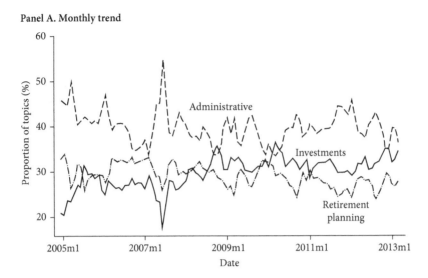

Panel B. Yearly trend

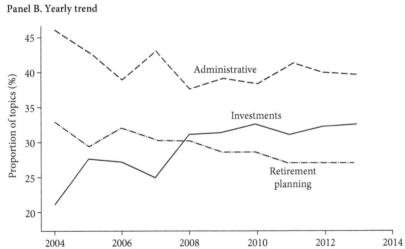

Figure 6.2. Proportion of topics raised on calls by category over time

Source: Authors' elaboration of Mercer Data.

economy, using quarterly data to represent macroeconomic conditions. A Tobit model was used to regress the percentage change in the volume of each topic category on a set of economic variables including change in employment, unemployment, gross domestic product, expectations of future economic conditions, and stock market performance.

To test whether the results were influenced by shocks occurring during the time period, three diagnostic tests were deployed. First, residuals were plotted vis-à-vis the time variable seeking evidence for possible outliers. These were found for investment and retirement planning topics; indeed, the first quarters of 2009 and 2013 were unusual with respect to average values. Second, winsorizing was used to smooth the effect of the outliers.[5] Third, yearly fixed effects were introduced to control for potential effects of heteroskedasticity induced by singular events.[6] As Table 6.1 shows, the change in employment was weakly but significantly related to the change in the volume of calls related to administrative and investment matters. Changes in call volume related to retirement planning were not significantly related to these variables, suggesting participants either recognized that the global financial crisis was of limited significance to Australia, or that retirement planning is a long-term matter not affected by short-term economic events.

To the extent that investment involves risk and uncertainty, it was hypothesized that changes in macroeconomic conditions would prompt reconsideration of investment strategies and their implementation. The positive sign on the coefficient (change in employment) suggests that, as the rate of increase in employment slowed, so too did the volume of calls related to administrative matters and investment matters. Participants may have adopted a wait-and-see strategy rather than responded by calling immediately for advice on either administrative or investment matters (and thereafter, changing some aspect of their investment strategy). This is consistent with Roy's (1950) notion of safety first and could be allied with Kahneman and Tversky's (1979) findings on loss aversion. It is also possible that participants may have thought there was more danger in responding quickly than in a wait-and-see strategy (O'Donoghue and Rabin 1999).

As for the sensitivity of calling in anticipation of retirement, Figure 6.3 displays the decomposition of the volume of calls into each category of advice-seeking distinguishing by gender and age at the time of calling, for those age 40+ (Figure 6.3, Panel A) and for those 54+ (Figure 6.3, Panel B). It was hypothesized that the volume of calls for advice on retirement planning would rise as participants neared the median Australian age of retirement (represented in Figure 6.1), and this was evident in Figure 6.3. Administrative calls dominated topics raised by participants in their 40s. Older cohorts shifted their focus to retirement planning matters, particularly investment matters. The turning point is at about age 55, when retirement planning issues become most salient. A breakdown of the year-by-year proportion of topics raised by those age 54+ (Figure 6.3, Panel B) confirms the reduction in the volume of calls raised on administrative matters and the increasing salience of retirement planning.

We also examined interactions between gender, age, salary, and account balance in terms of the topics raised in advice-seeking calls. Here, the

Panel A. Five-year age cohorts, over 40

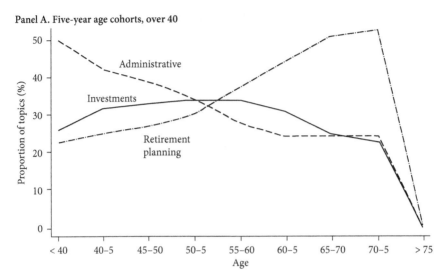

Panel B. Year-by-year, over 54 years old

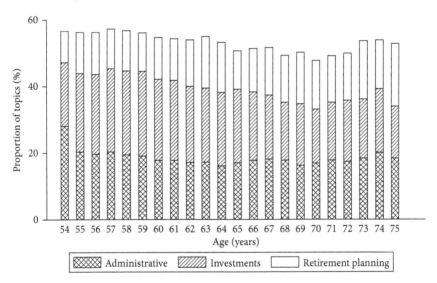

Figure 6.3. Frequency of calls by category and age over time

Source: Authors' elaboration on Mercer Data.

objective was to check for statistically significant differences across men and women when raising a topic. We plot the proportion of topics raised by gender and (i) age group, (ii) account balance, and (iii) salary, for each topic, and t-tests were computed for each possible combination. Results were in line with expectations: gender differences in every case were statistically significant (1 percent level), highlighting its role in driving the interests and attention of participants with respect to their pension plans.[7]

A closer look at the different topics by age showed that younger women asked more about administrative matters, whereas older women asked more about retirement planning. On investment matters, the proportion of men calling for advice increased for each age cohort over age 40. This is compatible with Barber and Odean's (2001) study finding that men churned their accounts more than women did.

With respect to account balances, participants with more money in their plans were most interested in how their future wealth would be managed and what they could expect from retirement. Conversely, they seemed to be less interested in administrative matters, whereas the latter were a main concern for participants with lower account balances.[8] Differences between men and women in their propensity to call about administrative matters declined as their salaries increased (with a marginal increase at the highest salary interval). This was also true for calls on investment topics, although the difference between men and women in calling propensity was more marked than in the case of administrative matters when taking into account average salaries over the previous five years. These results reinforce findings that men were more engaged in investment matters than women were.

Conclusions

In the Australian system, participation in a supplementary pension scheme is mandatory. Most participants are auto-enrolled into a target-date fund or similar investment vehicle. Once enrolled in an industry fund or related commercial organization, Australian DC plan participants rarely switch between providers; to the extent that switching takes place, more often than not it is the result of switching employers (who may be in a different industry with a different service provider) rather than making a choice in favor of a preferred provider. Participant inertia is reinforced by the time and opportunity costs involved in switching between providers and the upfront costs of learning about other providers and their respective virtues. Arguably, in these circumstances, service providers owe their participants a duty of care in terms of the nature and quality of services provided.

Our study has examined advice-seeking by such participants. Of those participants that did contact their funds, a large majority of younger participants called about administrative matters, rather than investment matters or retirement planning. Nevertheless it may behoove younger participants to engage in some form of retirement planning around the age of 40, so as to augment or take advantage of related retirement saving products. We also showed retirement planning advice is sought late in participants' working careers, perhaps too late to make an appreciable difference to their pension benefits. One way forward could be to link participants' advice-seeking on administrative matters to briefings on retirement planning (Thaler and Sunstein 2008).

Our results also showed that those seeking advice on investment matters were young and could also benefit from advice on retirement planning. These participants were often in their 40s and 50s, were more knowledge-able of the superannuation system and the services offered by funds, and could conceptualize the link between short-term investment considerations and long-term pension benefits. Advice on investment matters requires a higher level of knowledge and understanding of the issues by call handlers, so they are also subject to higher standards of certification by Australian authorities.

Linking advice on investment matters with retirement planning may require the upgrading of the call handlers' skills and, perhaps, hiring different kinds of call handlers than those that handle routine administra-tive matters. In practice, however, many super funds charge a fee to those seeking advice on investment matters, on the assumption that these matters are more complex, require higher levels of skill and expertise, and often incur follow-up calling and material provision. The fee-for-service model may be antithetical to engaging those active on investment issues with retirement planning.

Call centers, web access, and mail are crude mechanisms for engaging participants in retirement planning. In response, some employers have brought independent financial advisors to the workplace to counsel those seeking investment advice and retirement planning. While there is little in the way of published research on the value of this type of facility, experi-ence suggests that the take-up of this type of service depends upon the fee charged for the service, the degree to which an independent financial advisor is 'independent', and the age, gender, and incomes of employees. Also important, though less recognized, is the provision of expert advice by suitably qualified advisors without incurring (explicitly or by implication) long-term commitments by the employer. Many Australian employers have, in effect, given up responsibility for the retirement prospects of their employees, but providing this type of untaxed 'benefit' may well facilitate the engagement of employees with their retirement funds.

In some cases, Australian retirement funds have taken a more proactive stance by establishing drop-in centers in large retail parks, shopping malls, and in towns and cities with high participant concentrations. Local adver-tising, postcode leafleting, and sponsorship of local events can help establish the presence of these organizations in communities. While this is likely more effective than simply waiting for a participant to call on some matter of immediate interest, such engagement will be most effective when fund membership is geographically concentrated. By contrast, many of the largest funds are multi-employer, multi-jurisdictional, and multi-industry, where call centers, web access, and mail are the only ways to control costs and consequences of dispersed membership. New methods are needed to engage participants with advice that is category-specific, salient, and future-oriented, rather than simply servicing participant-initiated inquiries.

Acknowledgments

Research was supported by the CSIRO–Monash Superannuation Research Cluster, a collaborative project between the Commonwealth Scientific and Industrial Research Organization (CSIRO), Monash University, Griffith University, the University of Western Australia, the University of Warwick, and stakeholders of the Australian retirement system 'in the interest of better outcomes for all'. Support was also provided by Oxford's Fell Fund. Helpful comments and advice were received from the editors of this volume, Christine Brown, Huu Dong, David Knox, Paul Lajbcygier, Carly Moulang, Deborah Ralston, the late Maria Strydom, John Vaz, Victoria Wyllie de Echeverria, and Dane Rook. Preparation of the chapter was aided by Ailsa Allen, Rosanna Bartlett, Seth Collins, and Angela Sidaway and was made possible by data provided by Mercer (Australia).

Notes

1. This database has been analyzed to better understand the patterns of advice-seeking over time and in response to announced changes in pension policy and volatility in financial markets (see Clark et al. 2014).
2. Caplin and Martin (2011: 2899) show that individuals typically satisfice rather than optimize when searching for information. As a consequence, decisions are made without full examination of the available options indicating 'the best available options may be missed'. In response, individuals may outsource this function to those with the requisite skills and expertise and/or seek the advice of those they trust.
3. Superannuation funds have an interest in retaining fund participants (those that call and those that don't), especially those with large account balances. There are economies of scope and scale in the global funds' management industry.
4. The regulatory framework governing the provision of financial advice in Australia is complex, subject to overlapping and cross-cutting legislation and regulations,

and politically contested (see Hanrahan 2013; Latimer 2014; Serpell 2012). Further, debate about the proper provision of advice often focuses on distinctions between types of advice that the average person finds difficult to understand (Lindgren 2013).

5. Extreme values were capped to the 99th percentile (see Tukey 1962).

6. Plots of the residuals and full tables of the econometric results are available upon request.

7. These results and related graphs are available upon request.

8. We show, for the UK, that as a person's income rises and retirement account grows, this dependence on workplace pensions as the main source of future income declines. Furthermore, we show that the nature and number of a person's savings instruments change markedly. This is pronounced for higher-income male participants (see Clark et al. 2012). Here, we were unable to observe the other types of savings instruments available to participants.

References

Ainslie, G. (2012). 'Pure Hyperbolic Discount Curves Predict "Eyes Open" Self-Control'. *Theory and Decision* 73(1): 3–34.

Akerlof, G. A. (1970). 'The Market for "Lemons": Quality Uncertainty and the Market Mechanism'. *Quarterly Journal of Economics* 84(3): 488–500.

Akerlof, G. A., O. Blanchard, D. Romer, and J. Stiglitz (eds.) (2014). *What Have We Learned? Macroeconomic Policy after the Crisis*. Cambridge, MA: MIT Press.

Association of Superannuation Funds of Australia (2014). *ASFA Survey on the Provision of Financial Advice by Superannuation Funds*. Sydney: ASFA.

Australian Bureau of Statistics (2011). *Retirement and Retirement Intentions*. 6238.0. Canberra, ACT: Australian Government.

Barber, B. M. and T. Odean (2001). 'Boys Will Be Boys: Gender, Overconfidence, and Common Stock Investment'. *Quarterly Journal of Economics* 116(1): 261–92.

Baron, J. (2008). *Thinking and Deciding*, 4th edn. Cambridge: Cambridge University Press.

Beshears, J., J. J. Choi, D. Laibson, B. C. Madrian, and K. L. Milkman (2015). 'The Effect of Providing Peer Information on Retirement Saving Decisions'. *Journal of Finance* 70(3): 1161–201.

Bratman, M. E. (1987). *Intention, Plans, and Practical Reason*. Cambridge, MA: Harvard University Press.

Caliński, T. and J. Harabasz (1974). 'A Dendrite Method for Cluster Analysis'. *Communications in Statistics* 3(1): 1–27.

Campbell, J. C., H. Jackson, B. Madrian, and P. Tufano (2011). 'Consumer Financial Protection'. *Journal of Economic Perspectives* 25(1): 91–114.

Caplin, A. and D. Martin (2011). 'Search and Satisficing'. *American Economic Review* 101(7): 2899–922.

Clark, G. L. (2014). 'Roepke Lecture in Economic Geography: Financial Literacy in Context'. *Economic Geography* 90(1): 1–23.

Clark, G. L., E. Caerlewy-Smith, and J. C. Marshall (2006). 'Pension Fund Trustee Competence: Decision Making in Problems Relevant to Investment Practice'. *Journal of Pension Economics and Finance* 5(1): 91–110.

Clark, G. L., M. Faschetti, and P. Gerrans (2014). 'The Demand for Advice in Defined Contribution Pension Plans: Age, Gender, and the Size-of-Bet Effect'. CSIRO-Monash Superannuation Research Working Paper No. 2014-09.

Clark, G. L., K. Strauss, and J. Knox-Hayes (2012). *Saving for Retirement: Intention, Context, and Behavior*. Oxford: Oxford University Press.

Edey, M. (2009). 'The Global Financial Crisis and its Effects'. *Economic Papers* 28(3): 186–95.

Eslake, S. (2009). 'The Global Financial Crisis of 2007–2009: An Australian Perspective'. *Economic Papers* 28(3): 226–38.

Gabaix, X. and D. Laibson (2006). 'Shrouded Attributes, Consumer Myopia, and Information Suppression in Competitive Markets'. *Quarterly Journal of Economics* 121(2): 505–40.

Gabaix, X., D. Laibson, G. Moloche, and S. Weinberg (2006). 'Costly Information Acquisition: Experimental Analysis of a Boundedly Rational Model'. *American Economic Review* 96(4): 1043–68.

Gerrans, P. (2012). 'Retirement Savings Investment Choices in Response to the Global Financial Crisis: Australian Evidence'. *Australian Journal of Management* 37(3): 415–39.

Hanrahan, P. F. (2013). 'The Relationship between Equitable and Statutory "Best Interests" Obligations in Financial Services Law'. *Journal of Equity* 7(1): 46–73.

Harvey, N. (2012). 'Learning Judgement and Decision Making from Feedback'. In M. K. Dhami, A. Shlottmann, and M. R. Waldmann (eds.), *Judgement and Decision Making as a Skill: Learning, Development and Evolution*. Cambridge: Cambridge University Press, pp. 199–223.

Kahneman, D. (2011). *Thinking Fast and Slow*. London: Allen Lane.

Kahneman, D. and A. Tversky (1979). 'Prospect Theory: An Analysis of Decision Under Risk'. *Econometrica* 47(2): 263–91.

Laibson, D. (1997). 'Golden Eggs and Hyperbolic Discounting'. *Quarterly Journal of Economics* 112(2): 443–78.

Latimer, P. (2014). 'Protecting the Best Interests of the Client'. *Australian Journal of Corporate Law* 29: 8–22.

Lindgren, K. (2013). 'Administrative Law in the Superannuation Context'. *Australian Law Journal* 87(10): 688–98.

Lusardi, A. and O. S. Mitchell (2007). 'Baby Boomer Retirement Security: The Roles of Planning, Financial Literacy, and Housing Wealth'. *Journal of Monetary Economics* 54(1): 205–24.

Lusardi, A. and O. S. Mitchell (2011). 'Financial Literacy and Planning: Implications for Retirement Well-Being'. In O. S. Mitchell and A. Lusardi (eds.), *Financial Literacy: Implications for Retirement Security and the Financial Marketplace*. Oxford: Oxford University Press, pp. 17–39.

North, G. (2015). 'The Future of Financial Advice Reforms: Will They Achieve Their Long-Term Objectives?' *Competition and Consumer Law Journal* 22(1): 197–217.

O'Donoghue, T. and M. Rabin (1999). 'Doing it Now or Later'. *American Economic Review* 89(1): 103–24.

Roy, A. D. (1950). 'Introduction to the Distribution of Earnings and of Individual Output'. *Oxford Economic Papers* 125(583): 378–402.

Samuelson, W. A. and R. Zeckhauser (1988). 'Status Quo Bias in Decision Making'. *Journal of Risk and Uncertainty* 1(1): 7–59.

Serpell, A. J. (2012). 'The Future of Financial Advice Reforms'. *Company and Securities Law Journal* 30(4): 240–52.

Sharpe, W. F. (2007). *Investors and Markets: Portfolio Choices, Asset Prices and Investment Markets*. Princeton, NJ: Princeton University Press.

Simon, J. D. (1982). 'Political Risk Assessment: Past Trends and Future Prospects'. *Columbia Journal of World Business* 82(17): 62–71.

Spence, A. M. (1977). 'Consumer Misperceptions, Product Failure and Producer Liability'. *Review of Economic Studies* 44(3): 561–72.

Thaler, R. and C. Sunstein (2008). *Nudge: Improving Decisions about Health, Wealth and Happiness*. New Haven, CT: Yale University Press.

Tukey, J. W. (1962). 'The Future of Data Analysis'. *Annals of Mathematical Statistics* 33(1): 1–67.

UK Government, HM Treasury (2008). *Thoresen Review of Generic Financial Advice*. Final Report. London: UK Government.

Zeckhauser, R. (2010). 'Investing in the Unknown and the Unknowable'. In F. X. Diebold, N. A. Doherty, and R. J. Herring (eds.), *The Known, the Unknown, and the Unknowable in Financial Risk Management: Measurement and Theory Advancing Practice*. Princeton, NJ: Princeton University Press, pp. 304–46.

Chapter 7

Seven Life Priorities in Retirement

Surya Kolluri and Cynthia Hutchins

As Baby Boomers turn 65, issues pertaining to longevity, funding retirement, and discussions of life priorities in later life are coming to the fore. Our recent research is examining how Americans are preparing for retirement and reshaping their lifestyles during their later years. The goal is to discover what issues respondents are thinking and worrying about as they plan for retirement. In this chapter we review our findings.

The Americans' Perspectives on New Retirement Realities and the Longevity Bonus research study of July 2015 was conducted in partnership with Age Wave via an online data collection methodology. Our sample was nationally representative by age, gender, ethnicity, income, and geography. The survey was conducted among a total of 3,694 adult respondents age 25+, and it included the Silent Generation (age 70–90), Boomers (age 51–69), Generation Xers (age 39–50), and Millennials (age 25–38). Qualitative research—six focus groups among both pre-retirees and retirees, and interviews with national thought leaders on a variety of topics related to giving—was also conducted prior to the quantitative research.

This research with individuals living in the US led us to identify seven life priorities most important to today's pre-retirees and retirees: Health, Home, Family, Work, Giving, Finances, and Leisure. To summarize findings from our research on several of these priorities, we conclude that today's 'retirees' are not simply retiring; they are exploring new options, pursuing old dreams, and living life to the fullest. They are taking advantage of longer lifespans to devote energy to pursuits they may not have had the time or freedom to chase during the 'career' portion of their lives. They are staying active, engaging in new pastimes, and strengthening and expanding their social networks.

While our research found much reason for optimism around retirement, there is also cause for concern. Too many Americans are dying early on account of physical and mental health issues. Far too many have reached their retirement years with chronic diseases that are often associated with or caused by bad diet and poor exercise habits. And perhaps most importantly, many lack financial security.

The need for financial security is a common thread that runs throughout our research; each of the life priorities has financial implications that need to be thought through in planning discussions, from the increasing cost of health care to relocating expenses. With many already thinking differently about their lives, it is of utmost importance to make sure that their financial planning takes the above factors into consideration.

Health Challenges

As Baby Boomers move into retirement, health has become the ultimate retirement wildcard. Indeed, 81 percent of retirees cite health as the most important ingredient for a happy retirement (Merrill Lynch and Age Wave 2014a). For many, health can be the difference between a period of opportunity and independence, or one of worry and financial challenges. Health challenges are also a double threat to retirement financial security: between unpredictable and costly health care expenses, and unexpected early retirement due to health problems, planning ahead can become confusing and overwhelming. This underlines the importance of financial planning, as respondents increasingly seek guidance to help them make informed decisions for themselves and their families.

Although health care costs in retirement are a deep financial concern, a majority of respondents has not factored these costs into their retirement planning. For instance, we found that seven out of ten couples age 50+ had not discussed how much they might need to save to cover health care costs during retirement. Additionally, more than half of retirees retired earlier than they expected, and the number one reason for their early retirement was a health problem. Only 19 percent of current Medicare recipients felt they had a strong grasp of what health care costs their Medicare options cover.

Boomers' Approach to Health

On a positive note, we found that Baby Boomers are redefining the role of health care consumers by taking charge of their health and health care decisions (Merrill Lynch and Age Wave 2014b). Compared to their parents' generation, Boomers are more than twice as likely to say they are proactive about their health, and they are four times more likely to actively research health information. They are also far more likely to say they view their doctors as partners who work with them to optimize their health, as opposed to an authority who gives them a plan to follow. Boomers are also highly optimistic about their health, with nearly 80 percent expecting that their generation will be healthy and active at the age of 75.

The Threat of Health Costs

Regardless of their wealth levels, health care expenses rank as the most pressing financial concern in the stage we call retirement, exceeding even the fear of outliving one's money (Merrill Lynch and Age Wave 2014a). In fact, respondents age 50+ were nearly twice as worried about the cost of retirement health care as they were about the actual quality of care they might receive. This underlines the importance of preparing financially for the prospect of living longer and facing more health challenges with old age. Moreover, survey respondents were concerned about the financial impact of spousal serious illness, and some were more worried about this than their own illness. Women, who are likely to live longer and are more apt to spend savings on their spouse's health care, were more concerned than men about the financial impact of their spouse developing a serious health problem.

Early Retirement

Fewer than one in four (23 percent) of adults age 50+ said that they would be prepared financially if they or their spouse were forced to retire early because of a health problem, despite the fact that one-third of respondents in the US who retire early do so for health reasons. This stresses the importance of financial planning early on, as retirees not only have to consider their own health, but also that of their spouses.

Increasing life expectancy coupled with the aging of the large Boomer generation has also given rise to a growing number of older adults confronting chronic disease such as hypertension, heart disease, diabetes, cancer, Alzheimer's, and arthritis. In addition, as we live longer, the natural deterioration of cognitive capabilities will have an impact on how we live the additional twenty to thirty years and the quality of that time.

In fact, more survey respondents cited Alzheimer's as the disease about which they were most worried (see Figure 7.1). When asked what concerned them most about Alzheimer's, survey respondents cited becoming a burden on their family and loss of dignity.

Confidence, Knowledge, and Communication Gaps

Unfortunately, many retirement planners fail to factor in the cost of health care. Moreover, few people have attempted to forecast how much they might need to cover health care or long-term care expenses in retirement, and many felt the information available to them was overwhelming, confusing,

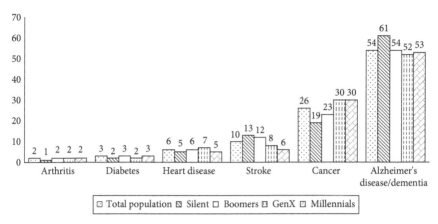

Figure 7.1. Percentage identifying the most frightening disabling prospect in later life

Source: Merrill Lynch and Age Wave (2013a).

and frustrating. One indicator of this profound challenge is the growing demand for elder care in the US.

Health and Home in Later Retirement

Though respondents said they enjoyed many new freedoms during retirement, health and health care can become significant factors when choosing where to live, particularly as people move into their 80s. Among our survey respondents age 85+, three-quarters had difficulties with daily activities including housework or getting around the home. While the average age of respondents entering assisted living is 85.7, respondents overwhelmingly preferred to receive extended care, if needed, in their own homes (NCAL 2009).

New Perspectives on the Home

With increasing longevity and greater freedom, it is not surprising that many retirees deserve to make their homes more fulfilling. Yet people must carefully consider expenses associated with current and future priorities, including potential frailty in later years. In the next decade, the number of age 65+ households will increase by nearly 11 million in the US, while growth in the number of households across all other age groups will be less than 2 million (Joint Center for Housing Studies 2016).

Over most people's lives, where they reside has been determined mainly by work and family responsibilities. Yet as people enter their late 50s and 60s, they approach the 'Freedom Threshold', with retirement representing a gateway to unprecedented freedom to choose where to live. How and where the nation's aging population chooses to live will have widespread implications on the way homes are designed, the resources people will need, and how communities and businesses nationwide should prepare.

Our research has found that (1) retirees are more than twice as likely to say they are free to choose where they want to live when compared to pre-retirees (67 vs. 30 percent), and (2) four out of five (81 percent) of the age 65+ are homeowners. Among them, 72 percent have fully paid off their mortgages (US Census Bureau 2014).

This freedom to decide where they want to live has led many retirees to move, with an estimated 4.2 million retirees moving to new homes each year. In our survey, 76 percent of the age 50+ retirees owned a home. Top motivations for moving included being closer to family (29 percent), reducing home expenses (26 percent), changes in health (17 percent), and changing marital status (12 percent) (see Figure 7.2).

Interestingly, while many survey respondents assume they will downsize once retired, we found that half (49 percent) of retirees did not downsize in their last move: in fact, 30 percent moved into larger homes. Retirees' top reasons for upsizing were to have a home large and comfortable enough for family members to visit (33 percent) or even live with them (20 percent). One of six retirees (16 percent) had a 'boomerang' child who had moved back in with them.

Of course, there are retirees who will not move during retirement for various reasons, the most popular being an emotional connection with their homes (Merrill Lynch and Age Wave 2015a). Prior to age 55, more homeowners say the financial value of their homes outweighs its emotional value.

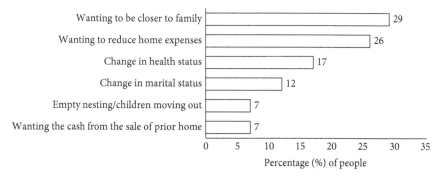

Figure 7.2. Reasons for moving in retirement

Source: Merrill Lynch and Age Wave (2015a).

As people age, however, they become far more likely to say their home's emotional value is more important; cited by nearly two out of three respondents age 75+ in our survey. Other reasons for not moving included staying in close proximity to family and friends, wanting to remain independent, or simply not being able to afford to move (Merrill Lynch and Age Wave 2015a).

Home Improvements

With age and retirement often come more flexibility, time, and financial resources for home improvements, as indicated by the fact that households age 55+ account for nearly half of all spending on home renovations (Merrill Lynch and Age Wave 2015b). While some retirees said they did modify their home to make it more age-friendly, many renovated to make it more attractive or versatile. For instance, renovations made by retiree homeowners age 50+ who planned to stay in their homes in retirement and wanted to create their dream home included (1) creating a home office for convenience, (2) improving curb appeal for enjoyment and ultimate resale, (3) upgrading a kitchen or bathroom to modify living arrangements, (4) adding safety features to accommodate aging concerns and mobility, and (5) modifying homes to live on one floor should there be trouble with stairs.

Many retirees were also interested in new technologies making their homes more convenient, connected, secure, and easier to maintain. For instance, 80 percent were interested in innovative ways of reducing their home expenses, such as smart thermostats or apps to control appliances, while 58 percent were interested in technologies to help maintain their homes such as cleaning robots or heated driveways (Merrill Lynch and Age Wave 2015b).

Family Support

Given the challenging economic climate during the past several years, it is not surprising that so many Americans have extended financial support to their loved ones. During the last five years, three out of five Americans age 50+ have provided financial assistance to members of their family, including adult children, parents, grandchildren, siblings, or other relatives (Merrill Lynch and Age Wave 2013b). But assistance can represent a hidden risk to retirement and place elders' long-term financial security in jeopardy.

The average level of financial assistance provided to family members during the last five years totaled nearly $15,000, and the figure was

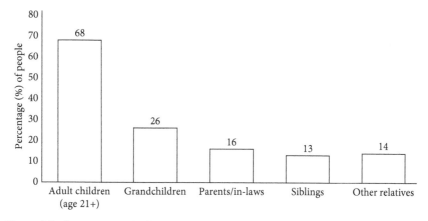

Figure 7.3. Percentage of older respondents providing financial support to family members in the last five years

Source: Merrill Lynch and Age Wave (2013b).

significantly higher among wealthy families (Figure 7.3; Merrill Lynch and Age Wave 2013b). Often this support helped relatives meet a one-time need or ongoing assistance, and it was generally given without expecting anything in return. But few respondents age 50+ had factored such support for family into their financial planning. Moreover, we also found a dangerous absence of proactive discussion among family members as they navigated these interdependencies.

Family Bank

Nearly three in five survey respondents age 50+ believed that a member of their family was the 'family bank', meaning someone their extended family was most likely to turn to for financial help. This person was often someone who was most financially responsible, had the most money, or was the easiest to approach (Merrill Lynch and Age Wave 2013a).

Generosity and Inheritance

Few of those helping family members financially did so because they expected future help or payback (Merrill Lynch and Age Wave 2013a). Respondents age 50+ were twenty times more likely to say they were helping family because 'it is the right thing to do' rather than because 'family members will help them in the future'; they were also five times more likely to stop support because a recipient did not use the money wisely, than because of worries about being paid back. More than one-third said they would accept a less comfortable retirement lifestyle to help family financially. Half of pre-retirees age 50+ said they would make major sacrifices to help family members that could impact their retirement. Among them, 60 percent said they would retire later and 40 percent would return to work after retiring to help out (Merrill Lynch and Age Wave 2013a).

Such individuals also expressed stress due to such family caregiving responsibilities. We found that the vast majority of respondents age 50+ had not prepared for potential family events and challenges which could affect their retirement, including remarriage and blended families (see Figure 7.4).

Family Structure Dynamics

Close to half of married retirees said that their marriages were more fulfilling and loving in retirement, and only 11 percent reported them being more boring or contentious (Merrill Lynch and Age Wave 2013b). Yet divorce has become increasingly common among older adults. One in seven respondents age 50+ who had married were now divorced and single—a seven-fold increase since 1960.

Rising divorce rates have also contributed significantly to a rise in blended families (Brown and Lin 2013). Nearly two in five respondents age 50+ are now part of a blended family (Merrill Lynch and Age Wave 2013b), and almost one-third of respondents age 50+ with stepchildren say this complicates financial planning. This percentage was equal to those who said they and their spouse had different financial priorities for their own children than they had for their stepchildren.

One in five parents age 50+ had at least one 'boomerang' adult child who moved back with them (Merrill Lynch and Age Wave 2013b). More than two-thirds of parents age 50+ had provided some form of financial support to their adult children during the last five years—among which, 36 percent did so without knowing how their money was being used.

The Changing Role of Work

Our research also found changes in retirees' willingness to continue working (Merrill Lynch and Age Wave 2014b), which will better equip respondents to pursue their goals. We found that nearly three out of four pre-retirees age 50+ said their ideal retirement included some work, often in new, more flexible, and fulfilling ways. With half of current retirees already having worked or planning to work in retirement, it will become increasingly

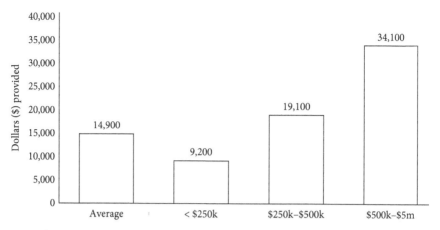

Figure 7.4. Financial support provided by people age 50+ to family members in the last five years, by investable assets

Notes: The data in this chart reflect the following number of survey respondents (by column): (1) 3,796 total respondents, (2) 71% with less than $250k in investable assets, (3) 12% with $250k–$500k in investable assets, and (4) 17% with $500k–$5m in investable assets.

Source: Merrill Lynch and Age Wave (2013b).

common for survey respondents to seek work during this stage of their lives (Munnell 2011).

The New Retirement Workscape

Previous generations viewed retirement as a permanent end of work, followed by continuous leisure. By contrast, modern-day reality for many pre-retirees and retirees can be defined as 'the new retirement workscape' (see Figure 7.5), represented by four different phases (Merrill Lynch and Age Wave 2014b):

Pre-Retirement

Five years before retiring, 37 percent of pre-retirees who wanted to work in retirement had already taken some meaningful steps to prepare for their post-retirement career; this rose to 54 percent among those within two years of retirement.

Career Intermission

Most pre-retirees do not seek to move directly from pre-retirement work to retirement work. Instead, they want a break or a sabbatical, giving them time to relax, recharge, and retool. More than half of working retirees said they took a break when they first retired, with such career intermissions averaging 2.5 years.

Re-engagement

We also found that the re-engagement phase lasted nine years and included a new balance of work and leisure. Compared to those in their pre-retirement careers, respondents working in 'FlexCareers' were nearly five times more likely to work part-time and three times more likely to be self-employed.

Leisure

In the fourth phase of retirement, respondents welcomed the opportunity to rest, relax, socialize, travel, and focus on other priorities. Leaving work was generally due to health challenges (77 percent) or simply not enjoying work as much (61 percent). When working retirees were asked to share their advice for respondents seeking work during retirement, the most popular advice was to 'be open to trying something new' and 'be willing to earn less to do something you truly enjoy'. Other tips to help prepare for a successful retirement career included keeping up with technology, with seven times as many working retirees citing the importance of this, versus trying to appear younger as a means of improving their ability to work in retirement.

Giving Opportunities

Today's retirees are in a position to make significant lasting contributions and define their legacies. We believe we are going to see older adults contributing to society in new and meaningful ways. We found that with more time, savings, and skills to contribute to the charities and causes they care about, 65 percent of retirees agree that retirement is the best time in life to give back. Over the next two decades there will be a giving surge in the US, valued at an estimated $8 trillion. This is due to the aging Baby Boomer generation, increasing life expectancy, and high rates of giving among retirees (Merrill Lynch and Age Wave 2015a).

We also found that more respondents age 65+ donated money or goods than any other age group, and gave the most (more than double that of younger adults, see Figure 7.6).

Retirees bring a lifetime of experience when they give back, and 84 percent of retirees reported that an important reason they can give more in

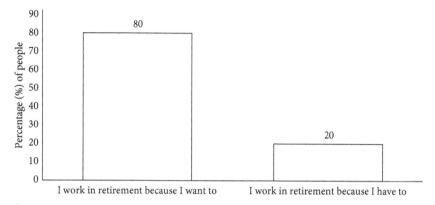

Figure 7.5. Percentage of working retirees who agree to each statement on working in retirement

Source: Merrill Lynch and Age Wave (2014b).

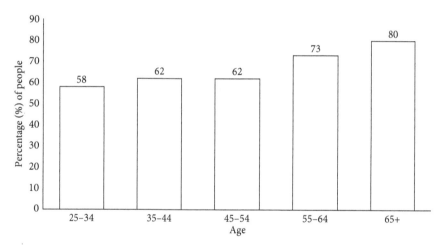

Figure 7.6. Percentage by age of respondents who give money/goods to charities, non-profits, or other causes

Source: Merrill Lynch and Age Wave (2015a).

retirement is that they have greater skills and talents compared to when they were younger. Although slightly fewer (24 percent) older adults volunteered compared to other age groups, those who did volunteer contributed more than twice as much time. The research found volunteers age 65+ gave an average of 133 hours per year, compared to those age 25–34 and 35–44 who volunteered an average of 55 and 58 hours per year, respectively. For this reason, retiring Boomers are a new and growing force in the giving space that cannot be ignored. Our study found that retirees not only give more but also believe they are able to give better by being more focused, hands-on, and impact-oriented (Merrill Lynch and Age Wave 2015a).

Moreover, retirees said they were positioned to give in ways that better matched their personal priorities and passions, were more thoughtful and focused (64 percent), and had a more meaningful impact (Merrill Lynch and Age Wave 2015a). Retirees were three times more likely to say helping others makes them happier than spending money on themselves. Retirees were also nearly six times more likely to say 'being generous' defines success for them than 'being wealthy'.

We also found that for many, giving was a key factor enhancing retirement. Compared to those who did not volunteer or donate, retirees who gave said they had a stronger sense of purpose, higher self-esteem, and were both happier and healthier, than those who did not contribute.

Giving can also be an important source of social connections in retirement. Although before retirement, people say they will miss a reliable income most after leaving the workforce, afterwards, retirees say that it is the social connections that they miss the most. Eighty-five percent of retiree volunteers in our study said they had developed important new friendships through their giving and volunteering activities (Merrill Lynch and Age Wave 2015b).

Our research also showed that retired women were more likely than men to say retirement was the best time to give back, and more retired women donated and volunteered to charitable causes than men. Additionally, women are increasingly taking control of inheritance and giving decisions to family and charitable causes, in part because of their superior longevity. Women are three times more likely than men to be widowed in later life and therefore often decide how and where to pass on assets. Among our respondents age 55+, unmarried women contributed nearly half of all charitable bequests (Merrill Lynch and Age Wave 2015a).

Challenges to Giving

Retirees worry about the trustworthiness of charitable organizations changing, too many options to choose from, and financial limitations as barriers limiting their giving. When seeking advice for how best to give, retirees reported needing a guide who understands their values and priorities, and someone to help them research and identify which charities and causes to support. When individuals and families did take the time to develop a giving strategy, they gave more and felt more fulfilled. We found that knowledgeable and engaged donors experienced greater personal fulfillment and gave larger amounts to charitable causes (Merrill Lynch and Age Wave 2015a).

Financial Goals

In previous decades, 'getting rich' and 'retiring early' were often heralded as the ideal retirement plan. Today, pre-retirees and retirees are more than seven times as likely to say their financial goal is 'saving enough to have financial peace of mind' versus 'accumulating as much wealth as possible'. This new focus on peace of mind is likely due to several factors. For instance, the fact that the 2008–9 financial crisis and recession was a financial wake-up call, exposing the dangers and risks of aggressive investment strategies. Another factor has been the movement of the Boomer generation from the accumulation years into the retirement years, when it is seeking to responsibly manage savings and income, while supplementing this with meaningful activity including work on its own terms. And finally, the rise in longevity is creating greater uncertainty regarding how much people need to save and prepare for retirement.

While a longer life is generally viewed positively, pre-retirees and retirees worry about unexpected life events due to a lengthier retirement. In fact, when asked what they worried about most, 70 percent of men and 68 percent of women said serious health problems, and 47 percent of men and 61 percent of women said running out of money. Many pre-retirees and retirees are seeking to adopt more conservative financial strategies. When considering investments or insurance, survey respondents age 45+ said that having guaranteed income and protecting assets was almost four times more important than achieving higher-risk returns (Merrill Lynch and Age Wave 2013a).

Troubling Lack of Discussion

We also found a significant lack of proactive discussion and engagement between family members on key financial topics, which can negatively impact retirement and financial well-being. Across all relationships, the most common catalyst for such discussions was usually the death or illness of a family member or friend, and the top barriers for having an open conversation included fear of family conflict and the fact that such topics were just too uncomfortable to discuss. Respondents who did have these discussions with family members were, on average, nearly twice as likely to say they would be well prepared financially if faced with a family challenge (Merrill Lynch and Age Wave 2013a).

Proactive discussions and coordination with family help alleviate the challenges of retirement. While such topics can be difficult to discuss, there is a clear benefit to having family conversations and planning ahead.

Conclusion

Population aging is creating the most powerful demographic revolution our nation has ever seen. Despite this, many respondents are poorly prepared for the possibility of longer retirement. Our nationally representative survey of Americans age 25+ has identified several key challenges to health, home life, family support, the measuring of work, giving, and finances. Each of these is shaping financial security at older ages.

Acknowledgments

Bank of America Merrill Lynch is a marketing name for the Retirement Services businesses of Bank of America Corporation ('BofA Corp.'). Banking and fiduciary activities are performed by wholly owned banking affiliates of BofA Corp., including Bank of America, N.A., member FDIC. Brokerage services are performed by wholly owned brokerage affiliates of BofA Corp., including Merrill Lynch, Pierce, Fenner & Smith Incorporated ('MLFP&S'), and a registered broker-dealer and member SIPC. Merrill Lynch Wealth Management makes available products and services offered by Merrill Lynch, Pierce, Fenner & Smith Incorporated, a registered broker-dealer and member SIPC, and other subsidiaries of Bank of America Corporation ('BofA Corp.'). Merrill Lynch Life Agency Inc. ('MLLA') is a licensed insurance agency and a wholly owned subsidiary of BofA Corp. MLPF&S and Bank of America, N.A. make available investment products sponsored, managed, distributed, or provided by companies that are affiliates of BofA Corp. or in which BofA Corp. has a substantial economic interest.

References

Brown, S. L. and I. Fen Lin (2013). 'The Gray Divorce: Rising Divorce among Middle-Aged and Older Adults, 1990–2010'. National Center for Family and Marriage Research Working Paper 13-03, March. <https://www.bgsu.edu/content/dam/BGSU/college-of-arts-and-sciences/NCFMR/documents/Lin/The-Gray-Divorce.pdf>.

Joint Center for Housing Studies of Harvard University (2016). 'The State of the Nation's Housing'. <http://www.jchs.harvard.edu/sites/jchs.harvard.edu/files/jchs_2016_state_of_the_nations_housing_lowres.pdf>.

Merrill Lynch and Age Wave (2013a). *Americans' Perspectives on New Retirement Realities and the Longevity Bonus.* New York, NY: Merrill Lynch. <https://mlaem.fs.ml.com/content/dam/ML/Articles/pdf/AR111544.pdf>.

Merrill Lynch and Age Wave (2013b). *Family & Retirement: The Elephant in the Room.* New York, NY: Merrill Lynch. <https://mlaem.fs.ml.com/content/dam/ML/Articles/pdf/family-and-retirement-elephant-in-the-room.pdf>.

Merrill Lynch and Age Wave (2014a). *Health and Retirement: Planning for the Great Unknown.* New York, NY: Merrill Lynch. <https://www.ml.com/publish/content/application/pdf/GWMOL/MLWM_Health-and-Retirement-2014.pdf>.

Merrill Lynch and Age Wave (2014b). *Work in Retirement: Myths and Motivations.* New York, NY: Merrill Lynch. <https://mlaem.fs.ml.com/content/dam/ML/Articles/pdf/ml_work-in-retirement-myths-motivations.pdf>.

Merrill Lynch and Age Wave (2015a). *Giving in Retirement: America's Longevity Bonus.* New York, NY: Merrill Lynch. <http://agewave.com/wp-content/uploads/2016/07/2015-ML-AW-Giving-in-Retirement_Americas-Longevity-Bonus.pdf>.

Merrill Lynch and Age Wave (2015b). *Home in Retirement: More Freedom, New Choices.* New York, NY: Merrill Lynch. <https://mlaem.fs.ml.com/content/dam/ML/Articles/pdf/ML_AgeWave_Giving_in_Retirement_Report.pdf>.

Munnell, A. (2011). 'What Is the Average Retirement Age?' CRR Working Paper No. 11-11. Boston, MA: Center for Retirement Research at Boston College.

National Center for Assisted Living (NCAL) (2009). 'Findings of the NCAL 2009 Assisted Living Staff Vacancy, Retention, and Turnover Survey'. <https://www.ahcancal.org/ncal/quality/Documents/2009NCALVacancyRetentionTurnoverSurveyReport.pdf>.

US Census Bureau (2014). *2014 National Population Projections: Summary Tables.* Washington, DC: BOC. <https://www.census.gov/population/projections/data/national/2014/summarytables.html>.

Chapter 8

Worker Choices About Payouts in Public Pensions

Robert L. Clark and Janet Raye Cowell

Public sector retirement plans need to be regularly evaluated and updated to ensure that they meet the needs of current and future public sector workers and retirees. This has not happened to the extent needed, in part because public pensions have been controversial in many places and recent debates on pension reform have focused on the retirement plans' costs. Even when a plan's fundamentals are strong, trustees have had to play defense concerning the generosity and cost of the plans rather than being able to direct their attention to managerial improvements. Incremental improvements in plan design nonetheless are vital to maintaining plans that match the needs of today's public sector employees.

This chapter investigates an important issue affecting almost all retirees in public employee retirement plans, namely the choice of annuity payment option. Most public sector plans are of the defined benefit (DB) variety, where benefits are a function of years of service, final average salary, and age at retirement. Nevertheless, most public retirement plans in the US offer retirees a menu of options for how their benefit can be paid. The annuity option that retiring employees elect will have significant long-term financial implications for retirees and their households.

In the private sector, concern has been expressed that pension partici-pants often request lump-sum distributions instead of selecting annuities provided by the plan (Mitchell et al. 1999; Brown 2001). When a lump-sum distribution is taken, retirees must manage their resources and bear both investment and longevity risk. This is less of an issue in the public sector, as most individuals who retire from public employment select one of the annuity options offered by the pension plan. They do so in part because selecting a lump-sum distribution may make them ineligible to remain in the employer's retiree health insurance plan. Therefore annuity options offered by public retirement plans serve many retirees well by providing lifetime benefits, thus eliminating the risk that people might outlive their retirement savings. An emerging question is whether the annuity options currently offered by public retirement plans will continue to be attractive as the population continues to age, life expectancy increases, and retirement patterns change. This chapter describes current annuity options offered by large public pension systems and then explores several modified annuity options to potentially address these emerging issues and improve public sector workers' utilization of retirement benefits.

We begin with a review of the annuity options offered by 85 large, state-managed retirement plans for public employees. The lifetime patterns of payments of these annuity options differ considerably. Next, we report the results of a survey sent to the state Treasurers (or comparable official) requesting information on the proportion of retirees selecting each option offered under the public plans in their states. We also examine how well the available annuity options serve the needs of public employees. Finally, we examine two new types of annuity payouts that could enhance the likelihood that public retirees will be able to achieve a reliable standard of living throughout their retirement.

Retirement Benefit Options in Public Retirement Plans

We explore the current options offered by public sector retirement plans, focusing on 85 state-managed retirement plans included in the 2012 Comparative Study of Major Public Employee Retirement Systems prepared by the Wisconsin Legislative Council (2013).[1] We reviewed the websites of each of these plans and created a list of the various annuity options offered in each case. The plans included in this review cover general employees and teachers; pensions offered to police, firefighters, and elected officials are excluded from our analysis (see Appendix Table 8A.1).[2] Among the 85 plans, 13 cover only state employees, 27 cover only teachers, 8 cover only local employees, 14 cover state and local employees, 3 cover state employees and teachers, and 20 include state employees, local employees, and teachers.

Figure 8.1 depicts the number of plans that offer each of the most frequently available annuity options.[3] Using assumptions concerning age-specific life expectancies of the retirees and beneficiaries, as well as the plan's assumed discount rate or rate of return, each retirement system attempts to calculate the benefits under each of the payment options so that the expected present value of each annuity option is the same. For example, the monthly benefit is higher if the retiree selects a single life annuity (often referred to as the maximum allowance), and it is lower if a joint and survivor benefit is chosen.[4] Public plans usually offer separating employees the option to request a lump-sum distribution. Unlike lump-sum options in

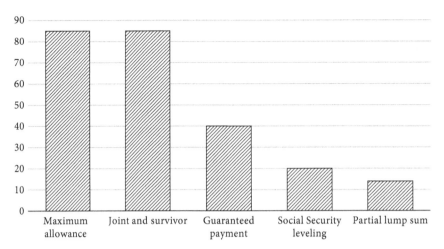

Figure 8.1. Annuity options in state-managed retirement plans: number of plans with each option

Notes: Maximum allowance refers to the option that pays the highest monthly benefit to a retiring member of a plan. This benefit is a lifetime benefit paid to the retiree on a monthly basis. At the death of the retiree, all monthly benefits cease. This type of benefit is often called a single life annuity. In some plans, the remaining balance due to employee contributions may be paid out in a lump sum to a designated beneficiary at the death of the retiree. Joint and survivor refers to the option that pays a reduced benefit over the life of a retiree in return for allowing a designated beneficiary to receive a percentage of the benefit after the retiree's death. Plans often have various options with the survivor benefit being equal to 100%, 75%, 50%, or 25% of the benefit payable during the life of the retiree. Modified joint and survivor is an available provision for some of these plans where monthly payments increase to the amount payable under the maximum allowance upon the death of the beneficiary. Guaranteed payment refers to the option that guarantees a certain number of payments to the retiree. If the retiree's death occurs before receiving all of the monthly payments, the remaining payments are made to the beneficiary until all payments have been made. Social Security leveling refers to the option that pays larger monthly payments until the retiree is eligible for Social Security at age 62. When the retiree becomes eligible to claim an early Social Security benefit the monthly payments from the pension are reduced to a lower amount so the total retirement income (pension + Social Security) remains the same. Finally, partial lump sum refers to the option that pays a one-time lump-sum payment of a portion of the retiree's retirement benefit, plus a reduced monthly benefit payable for the retiree's lifetime. The number of state plans with each option is shown above each bar.

Source: Authors' computations using data derived from state plan websites.

the private sector, this distribution option in most public plans is based on employee contributions compounded over time using a specified interest rate.[5] Public sector employees who are eligible for an immediate benefit upon terminating employment rarely request a lump-sum distribution.

Each plan offers an annuity in which the retiree is paid a monthly benefit based on a formula specified in the plan. In Figure 8.1, this option is labeled the maximum allowance and is basically a single life annuity where all payments cease with the death of the retiree.[6] Each plan also offers some type of joint and survivor annuity option (J&S). These annuities provide a lower income stream than the maximum allowance during the retiree's life but then they continue to pay monthly benefits for the remaining lifetime of the beneficiary. Plans usually offer several versions of the J&S benefits. The options specify the benefit of the survivor as a percentage of the benefit paid to the retiree prior to her death. Typically, the benefit paid to the survivor represents a specified percentage of the benefit paid to the retiree during her lifetime. Most retirement systems offer a range of J&S payout options (see Appendix Table 8A.2). Among the plans in our sample, 77 plans allow retirees to select a 100 percent benefit for the beneficiary while 78 plans have a 50 percent option. In addition, 33 plans have a 75 percent option and 7 plans have a 25 percent survivor option. Finally, 16 plans have additional J&S options. For example, Virginia's SRS allows retirees to choose any whole percentage of the retiree benefit to be paid to the survivor between 10 and 100 percent. The larger the benefit paid to the survivor, the lower the initial benefit that is paid during the life of the retiree.

Slightly fewer than half of the plans have an annuity option that provides a single life annuity with a guaranteed number of payments. If the retiree were to die before all of the guaranteed payments are made, the remaining payments will be made to the named beneficiary; however, after the specified number of payments, the survivor receives no further benefits from the retirement system. Of course, this option provides lower monthly benefits than those of the maximum benefit option.

Another option offered by 14 plans allows retirees to select a partial lump-sum distribution. These retirees then receive an immediate payout reflecting some portion of the present value of their benefit, and by accepting this distribution, retirees agree to permanently lower monthly benefits from the retirement system in the form of single life annuities. The lump-sum payments are typically specified as a percentage of the annuity or a number of months of benefits. For example, Georgia ERS restricts the lump sum to between 1 and 36 months of the normal benefit, and Ohio PERS/ STRS, Mississippi PERS, Virginia SRS, and Texas ERS have similar options. Kansas PERS Tier 2 allows the retiree to select a 10, 20, or 30 percent option which provides a lump sum equal to the percentage of the present value of the maximum allowance and requires a corresponding reduction in the size of the monthly benefit. Some states limit eligibility for this option to individuals retiring at or after their full retirement date.

Twenty plans have an annuity option called 'Social Security Leveling'.[7] This option requires retirees to report to the retirement system their expected Social Security benefit at a specified age. Most state plans with the Social Security leveling options stipulate that age 62 be used to determine the Social Security benefit. However, Idaho PERS and Illinois SRS specify that the leveling age is the full retirement age for Social Security, and North Dakota TRF allows either age 62 or the full retirement age to be used in the calculation. Virginia SRS allows the worker to choose any age between 62 and the Social Security full retirement age in this option, while Alaska PERS uses age 65 in its calculation; however, that option is only available to individuals who entered the system prior to July 1, 1996. Workers selecting the option receive a higher initial benefit from their state pension, compared to the maximum benefit option, and the annual pension benefit is reduced when the individual reaches the specified leveling age, at which time the retiree is expected to claim a Social Security benefit. The idea is that the retiree will receive the same total retirement benefit (pension plus Social Security) before and after the age given for claiming Social Security benefits.

This option may appeal to some retirees because many public sector workers retire prior to age 62 and hence before becoming eligible for Social Security. To these early retirees, the higher initial pension benefit can seem attractive. A concern with this option is that, by linking the reduction in the pension benefit to age 62, retirees are encouraged to claim Social Security benefits as soon as they become available at age 62. This may not be optimal for all retirees (Goda et al. 2015). The pension benefit in the leveling option is also based on the single life of the retiree and provides no beneficiary payments after the death of the retiree.

Choice of Annuity Options by Recent Retirees

Figure 8.1 shows that public pension plans offer retirees a menu of payment options. The key question for our study is whether even better options could be designed for workers in the twenty-first century, in the context of an aging population and increasing life expectancy. To understand the implications of current annuity options and their impact on well-being in retirement, we refine data on the proportion of retirees selecting each of these annuity options. To obtain this information, we sent an email request to the 50 state Treasurers and comparable officials requesting data on the proportion of recent retirees who selected each of the options offered by the plans in their state. The email provided a link to an online page where the plan administrator could report the distribution of retirees across the options.[8]

Ten states covering 13 plans responded to our request for information on the annuity options selected by their retirees. Table 8.1 presents the responses from the survey of plan managers by showing the proportion of recent retirees that selected each of the options provided by their retirement plans. In general, the most popular annuity option in most of the plans

TABLE 8.1 Percentage of state retirees selecting annuity options

State	Plan	Maximum allowance	Joint and survivor	Social Security leveling	Guaranteed payment	Partial lump sum
California	PERS	44.5	37.3	1.3	N/A	N/A
California	TRS	52.1	46.9	N/A	N/A	N/A
Delaware	SEPP		100	N/A	N/A	N/A
Iowa	PERS	9.4	38.2	0.4	32.8	19.2
Maryland	SRPS	40.0	34.0	N/A	N/A	N/A
Mississippi	PERS	65.8	22.0	N/A	7.6	21.1
Nebraska	SPP	14.1	38.8	N/A	30.2	N/A
North Carolina	TSERS	56.2	25.9	17.9	N/A	N/A
North Carolina	LGERS	55.7	34.6	9.7	N/A	N/A
South Carolina	SCRS	64.3	30.4	4.6	0.4	N/A
Washington	PERS	65.2	34.8	N/A	N/A	N/A
Washington	TRS	38.8	21.4	N/A	N/A	39.8
Wyoming	WRS	43.1	52.9	N/A	4.1	N/A

Notes: In some cases, plan managers reported retirees selecting annuity options that are not shown on websites as being available to current retirees. This difference could be due to annuity options that were offered to individuals hired at earlier dates. Plans often have various tiers that cover individuals hired at various times. The request to the Treasurers was to provide information on the proportion of retirees selecting each of the options. California TRS participants are not included in Social Security.

Source: Data provided by state plans in response to Janet Cowell's email to state Treasurers.

is the maximum allowance. Over 60 percent of retirees in the Mississippi PERS, South Carolina SCRS, and Washington PERS have elected this single life annuity, while between 50 and 60 percent of retirees opted for this annuity type in California TRS, North Carolina TSERS, and North Carolina LGERS. With the exception of Delaware, which reported that 100 percent of its retirees selected a J&S annuity, the lowest proportions of retirees selecting the maximum allowance were in Iowa and Nebraska. In those states, almost one-third of retirees selected the guaranteed payment period and about 20 percent chose the partial lump-sum option. Each of these options requires the retiree to select the single life annuity and then adjusts the monthly payment to offset the expected payments associated with the option. Neither of these options provide a retiree's surviving beneficiary a benefit for life.

All of these options provide a retirement benefit to retirees for the duration of their lives but, in general, they do not provide any benefit to survivors. The J&S options enable retirees to engage in long-term planning for a beneficiary, typically a surviving spouse.[9] With the exception of Delaware SEPP that reported 100 percent of its retirees selecting a J&S option, only in Wyoming WRS and California TRS does the proportion of retirees selecting a J&S option approach 50 percent. All of the other benefit options are based on single life annuities and provide little in the way of expected lifetime income protection to surviving spouses. Since public retirement plans are not subject to ERISA, there has been no requirement that the interest of a spouse be considered when the retiree is selecting a distributional option.

Five of the 12 plans in which workers are also covered by Social Security offer a Social Security leveling option. Among these plans, only in North Carolina is the incidence of this option greater than 10 percent of retirees.[10] The partial lump-sum option seems to be a desirable choice for some but by no means all retirees. Only Iowa PERS, Mississippi PERS, and Washington TRS offer retirees the option of partial lump-sum distributions where 20 to 40 percent of retirees in each of these plans select this option. Five states offer a guaranteed payment period annuity option. This distribution option is popular in Iowa and Nebraska, where almost one-third of retirees select it; however, the proportion of retirees in Mississippi, South Carolina, and Wyoming selecting this option is under 10 percent.

Do these options represent the best payout choices for public sector retirees, given the early ages at which many retire and the rising number of years that many will spend in retirement? Since many public retirees find new employment shortly after leaving their career jobs, their need for immediate income from their pension may be less pressing compared to older persons who do not work after retirement. Moreover, delaying the start of Social Security benefits is an excellent method of enhancing retirement income, but the Social Security leveling option encourages people to take their benefits as soon as they are eligible. In what follows, we develop two annuity options that could enhance the probability that public retirees will achieve their retirement goals.

New Annuity Options for Public Retirement Plans

We now examine two potential new annuity options that could improve retirement well-being for some households. One would be to allow retirees to defer receiving their retirement benefits to a specified age, with the proviso that the retirement system would recalculate the monthly benefit so that the lifetime expected present value would be the same as if benefits had begun at the time of retirement. In the following, we refer to this option as a 'deferred annuity'. This could appeal to young retirees in good health and who expect to shift from their career public job to new employment.[11] The second option would be for public retirement systems to modify the Social Security leveling options so workers could elect later target ages for claiming Social Security. We call this a 'flexible Social Security leveling'. This second approach could appeal to young retirees who do not plan to re-enter the labor force after retirement but who would like to maximize their retirement income. Both options should provide increased income in the later years of retirement compared to currently available options.

Deferred Annuity

Many career public employees retire from their state or local jobs at relatively young ages, in their 50s or early 60s.[12] Many of these young retirees move directly, or after a short period, into bridge jobs or new careers.[13] Clark et al. (2015) reported that 85 percent of public employees age 50–9 in North Carolina planned to work after retiring from their current state or local government job. Younger retirees are much more likely to anticipate a period of employment following retirement from their public sector jobs. Depending on whether they work full- or part-time, these individuals may not need to draw their pension immediately after leaving the public sector.

A deferred annuity option would offer public sector retirees the opportunity to select some future year to start retirement benefits with the annual benefit being recalculated, so that the expected present value of lifetime retirement benefits remained the same regardless of when they were initiated. Using the restriction that the new option would be cost-neutral to the system, the increase in annual benefits would be an easy calculation using the same assumptions currently used by the system to determine other benefit calculations. This new annuity option should be cost-neutral to the system in the same manner as joint and survivor annuities are cost-neutral relative to the maximum benefit options in public sector retirement plans.

A simple example helps illustrate the impact on annual retirement benefits of postponing the start of annual payouts based on a deferred annuity option. Assume that a worker leaves public employment at age 55 with the option to start receiving a benefit of $30,000 immediately (the maximum allowance), or a higher annual benefit beginning at some point in the future. She can expect to live until age 85, for 30 years of benefits in retirement. Table 8.2 shows the benefit if the worker selected the deferred annuity option and delayed the start of benefits for five years until age 60, or 10 years until age 65.

If the retiree deferred the start of benefits under the deferred annuity option until age 60, she could anticipate a life annuity beginning at that time of approximately $39,233 (using a real interest rate of 3 percent).[14] If benefits were delayed further until age 65, the annual benefit would increase to $53,351. Of course, the retiree does not have access to any benefits during the first five or ten years while the benefit is being deferred. For public employees who leave their career job in their 50s and shift to new

TABLE 8.2 Impact of deferred annuity on annual payouts and pension present values (PV)

Annuity option	Annual payout	PV@55	PV@60	PV@65
Maximum allowance				
3% interest	$30,000	$588,013		
7.25% interest	$30,000	$363,110		
Deferred annuity: first benefit deferred until age 60				
3% interest				
Ages 55–64	$0	$588,013	$683,174	
Ages 65–84	$39,233			
7.25% interest				
Ages 55–64	$0	$363,110	$522,878	
Ages 65–84	$45,884			
Deferred annuity: first benefit deferred until age 65				
3% interest				
Ages 55–64	$0	$588,013		$793,735
Ages 65–84	$53,351			
7.25% interest				
Ages 55–64	$0	$363,110		$749,724
Ages 65–84	$72,150			

Notes: Values in table assume that the individual retires at age 55 and dies at age 85. Selecting the maximum benefit allowance, the annual pension benefit is $30,000 if the retiree begins receiving payments at age 55. The present value of $30,000 per year for 30 years at a 3% discount rate is $588,013 and $363,110 using a discount rate of 7.25%. Next, we assume that if benefits are deferred, the retirement system pays an implicit annual return on the present value equal to the assumed interest rate. The annual payouts at age 60 and 65 are derived by using the annuity formula and the implied present value of the account balance at these ages. Calculations are based on annual pension benefit paid at the end of each year. Values are derived using a real interest rate of 3% per year and an interest rate in the range of that assumed by many state retirement plans of 7.25% per year.

Source: Authors' calculations.

employment, the deferred annuity could be an effective means of enhancing retirement income. Table 8.2 shows that the increase in annual benefits will be greater when the system uses an interest rate consistent with its assumed rate of return or discount rate used in calculating the present value of liabilities.

The deferred annuity option would give retirees more flexibility in their retirement planning and allow some to shift income from a period of continued employment in bridge jobs to later ages. Clark et al. (2015) illustrate the importance of bridge jobs and work after retirement for public retirees in North Carolina. This adjustment to the timing of retirement income could also help retirees finance health care costs, which often rise with advancing age, and provide increased protection against the erosive effect of inflation over 20 or 30 years in retirement.

Flexible Social Security Leveling

Another group of public sector employees retires at relatively young ages and leaves the labor force permanently. Such individuals need to access their pension benefits immediately on retiring from their career jobs. The Social Security leveling option currently included in 20 public pension plans allows retirees to receive an annual benefit larger than the maximum benefit option prior to the specified age, typically age 62, but then the pension benefit declines when the individual is eligible to claim early Social Security benefits. The idea is to provide retirees with a constant total annual benefit (pension plus Social Security) from retirement until death. While retirees are not required to claim Social Security at age 62, if they do not, their annual incomes will fall. Thus there is a strong incentive for retirees who have chosen the Social Security leveling option to claim benefits at age 62.

It is worth noting, however, that Social Security currently specifies age 66 as the age for full retirement benefits and imposes penalties for claiming benefits between 62, the early retirement age, and 66. Similarly, the system currently provides delayed retirement credits for postponing the start of benefits up to age 70.[15] Claiming benefits prior to age 66 results in a reduction in monthly benefits of five-ninths of 1 percent per month for the first 36 months and five-twelfths of 1 percent for each additional month.[16] Delaying claiming benefits after age 66 increases benefits by 8 percent per year up to age 70. Assume that if benefits are begun at the full retirement age of 66, the monthly benefit will be $1,000. If benefits are claimed at 62, the earliest age of eligibility, the monthly benefit is only $750 per month or a 25 percent reduction in monthly benefits for the rest of one's life. Despite these penalties for early claiming, almost half of all individuals claim benefits at age 62.[17] In contrast, if benefit claiming is delayed until age 70, the monthly benefit would be $1,320 or 32 percent greater than would be true if benefits are begun at age 66. Comparing the benefit at age 70 to the benefit at 62, the monthly benefit is 76 percent greater when benefits are claimed at age 70.[18]

Experts examining the Social Security rules have also argued that, for most households, delaying the start of Social Security benefits results in a higher lifetime present value of these benefits (Shoven and Slavov 2014a, 2014b). Moreover, the rise in lifetime benefits resulting from a claiming delay has been increasing due to changes in Social Security rules.[19] Shoven and Slavov (2013: 1) state that 'with today's life expectancies and today's extremely low interest rates, it is in almost everyone's interest to delay the commencement of Social Security. For many people, delaying to 70 is the value maximizing strategy.'[20]

Instead of claiming Social Security benefits at age 62, Goda et al. (2015) examine how retirees could draw on their assets in retirement saving accounts (IRAs and 401(k) accounts) to fund consumption for several years prior to claiming Social Security benefits. Because the lifetime expected present value of Social Security benefits is greater when individuals wait to begin claiming their benefit until an older age, drawing on personal savings, such as the retirement savings accounts mentioned earlier, after age 62 and waiting to claim Social Security benefits at older ages will yield higher annual retirement income.

A flexible Social Security leveling annuity would allow public sector retirees to select any age between 62 and 70 for the target date on which the pension annuity would decline and Social Security benefits would begin.[21] This option would use the same assumptions currently used to derive the pension annuity before and after age 62, and thus should be cost-neutral to the system. If the lifetime present value of Social Security benefits rises with delayed claiming while the present value of the pension benefits is held constant, then total annual income will be higher if Social Security leveling were based on a later retirement age.

Conclusions

State and local retirement plans typically offer retirees a range of annuity options. Nevertheless, increasing life expectancy and delayed retirement suggest some new options are needed. Specifically, the deferred annuity option we outline here would allow young retirees who are moving to new jobs the ability to defer the start of their pension, providing for a greater benefit in future years. A flexible Social Security leveling option would provide greater annual benefits for early retirees throughout their retirement. This second innovation would take advantage of the fact that the present value of Social Security benefits increases if claiming is delayed for most individuals.

In the wake of the economic downturn, many public pension plan administrators and lawmakers came to the conclusion that modifying or even terminating existing public sector DB plans would provide cheaper, more sustainable retirement benefits. Pension reforms have ranged from simple reductions in benefit generosity, including benefit multiplier reductions or increased normal retirement ages, to a more drastic restructuring of benefit design. Such changes have typically aimed to shift some or all of the investment and longevity risk on to employees while protecting the employers against risk, market volatility, and further increases in pension costs. But the efficacy of these pension reforms in minimizing employer costs and risks, as well as the broader impact on public sector retirement security and human resource needs, remain to be seen.

Meanwhile, we have outlined two ways to restructure the traditional DB plans to ensure that these plans can meet the needs of current and future public sector workers and retirees. Ultimately, the true value of a public employee benefits system is that retirement benefits help government employers recruit and retain qualified personnel to deliver essential services and then provide adequate retirement income to career employees. This policy goal reflects a trade-off between the cost of funding the plan and the benefit of maintaining a quality labor force that is able to produce the goods and services that its citizens desire. To this end, it is essential to administer the plan benefits in a manner that encourages sensible public employee choices in the face of evolving economic circumstances and preferences. Modernization of this benefit structure will build the continued value, equity, and cost effectiveness of these plans. Reforming traditional DB plans instead of shifting to defined contribution plans or hybrid plans is a viable path forward for some state and local governments.

Our study highlights one important plan characteristic within the larger design of DB plans that demonstrates the valuable role that independent policy and economic research can play in pension reforms. Reinventing pension administration requires that adequate time and resources be devoted to understand the costs, benefits, efficiencies, and opportunities with the current system. Changing public sector retirement plans without such analysis could yield undesirable outcomes and produce unanticipated, and even potentially harmful, fallout for public employers, employees, and taxpayers.

Acknowledgments

The authors acknowledge the helpful suggestions and comments of Emma Hanson Turner, Christelle Khalaf, Sam Watts, and Matthew Leatherman. Partial support for Clark in the preparation of this chapter was provided by the Sloan Foundation, Grant Number 2013-10-20.

Appendix

TABLE 8A.1 Percentage of state plan retirees selecting annuity options

State	Plan	Maximum allowance	Joint and survivor	Social Security leveling	Guaranteed payment	Partial lump sum
Mississippi	MHSPRS	26.81	70.28		2.08	22.92
Mississippi	SLRP	42.78	36.36		14.44	16.04
South Carolina	GARS	36.74	63.26			
South Carolina	JSRS	90.34	9.66			
South Carolina	PORS	59.65	34.66	5.69		
South Carolina	SCNG	100				
Washington	LEOFF	12.80	87.20			
Washington	PSERS	71	29			
Washington	SERS	72.70	27.30			
Washington	WSPRS		100			
Wyoming	Air Guards	20	80			
Wyoming	Law	25.03	72.16		2.81	
Wyoming	Firefighters	30.38	60.75		8.86	
Wyoming	Warden	44.9	51.43		3.67	

Source: Data provided by state plans in response to Janet Cowell's email sent to state Treasurers.

TABLE 8.2 Annuity payout options offered by state retirement plans

State	Plan	Maximum allowance	Joint and survivor	Social Security leveling	Guaranteed payment period	Lump sum + benefit
Alabama	ERS	2 options	100%–50%	No	No	No
Alabama	TRS	2 options	100%–50%	No	No	No
Alaska	**PERS**	Yes	75%–50%	Yes	No	No
Alaska	**TRS**	Yes	75%–50%	No	No	No
Arizona	SRS	Remaining balance paid to beneficiary	100%–66%–50%	No	5Y–10Y–15Y	No
Arkansas	PERS	Remaining balance paid to beneficiary	75%–50%	No	60P–120P	No
Arkansas	TRS	Remaining balance paid to beneficiary	75%–50%	No	60P–120P	No
California	PERS	2 options*	100%–50%	No	No	No
California	**TRS**	Yes	100%–75%–50%	No	No	No
Colorado	**PERA**	Remaining balance paid to beneficiary	100%–50%	No	Yes+	No
Connecticut	SERS	Yes	100%–75%–50%	No	10Y–20Y	No
Connecticut	**TRS**	Remaining balance paid to beneficiary	100%–66%–50%–33%	No	5Y–10Y–15Y–20Y–25Y	No
Delaware	SEPP	Remaining balance paid to beneficiary	100%–75%–66%–50%	No	No	No
Florida	FRS	Remaining balance paid to beneficiary	100%–75%	No	10Y	No
Georgia	ERS	Remaining balance paid to beneficiary	100%–50%	No	Yes	Yes
Georgia	TRS	Remaining balance paid to beneficiary	100%–50%	No	No	No
Hawaii	ERS	Remaining balance paid to beneficiary	100%–50%	No	No	No

(continued)

TABLE 8A.2 Continued

State	Plan	Maximum allowance	Joint and survivor	Social Security leveling	Guaranteed payment period	Lump sum + benefit
Idaho	PERS	Yes	100%–50%	Yes	No	No
Illinois	SRS	Remaining balance paid to beneficiary	100%–50%	Yes	No	No
Illinois	**TRS**	Remaining balance paid to beneficiary	100%–75%	No	10Y–15Y–20Y	No
Illinois	MRF	Remaining balance paid to beneficiary	100%–75%–50%	Yes	No	Yes
Indiana	PERF	Remaining balance paid to beneficiary	100%–66%–50%	Yes	5Y	No
Indiana	TRF	Remaining balance paid to beneficiary	100%–66%–50%	Yes	Yes	No
Iowa	PERS	2 options*	100%–75%–50%–25%	No	120P	No
Kansas	PERS	Yes	100%–75%–50%	No	5Y–10Y–15Y	Yes
Kentucky	KERS	Remaining balance paid to beneficiary	100%–66%–50%	Yes	5Y–10Y–15Y	Yes
Kentucky	CERS	Yes	100%–66%–50%	Yes	5Y–10Y–15Y	Yes
Kentucky	**TRS**	Remaining balance paid to beneficiary	100%–50%	No	10Y	No
Louisiana	**SERS**	Remaining balance paid to beneficiary	100%–50%	No	No	No
Louisiana	**TRSL**	2 options*	100%–66%–50%	No	No	No
Maine	**PERS**	2 options*	100%–50%	No	No	No
Maryland	SRPS	Remaining balance paid to beneficiary	100%–50%	No	No	No
Massachusetts	**SERS**	2 options*	66%	No	No	No
Massachusetts	**TRS**	2 options*	66%	No	No	No
Michigan	SERS	Remaining balance paid to beneficiary	100%–75%	Yes	No	No

State	System	Benefit option				
Michigan	MERS	Remaining balance paid to beneficiary	100%–75%–50%	No	5Y–10Y–15Y–20Y	No
Michigan	PSERS	Remaining balance paid to beneficiary	100%–75%–50%	Yes	No	No
Minnesota	MSRS	Remaining balance paid to beneficiary	100%–75%–50%	No	15Y	No
Minnesota	PERA	Remaining balance paid to beneficiary	100%–75%–50%–25%	No	No	No
Minnesota	TRA	2 options*	100%–75%–50%	No	15Y	No
Mississippi	PERS	Remaining balance paid to beneficiary	100%–75%–50%	No	10Y–15Y–20Y	No
Missouri	SERS	Remaining balance paid to beneficiary	100%–50%	No	60P–120P	No
Missouri	LAGERS	Yes	100%–75%–50%	No	No	No
Missouri	**PSRS**	Remaining balance paid to beneficiary	100%–75%–50%	No	60P–120P	No
Montana	PERS	Remaining balance paid to beneficiary	100%–50%	No	10Y–20Y	No
Montana	TRS	Remaining balance paid to beneficiary	100%–66%–50%	No	10Y–20Y	No
Nebraska	SEPP	2 options*	100%–75%–50%	No	5Y–10Y–15Y	No
Nebraska	CEPP	2 options*	100%–75%–50%	No	5Y–10Y–15Y	No
Nebraska	SPP	2 options*	100%–75%–50%	No	5Y–10Y–15Y	No
Nevada	**PERS**	Yes	100%–50%	No	No	No
New Hampshire	NHRS	Remaining balance paid to beneficiary	100%–50%	No	No	No
New Jersey	PERS	2 options*	100%–75%–50%–25%	No	No	No
New Jersey	TPAF	2 options*	100%–75%–50%–25%	No	No	No
New Mexico	PERA	Remaining balance paid to beneficiary	100%–50%	No	No	No
New Mexico	ERA	Remaining balance paid to beneficiary	100%–50%	No	No	No

(continued)

State	Plan	Maximum allowance	Joint and survivor	Social Security leveling	Guaranteed payment period	Lump sum + benefit
New York	ERS	Yes	100%–75%–50%–25%	No	5Y–10Y	No
New York	TRS	2 options*	50%	No	5Y–10Y	No
North Carolina	TSERS	Yes	100%–50%	Yes	No	No
North Carolina	LGERS	Yes	100%–50%	Yes	No	No
North Dakota	PERS	Remaining balance paid to beneficiary	100%–50%	No	10Y–20Y	Yes
North Dakota	TRF	Remaining balance paid to beneficiary	100%–50%	Yes	10Y–20Y	Yes
Ohio	**PERS**	Remaining balance paid to beneficiary	100%–75%–66%–50%–25%	No	No	Yes
Ohio	**STRS**	Remaining balance paid to beneficiary	100%–50%	No	Yes+	Yes
Oklahoma	PERS	Yes	100%–50%	No	10Y	No
Oklahoma	TRS	Remaining balance paid to beneficiary	100%–50%	No	120P	Yes
Oregon	PERS	2 options*	100%–50%	No	15Y	Yes
Pennsylvania	SERS	Remaining balance paid to beneficiary	100%–50%	No	No	No
Pennsylvania	PSERS	Remaining balance paid to beneficiary	100%–50%	No	No	Yes
Rhode Island	ERS	Yes	100%–50%	Yes	No	No
South Carolina	SCRS	Remaining balance paid to beneficiary	100%–50%	No	No	No
South Dakota	SRS	Remaining balance paid to beneficiary	66%	Yes	No	No
Tennessee	CRS	Remaining balance paid to beneficiary	100%–50%	Yes	No	No

Texas	ERS	Remaining balance paid to beneficiary	100%–75%–50%	No	60P–120P	Yes
Texas	**TRS**	Remaining balance paid to beneficiary	100%–75%–50%	No	No	No
Texas	MRS	Remaining balance paid to beneficiary	100%–75%–50%	No	60P–120P	No
Utah	SRS	2 options*	100%–50%	No	No	No
Vermont	SRS	2 options*	100%–50%	Yes	No	No
Vermont	TRS	2 options*	100%–50%	Yes	No	No
Virginia	SRS	Remaining balance paid to beneficiary	100%–75%–66%–50%–25%	Yes	No	Yes
Washington	PERS	Remaining balance paid to beneficiary	100%–66%–50%	No	No	No
Washington	TRS	2 options*	100%–66%–50%	No	No	No
West Virginia	PERS	Yes	100%–50%	No	No	No
West Virginia	TRS	Yes	100%–50%	No	120P	No
Wisconsin	WRS	Yes	100%–75%	Yes	60P–180P	No
Wyoming	WRS	2 options*	100%–50%	No	10Y–20Y	No

Notes: Alaska also offers a 66% last survivor plan. The last survivor (retiree or beneficiary) gets 66% of the benefit. Employees in state plans in bold are not covered by social security. Employees covered by plans shown in bold are not included in the Social Security system.

Source: Authors' derivations using data from all plan websites.

Notes

1. The Wisconsin report compares important characteristics of retirement plans covering major state and local retirement systems in the US. Similar reports have been prepared bi-annually since 1982 and are a useful source of pension characteristics and how they have evolved over the past 30 years. Key characteristics of plans include normal and early retirement provisions, contribution rates, vesting requirements, benefit formulas, COLAs, and actuarial methods and assumptions. Many public plans have specific features that vary by when employees were hired. For these plans, the report describes the features that apply to the most recently hired employees.

2. While these plans for specific types of employees are not included in the Wisconsin survey, we did receive information from some of the states indicating the proportion of retirees in these plans that selected specific types of annuities.

3. The options available to current retirees in each of the plans are reported in Appendix Table 8A.2.

4. The benefit paid to the retiree who selects a J&S option will depend on the age of the beneficiary and benefit paid to the survivor relative to the benefit payable while the retiree was alive.

5. In the private sector, most DB plans do not require employee contributions. The lump-sum distribution is based on a calculation of the discounted present value of the promised annuity.

6. The maximum benefit allowance in some plans includes a provision to provide a payment to the survivor if the total pension payout has not exceeded the worker's contributions to the plan.

7. Workers in 17 of the 85 plans are not covered by Social Security. Ten of these plans in which participants are not included in Social Security cover only teachers.

8. The email requested information on the proportion of retirees selecting each of the annuity options. In some cases, certain options may no longer be offered so we observe some differences in the annuity options that are shown in Appendix Table 8A.2 and the responses to the survey presented in Table 8.1.

9. Brown and Poterba (2000) examine the importance of joint life annuities and the demand for this type of annuity by married couples.

10. It is important to remember that only individuals who retire prior to the specified age in the leveling options would be able to select Social Security leveling. Thus, the proportion of eligible retirees selecting Social Security leveling will be higher than the proportion of all retirees choosing this annuity.

11. Cahill et al. (2012, 2015) use the Health and Retirement Survey to document this type of return to work after retirement from a career job.

12. The retirement plans included in this study typically have several age and service requirements that allow career employees to retire in their 50s with unreduced benefits. In 2012, 40 plans had normal retirement requirements

that allowed workers with 30 or fewer years of service to retire at age 55 with unreduced benefits. Another 11 plans determine eligibility by the sum of an individual's age and service ('Rule of 85' or 'Rule of 80') which allows career employees who began their employment in their 20s to receive unreduced benefits in their 50s. Public retirement plans are now moving to increase normal retirement ages. According to the Wisconsin Comparative Study of major plans, between 2010 and 2012, 29 plans increased the requirements for normal retirement.

13. Clark and Morrill (2016) provide a comprehensive review of retirement transitions including workers remaining on career jobs until complete retirement, shifts into phased retirement, and movement into bridge jobs or self-employment.

14. This calculation is based on the present value of $30,000 per year for 30 years which is $588,013. If the retirement system credits this balance with a 3 percent per year return for 10 years, the account balance would be $793,734 at age 65. Again using a discount rate of 3 percent, the annual payout for an expected 20 years would be $53,351. Thus, the increase in the annual retirement benefit is due to the increase in the account balance from delaying the start of the annuity and the shorter payout period associated with a higher age for starting the annuity. A 3 percent discount rate is consistent with the rate that most economists would recommend as an approximation of the real interest rate. Most public pension plans use a much higher rate, typically between 7 and 8 percent. Thus, we also provide the impact of using a higher interest rate consistent with the assumption adopted by most plans.

15. Under current law, the full retirement age is scheduled to rise to 67 for individuals born in 1960 or thereafter.

16. Knoll and Olsen (2014) describe how these reductions for claiming early and increases for delaying claiming after the full retirement age have changed over time to provide increased incentives for delaying the start of benefits. Based on their analysis and review of the literature, they conclude that delaying the claiming of Social Security retirement benefits is now recognized as an important way to enhance retirement security.

17. Munnell and Chen (2015) find, using a cohort analysis, that the proportion of recent cohorts claiming benefits at age 62 has fallen to 36 percent for men and 40 percent for women.

18. The impact of claiming age on monthly benefits is nicely shown in 'When to Start Receiving Retirement Benefits', https://www.ssa.gov/pubs/EN-05-10147.pdf

19. For instance, the increase in the delayed retirement credit after the full retirement age, lower real interest rates, and increases in life expectancy for individuals in their 60s.

20. Shoven and Slavov (2013) provide a detailed review of claiming options and how delaying the start of Social Security benefits increases lifetime benefits.

21. This option is similar to the one used by Virginia SRS except we would allow the individual to specify any age between 62 and 70 for the calculation of retirement benefit.

References

Brown, J. (2001). 'Private Pensions, Mortality Risk, and the Decision to Annuitize'. *Journal of Public Economics* 82(1): 29–62.

Brown, J. and J. Poterba (2000). 'Joint Life Annuities and the Demand for Annuities by Married Couples'. *Journal of Risk and Insurance* 67(4): 527–53.

Cahill, K., M. Giandrea, and J. Quinn (2012). 'Older Workers and Short-Term Jobs: Patterns and Determinants'. *Monthly Labor Review* 135(5): 19–32.

Cahill, K., M. Giandrea, and J. Quinn (2015). 'Retirement Patterns and the Macroeconomy, 1992–2010: The Prevalence and Determinants of Bridge Jobs, Phased Retirement, and Re-Entry among Different Cohorts of Older Americans'. *The Gerontologist* 55(3): 384–403.

Clark, R., R. Hammond, M. Morrill, and A. Pathak (2015). 'Working after Retiring from Career Jobs: Worklife Transitions of Public Employees in North Carolina'. Paper presented to 2015 SIEPR Conference Working Longer and Retirement, Stanford University, October.

Clark, R. and M. Morrill (2016). 'Extending Worklife: Employer Interest and Concerns'. North Carolina State University Working Paper.

Goda, G. S., S. Ramnath, J. Shoven, and S. Slavov (2015). 'The Financial Feasibility of Delaying Social Security: Evidence from Administrative Tax Data'. NBER Working Paper No. 21544. Cambridge, MA: National Bureau of Economic Research.

Knoll, M. and A. Olsen (2014). 'Incentivizing Delayed Claiming of Social Security Retirement Benefits before Reaching the Full Retirement Age'. *Social Security Bulletin* 74(4): 1–31.

Mitchell, O. S., J. Poterba, M. Warshawsky, and J. Brown (1999). 'New Evidence on the Money's Worth of Individual Annuities'. *American Economic Review* 89(5): 1299–318.

Munnell, A. and A. Chen (2015). 'Trends in Social Security Claiming'. Center for Retirement Research at Boston College Working Paper No. 15-8.

Shoven, J. and S. Slavov (2013). 'Efficient Retirement Design: Combining Private Assets and Social Security to Maximize Retirement Resources'. Stanford Institute for Economic Policy Research Policy Brief. Stanford, CA: SEPR.

Shoven, J. and S. Slavov (2014a). 'Does It Pay to Delay Social Security?' *Journal of Pension Economics and Finance* 13(2): 121–44.

Shoven, J. and S. Slavov (2014b). 'Recent Changes in the Gains from Delaying Social Security'. *Journal of Financial Planning* 27(3): 32–41.

Wisconsin Legislative Council (2013). '2012 Comparative Study of Major Public Employee Retirement Systems'. Wisconsin Legislative Council Issue Brief. Madison, WI: WLC.

Part III
Solutions and Opportunities

Chapter 9

Aging and Exploitation: How Should the Financial Service Industry Respond?

Marguerite DeLiema and Martha Deevy

Elder financial victimization encompasses fraud targeting vulnerable older adults and financial exploitation by someone in a position of trust, yet it is difficult to define. This is partly due to the diverse mechanisms of financial victimization, the various actors involved, and the different types of relationships between perpetrators and their targets (Jackson 2015). The National Center on Elder Abuse (1998) defines elder financial exploitation as the illegal or improper use of an elder's funds, property, or assets. An 'elder' is typically defined as an adult over the age of 60 or 65, although legal statutes and social programs for the elderly may differ.

Financial victimization includes crimes such as scams and fraud, use of an older person's checks, credit, or debit cards without permission, wrongful transfer of property or assets, misappropriation of funds, and abuse of fiduciary duty by a trusted representative (Bonnie and Wallace 2003). Friends, relatives, and caregivers who financially exploit vulnerable people take advantage of their trust to gain control of bank accounts, checkbooks, and payment cards, often under the guise of 'helping' elders manage their finances. The abuser may be an appointed power of attorney, a legal guardian, a trustee, or someone else in a fiduciary role, or have informal access to the elder's money through a familial bond. Fraud perpetrators, by contrast, are predatory strangers who earn their target's trust by promising a future benefit or reward in exchange for money or personal information upfront.

Compared to younger persons, seniors may be disproportionately targeted by fraud perpetrators based on assumptions that they are more trusting of strangers, socially isolated, cognitively impaired, and have more financial resources to exploit. Older adults generally have higher credit scores, fixed Social Security or pension income, and more established savings, which also makes them more attractive targets for identity thieves and hackers (Comizio et al. 2015). Although people of all ages can be victims of fraud regardless of cognitive status or financial sophistication, common scams targeting seniors include bogus sweepstakes and prize promotions, unnecessary health care products, imposter scams, bogus investments, tech support scams, and fake charities (National Council on Aging 2015). To elicit compliance, perpetrators use tactics such as false affiliation with a trusted authority, social consensus, emotional arousal, enticement, intimidation, undue influence, and other persuasion methods. Victims ultimately never receive the promised rewards because they do not exist, were never intended to be provided, or were grossly misrepresented (Titus et al. 1995). In this chapter we focus on *financial exploitation*, where an older person is taken advantage of by friends and/or family members (people in positions of trust), as well as *elder fraud*, where a vulnerable older adult willingly agrees to give the perpetrator money in exchange for a promised future benefit or reward. Crimes in which the victim has no active role in the fraudulent transaction or where there is no interaction with the perpetrator (such as credit card theft or identity theft) are outside the scope of this chapter.

In what follows, we describe what the financial service industry is doing to adjust to an aging client population frequently targeted by predatory scam artists and greedy family members. We describe new approaches to financial victimization detection, prevention, and intervention by wealth advisory and banking firms, and we also outline the current regulatory landscape under which these firms are operating. We highlight the limitations of current regulations and practices, identify regulatory/legislative solutions, and offer options for improving protection.

Background and Significance

As the number of adults age 65+ grows in the US, so too will the incidence and cost of financial victimization. A study by Holtfreter et al. (2014) found that annual prevalence of elder financial fraud was approximately 14 percent among those age 60+ in Florida and Arizona. This is higher than the rate of elder financial exploitation by a family member of 5.2 percent among community-residing adults age 60+ (Acierno et al. 2010). Both numbers may be underestimates given the low rates of reporting among older people (Pak and Shadel 2011). Estimates of direct losses from elder financial victimization range from $2.9 to $36.5 billion a year (MetLife Mature Market Institute 2009; True Link 2015), and total fraud losses for all US adults may be well over $50 billion annually (Deevy and Beals 2013). In addition to direct losses, other costs include legal fees and time off work to resolve the cases; as well as emotional consequences such as shame, frustration, depression, and feelings of betrayal (Button et al. 2010; Deem 2000; FINRA Foundation 2015). Among victims who experienced indirect losses from fraud, 45 percent of survey respondents paid $100–$1,000 in additional costs associated with the incident, and 29 percent paid over $1,000 in indirect costs (FINRA Foundation 2015).

The financial industry has a pivotal role to play in reducing fraud and financial exploitation. Financial professionals are well-positioned to recognize the hallmarks of fraud and financial exploitation which include uncharacteristic withdrawals from checking, savings, or investment accounts; forged signatures on checks or financial documents; abrupt changes in powers of attorney; unexplained asset transfers; large checks written out to cash; and strangers becoming involved in the client's financial affairs (Conrad et al. 2011). A majority of financial professionals have witnessed these and other indicators during their careers. The Certified Financial Planner (CFP) Board of Standards found that 56 percent of CFPs stated they had clients who had been subject to unfair, deceptive, or abusive practices, with an average loss of $50,000 per victim (CFP Board of Standards 2012).

Financial sector firms face increasing pressure from regulators to ramp up their financial protection efforts. They can suffer customer litigation liability and enforcement actions for failing to address the risk of fraud in their compliance and employee training programs (Comizio et al. 2015). In the 2015 White House Conference on Aging, financial service firms were called on by the Director of the Consumer Financial Protection Bureau to educate employees and consumers on identifying crimes against the elderly (Cordray 2015). Due to the increased scrutiny around the issue, many firms are investing in programs to better detect customer vulnerability before funds are stolen and are developing protocols to respond quickly and effectively if prevention attempts fail. These practices help secure client assets, restore confidence in the institution, and strengthen brand value (Gunther 2016).

Though these are powerful motivators, preventing financial victimization is fraught with risks. Regulations designed to uphold consumer rights to privacy and autonomy sometimes interfere with a firm's financial protection efforts. For example, consumers have a right to make decisions about how and where they spend and invest their money, even if these choices are not in their best interests. So although firms have relationship management and risk management reasons to intervene when fraud is suspected, they must also be cautious not to infringe on their clients' autonomy (Lichtenberg 2016; Lock 2016). This means they must attempt to differentiate when losses are due to financial victimization versus when they result from poor consumer decision making in risky financial markets. This is a significant challenge given the ambiguity of many situations.

Analyses

Our approach was to conduct semi-structured interviews with a range of representatives from financial service firms and regulatory agencies. We agreed that data from written questionnaires would be less informative given the dearth of research that exists in this area to help design survey items and the challenge of recruiting enough representatives who are knowledgeable about the topic and their organizations' activities. Our findings were further informed by research from the AARP Public Policy Institute's BankSafe Initiative, policy briefs, financial institution trade organizations, and academic researchers. We focus exclusively on financial advisors and depository institutions because they have high customer contact and serve a sizeable proportion of the older adult population.[1]

In selecting participants to interview, our goal was to survey firms that varied in size and market share to identify the scope of detection, intervention, and prevention practices. Accordingly, we spoke to two large banks with over 70 million customers that manage $1.8 and $2.1 trillion in assets, respectively, and employ an average of 244,000 full-time employees. We also interviewed midsize regional banks with approximately $74 billion in assets and 10,000 employees, as well as small community banks with fewer than fifteen branches, less than $1 billion in assets, and under 350 employees. To report on the broker-dealer side of the industry, we also interviewed large and medium-sized wealth management firms. The largest had approximately $2.5 trillion in assets and over 15,000 financial advisors, and the smallest had nearly $650 billion in assets and a few thousand contracted financial advisors. No small brokers or registered investment advisors were interviewed for this chapter, a limitation that may be addressed in later research. We also sought perspectives from regulatory bodies that oversee financial service industries including the Financial Industry Regulatory Authority (FINRA) (the largest broker-dealer self-regulatory organization), the North American Securities Administrators Association (NASAA), the Consumer Financial Protection Bureau (CFPB), and the Securities and Exchange Commission (SEC).[2]

Questions posed to the financial service firms included: (1) What is your firm doing to detect and prevent fraud and financial exploitation? (2) What regulations govern your detection/prevention policies? (3) How do you train your employees to recognize the signs of financial victimization by the clients' friends, family, or strangers? (4) What are your policies for reporting concerns that a client is being victimized? (5) Are there any actions you wish you could take to intervene, but can't because of regulatory/legal issues? (6) Is your firm going beyond regulatory requirements? (7) Are there any other barriers to detection and intervention that you would like to share? (8) Do you wish you could do more?

Questions posed to the state, federal, and local regulatory bodies/law enforcement agencies were: (1) Under current rules and regulations, what are [banks/financial advisors] obligated to do to protect their clients from fraud and financial abuse? (2) Do these regulations conflict with what firms are actually doing or not doing? If so, how? (3) What would you like to see firms doing better to protect their clients against financial victimization? (4) What do you see as the future of regulation in this area?

All participants were informed that no comments would be attributed to particular informants unless special permission was requested. These steps were taken to encourage the entities to speak candidly about sensitive topics typically not discussed with researchers because of concerns about brand reputation and potential liability issues.

Findings

A key priority across the financial service sector was to reduce the incidence of fraud and financial exploitation. Our respondents expressed that the interest in elder financial abuse has grown exponentially of late, starting in the broker-dealer side of the industry. Interest was driven by increasing referrals to compliance departments and demand by frontline staff to receive more guidance on how to address potential financial victimization of older clients.

We found significant variations in approaches for resolving financial victimization that were based on differences between bank and financial advisory firms' customer relationship models. Financial advisors have personal relationships with their clients and often work with the same individuals for decades and through multiple life stages. Therefore they tend to be more familiar with their clients' finances, risk preferences, and short- and long-term financial goals. By contrast, bank employees have transaction-based relationships with their customers. Their interactions are typically very brief and they do not assist customers with financial planning. Employees of small community banks may know some customers personally, but large national bank employees have thousands of customers who may visit multiple branches across different locations. These different client relationship models have produced somewhat different strategies for detecting and preventing financial victimization.

Borrowing terms sometimes used to classify the stages of patient care, we suggest that financial victimization can be addressed using both *primary* and *secondary* intervention. *Primary* interventions focus on stopping losses before they occur, such as by training frontline staff to recognize red flags, blocking suspicious transactions, and educating customers about avoiding scams and protecting their assets through estate planning. The primary interventions that we discuss in this chapter include: (1) employee training, (2) community outreach, (3) early financial planning, (4) financial tools, products, and account features, and (5) data-driven fraud detection strategies. *Secondary* interventions are those used to 'treat' the problem once it has already occurred, such as recovery of lost funds and/or criminal prosecution of offenders. The secondary interventions that we discuss in this chapter include: (1) federal reporting of elder financial victimization, (2) reporting to adult protective services (APS), and (3) working with local law enforcement agencies. Systematic research on the effectiveness of specific primary and secondary intervention practices is lacking in this area, so while various programs are described in this chapter, their outcomes are not presented. Evaluations of program effectiveness are sorely needed and should be addressed in future research. Because intervention approaches differ between banks and wealth advisors due to different client relationship models and different regulations, their unique approaches are presented separately in the following.

Primary Interventions

Training Financial Advisors

Training wealth advisors on issues related to elder financial victimization is required at all the firms we interviewed, although the focus, frequency, duration, and modality of training programs differ. All businesses require new employees to be trained to identify the signs of financial exploitation and the steps to take when exploitation or fraud is suspected. Some firms require employees to complete training one time only, generally when they are first hired, whereas others require re-training each year or whenever new guidelines and protocols are implemented.

While most firms state that their training programs are computer-based, two wealth advisory firms indicated that instructor-led training is more effective at increasing retention and conveying the complexity of financial exploitation scenarios. For example, Wells Fargo Advisors has a training program that uses hypothetical video-based vignettes to guide advisors and client associates through group discussions about elder financial abuse (Long 2014). This training is mandatory for all advisors. Employees are also given instructions on how to *OWN IT*, which involves five steps:

(1) *Observe*: Notice unusual patterns or changes in a client's behavior. Are there recent changes in the client's health or mental status that may explain the unusual behavior? Is a stranger accompanying the client to meetings, coaching him over the phone, or overly interested in the client's financial affairs?

(2) *Wonder Why*: Question these unusual behaviors. For example, why is the client suddenly requesting a large disbursement of funds? Who is the unknown third party that will receive the funds?

(3) *Negotiate*: Try to convince the client to delay the transaction or to withdraw a smaller amount until the request can be investigated by the firm.

(4) *Isolate*: Speak with the client privately so that the suspected abuser cannot influence the client's responses.

(5) *Tattle*: Report concerns to a supervisor so that the situation can be investigated further and a report made to APS and/or law enforcement if necessary.

In addition to these programs, financial service professionals are also being educated about issues related to aging and how declines in cognitive functioning may increase the risk of financial exploitation (Marson 2016; Little and Timmerman 2015). This has been identified as a key area of interest among the firms we interviewed. Problems managing money are one of the initial areas of cognition to be impaired with age, and wealth advisors are sometimes the first professionals to notice diminished capacity in their clients (Marson and Sabatino 2012). Signs to look for include repeated phone calls to the advisor, inability to recall signing paperwork, forgetting prior conversations, losing track of important documents, trouble understanding financial concepts, and impaired financial judgment such as showing atypical interest in risky investment options (Triebel and Marson 2012). If diminished capacity is suspected, Little and Timmerman (2015) recommend asking the client to bring a trusted family member to the next meeting and to determine if the client has granted anyone financial power of attorney. They also recommend carefully documenting the conversation and following up via a phone call or email.

Training Bank Employees

Most Americans do not have personal wealth advisors, but the vast majority do have bank accounts (Survey of Consumer Finances 2013). Large depository institutions and payment card retailers are at the forefront of fraud detection using sophisticated algorithms that flag suspicious transfers; however, signs of financial abuse, such as unusual signatures on checks or strangers who accompany an older customer to the bank, are not flagged by automated fraud detection systems. In such situations, customer-facing employees are in the best position to notice exploitation and to get others involved.

A recent AARP study found that 70 percent of adults age 50+ reported that bank employees recognized them when they visited their local branch, and 32 percent saw an employee they knew (Gunther 2016). A Federal Deposit Insurance Corporation (FDIC 2014) survey found that over half of households age 65+ relied primarily on bank tellers to access their accounts, compared to less than 20 percent of households younger than age 45 (FDIC 2014). As a result, in-person interactions with bank employees are still common among older cohorts, and educating frontline staff may curb rates of exploitation. One bank prevented $2.2 million in potential losses through situational training where frontline employees learned the red flags of exploitation and how to report suspicious activity (Swett and Millstein 2002).

Our respondents noted that developing financial exploitation training programs is costly, particularly for small banks with limited development funds. To address such cost issues, financial institution trade organizations are helping their member firms create training materials and other media. For example, with support from the Oregon Department of Human Services, the Oregon Department of Justice, and AARP, the Oregon Bankers Association developed a training manual and DVD for frontline staff. The Oregon Bank Project toolkit and training manual outlines warning signs such as sudden changes in beneficiaries or increases in debt, adding third parties to personal accounts, multiple requests to wire money, and unrecognizable handwriting on checks, deposit slips, or loan applications (Oregon Bankers Association 2013). This toolkit advises staff on what to look for when interacting with customers face-to-face. Such warning signs include the following indicators: the customer is accompanied to the bank by a 'new best friend'; another person speaks on the customer's behalf without authorization; and the customer is confused and cannot give plausible explanations for unusually large withdrawals. This training manual also features information on relevant laws and response protocols. It is freely accessible online and has been distributed to banks throughout the country. Oregon banks are now the second highest reporters of abuse to APS in the state even though reporting is not mandatory for financial institutions (Gunther and Neill 2015).

Several innovative companies are using gamification strategies to make online training more interactive and to incent employees to participate. Barclays, one of the UK's largest banks, created an interactive web-based training tool called *Community Driving Licence*. Employees can earn points by taking short quizzes after each module and then post their points on the company's internal social media platform. The accredited program features modules on how to recognize cognitive impairment and how to make the banking experience more accessible to seniors (Gunther and Neill 2015). Employees can even earn continuing education credits for enrolling in the voluntary program. Such incentives have increased participation.

Acknowledging employees who successfully stop unauthorized transactions also improves motivation and reinforces their training. First Financial Bank in Texas instituted a Fraud Busters program to teach 1,200 frontline staff how to recognize and report signs of financial exploitation. This program is based on three principles: prevention, apprehension, and education. Employees who successfully spot and report elder financial exploitation receive public recognition from the CEO and a Fraud Busters pin to wear to signify their commitment to fighting exploitation. So far, First Financial Bank has saved its customers over $1 million by intercepting fraud and financial exploitation attempts (Gunther and Neill 2015).

Bank of American Fork, a small community bank in Utah, selects one full-time employee at each of its retail locations to be the branch's *Age-Friendly Champion*. While all employees receive yearly mandatory training on elder financial exploitation, the Age-Friendly Champion attends quarterly workshops at the firm's headquarters and receives leadership training on issues pertaining to older adults. Dementia, sensory changes, and financial victimization are all part of the curriculum. These team members are encouraged to share their knowledge with co-workers at the local branch and to foster a culture that emphasizes reporting elder mistreatment to the appropriate authorities (Gunther and Neill 2015). This program is perceived as successful at cultivating heightened sensitivity to older customers' needs, and it has generated attention and praise from the media.

Some employee training is virtually free to implement. For example, screen savers throughout the Hong Kong and Shanghai Banking Corporation (HSBC) display pictures of older adults alongside information on the warning signs of financial victimization. These messages raise awareness and remind frontline staff to be vigilant. AARP is planning to create a similar screen saver and distribute it to banks across the US. The screen saver will be customizable so that companies can add their logos and other branding.

Preventing Exploitation through Community Outreach

Education efforts have moved beyond frontline staff. Three firms reported that they are hosting events to educate older customers and their family caregivers about fraud. Outreach events are typically held at local senior and community centers, churches, local businesses, libraries, police departments, and civic centers. Allianz Life has partnered with the Better Business Bureau to create the *Safeguarding Our Seniors* volunteer program for employees and community members. Volunteers go to community and senior centers to speak about exploitation and the importance of financial planning. Collaborating with community groups brings credibility to firms, builds relationships, and brings positive media attention (Barbic 2016).

Several community outreach and education initiatives are led by financial institution trade organizations. For instance, the American Bankers Association

(ABA) Foundation launched the *Safe Banking for Seniors* campaign, with the goal of helping firms improve fraud prevention and education programs (Barbic 2016). Any bank can participate and download communication resources such as ready-made presentations, handouts on financial exploitation, and 'how-to' guides for hosting educational events. The ABA Foundation also encourages banks to network with local groups that serve the needs of seniors, like Area Agencies on Aging (AoA) and APS. ABA also recognizes banks leading the way in community outreach and age-friendly practices through their *Community Commitment Awards*. So far, small and medium-sized banks have received the most recognition. For example, Bank of the West received an Honorable Mention for its partnership with non-profit organizations to host financial exploitation seminars aimed at low- and middle-income seniors and those who live in rural areas. They also support broad consumer awareness initiatives by collaborating with aging advocacy groups to create educational films/projects and publicize information about scams on social media. Other banks have also received recognition from ABA for their toolkits designed to help seniors and caregivers avoid financial victimization.

Preventing Exploitation through Early Financial Planning

To limit opportunities for fraud and financial abuse, Lichtenberg (2016) has recommended proactive estate planning between financial service professionals and their customers. Some firms reported using the educational outreach materials developed by their companies as conversation starters to encourage clients to think about whom they would appoint as authorized representatives should they be unable to make financial decisions independently. DaDalt and Coughlin (2016) present five financial planning actions that should be addressed sequentially by families and advisors to support an older person. These include: (1) assess current assets, (2) review income and insurance, (3) discuss future care preferences, (4) manage daily expenses, and (5) plan care management.

Initiating delicate conversations about aging and cognitive decline has been identified as a key challenge by the professionals interviewed. Older clients may feel threatened when their advisors seek to discuss the risks associated with cognitive impairment, particularly those who value autonomy in financial decision making or who feel anxious about their cognitive abilities. Advisors recommended that such conversations should occur early in the client–advisor relationship, long before any signs of impairment emerge.

As part of FINRA's *Know Your Customer* rules (FINRA 2011), broker-dealers (individuals that can buy and sell securities) are required to know essential facts about their clients and who has authority to act on behalf of the client. To comply, most firms require their advisors to have a conversation with the client every three years (at a minimum). One interview respondent stated that discussions about estate planning can be integrated into these conversations, particularly when the client reaches a particular age or life milestone. This respondent also recommended that firms institute a 'financial checkup' policy for clients once they turn age 75 and 80. If instituted within *Know Your Customer* policies, routine checkups may help normalize discussions around how and when to transition financial responsibilities to an adult child, a close friend, or other relative.

All of the firms interviewed recognized that it can be more difficult to intervene when financial abuse is committed by someone close to the client, particularly when this individual already has control over the client's assets. Victims may deny exploitation to protect those they depend on for care and emotional support, and they may not want the offender (often an adult child) to be penalized by law enforcement (Enguidanos et al. 2014). Two firms we interviewed recommended that, to prevent financial abuse by friends and family, advisors should encourage clients to name multiple individuals to oversee their finances. Assigning co-trustees and joint powers of attorney ensures that no single person has full decision making control and reduces the risk of financial abuse.

NASAA has also created power of attorney guidelines and best practices with instructions on what financial advisors should do if an appointed agent takes advantage of a client. Additionally, the CFPB has issued instructions on how to manage someone else's money. These guides specify the rules and responsibilities of powers of attorney, trustees, and legal guardians, and they are publicly available for download.

As more people age without children or with children who live far away, financial advisors may find themselves isolated when working with impaired older clients who have no trusted people to help. One option is to recommend that the client work with a corporate trustee from a bank trust department or an independent trust company (Little and Timmerman 2015). Corporate trustees, though costly, are experts in trust administration and tax considerations. Another option for financial advisors is to contact APS, particularly if the client is cognitively impaired and appears to be neglecting personal needs. FINRA (2015a) has recommended that financial advisors not act as their clients' power of attorney, trustee, representative payee, or legal guardian, as this gives the advisors too much discretionary control over client assets and may lead to abuse.

Financial Tools, Products, and Account Features that Prevent Financial Victimization

To prevent financial victimization of older adults who depend on others for care and support, some companies have introduced products that allow caregivers to help elders with shopping, transportation, and paying bills, while limiting how much total money can be spent. For example, True Link is a debit card designed for families caring for seniors with mild cognitive impairment. The primary caregiver—usually the elder's son or daughter—can set spending limits and restrict the card's functionality to specific venues and retailers, such as the elder's favorite restaurant, a movie theater, or store. The card is meant to preserve the older person's autonomy by providing some financial independence, but it prevents others, such as hired personal caregivers, from misusing the funds. Prepaid debit cards can also help caregivers purchase needed items, but this system can be exploited by an individual who loads money onto the prepaid cards from the elder's account, so they should be used with caution.

Nearly every bank offers its customers the option to set up recurring automatic transfers from their main accounts into joint accounts they hold with others. Caregivers can use these joint accounts with lower balances to pay for groceries, medications, utilities, and other services, but they cannot access the rest of the elders' money. Convenience accounts are safer than traditional joint accounts and are recommended by the CFPB. These accounts do not have the right of survivorship and caregivers can only use them for the benefit of the elder in accordance with the elder's wishes (CFPB 2016). Upon the death of the elder, the money is distributed according to the will, rather than going to the secondary account holder by default. Third-party account monitoring is another popular online banking service whereby designated individuals have read-only privileges and may receive fraud and/or spending alerts on behalf of the primary account holders, but they cannot withdraw funds or transact business on the accounts. These are simple and low-cost interventions which financial institutions are promoting to older customers and their caregivers.

Data-Driven Strategies to Detect Financial Exploitation

Spurred by advances in mobile and online payment technology (Heintjes 2014), retail banks have invested in sophisticated fraud management systems to identify suspicious transactions. Some systems rely on user-defined criteria to predict which transactions are fraudulent, whereas others use advanced machine learning algorithms (Joyner 2011). Data gathered might include customer demographic information, the amount of money transferred, the location and IP address of the device used, and the pattern-ing of transactions. More advanced algorithms can now integrate unstruc-tured qualitative data from consumers' social media accounts like Twitter, Yelp, and Facebook. The hope is that by modeling typical patterns of online activity, financial institutions can flag deviations in behavior that signal financial victimization of customers of any age, not just older adults. To stay ahead of scam artists, these fraud detection algorithms must continu-ously evolve and incorporate new types of data.

If suspicious activity is detected in a customer's account, the banks inter-viewed seek to alert customers to potential fraud, usually via email, a letter, or a phone call. Often customers will notice the unauthorized transaction before the bank and will call customer service directly to report it. At Wells Fargo and other large banks, complaints are forwarded to an internal claims department for further investigation. The bank can stop the transaction if it is still in progress and reimburse losses depending on the outcome of the claims investigation. Wells Fargo instructs its customer service representa-tives to use the interaction as an opportunity to educate customers about how to protect themselves from future fraud attempts. Strategies recom-mended include ensuring that all access devices are password protected, and that customers inform the bank in advance about international travel plans and changes in address.

When accounts are held at different companies, it is challenging for any single institution to model patterns in customer financial behaviors and alert them to questionable transactions. One new company, EverSafe, seeks to solve this problem by consolidating customer account information across institutions and by providing daily fraud monitoring. EverSafe ana-lyzes signs such as abnormal cash withdrawals, missing deposits, possible identity theft, and unusual credit bureau activity. Some fraud alerts are based on common signs of financial exploitation, while others are tailored to client financial history and spending patterns. The company also helps older clients select a trusted advocate who can help monitor accounts and receive alerts if abnormal activity is detected.

Transaction history data can also be used to proactively protect clients from fraud and financial abuse. For example, based on the profiles of elders exploited in the past, Barclays has applied specific search criteria to identify others with similar risk factors. One of the parameters selected was whether the customer issued an abnormally high number of checks in a very short period. Once such high-risk customers are identified, the bank places notifications on these accounts as an indication to frontline staff to educate these customers on reducing fraud risk during subsequent phone calls or visits to a branch. The firm is currently exploring a more direct approach, whereby bank staff contact the customer proactively to discuss fraud rather than waiting for the customer to initiate the conversation (Gunther and Neill 2015).

Secondary Interventions

Federal Reporting of Elder Financial Victimization

In addition to detecting elder financial exploitation, financial service professionals receive training in reporting procedures. All depository institutions and securities firms must submit a Suspicious Activity Report (SAR) to the Treasury Department's Financial Crimes Enforcement Network (Fin-CEN) within thirty days following an incident. SAR filings help law enforcement agencies identify individuals, groups, and organizations involved in committing fraud, money laundering, and other crimes. In February 2011, a new category, 'Elder Financial Exploitation', was added to the reporting form following advisory notice FIN-2011-A003. In the eighteen months following the release of the new guidance, there was a 382 percent increase in the number of reports containing the terms 'elder financial abuse' and 'elder financial exploitation' (FinCEN 2013). This increase is depicted in Figure 9.1.

The reporting trend has continued to rise, particularly among banks. In 2015, depository institutions filed over 19,000 elder financial exploitation SARs, compared to 10,923 in 2013. Figure 9.2 shows that only 568 elder financial exploitation SARs were filed by securities firms in 2013, compared to 1,763 in 2015, or an increase of over 210 percent in just two years.

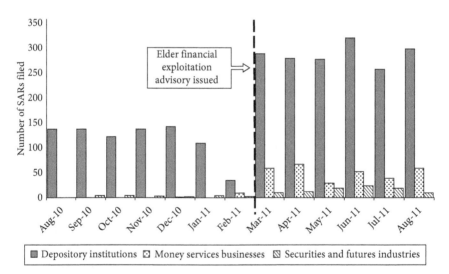

Figure 9.1. Increase in SAR filings containing the phrase 'elder financial exploitation' following FinCEN Advisory FIN-2011-A003 (August 2010–August 2011)

Notes: SAR Activity Review: Trends, Tips & Issues. *BSA Advisory Group.* Issue 23. Available at <https://www.fincen.gov/news_room/rp/files/sar_tti_23.pdf>.

Source: FinCEN (2013).

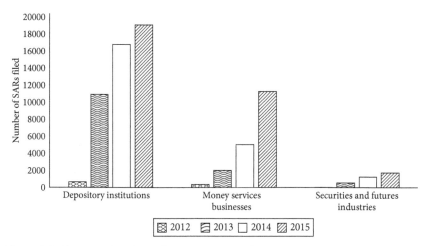

Figure 9.2. Increase in SARs filings containing the phrase 'elder financial exploitation' from 2012 to 2015 by type of financial service institution

Source: Author calculations using FinCEN (2016) data publicly available at <https://www.fincen.gov/Reports/SARStats>.

Financial exploitation by a relative or caregiver has been the most common type of elder financial victimization reported by depository institutions, which, compared to other types of financial institutions, file the highest number of financial exploitation SARs. Misuse of funds by an appointed power of attorney and the use of coercion to manipulate the client have also been frequently cited. Among filers with securities and futures firms, the most common type of activities reported were sweetheart scams, suspicious identification, embezzlement, identity theft, and mail fraud (FinCEN 2013).

The addition of elder financial exploitation as a new SAR filing category has helped protect at-risk seniors (FinCEN 2013). Money service businesses have identified and blocked the majority of suspicious transactions that were filed. FinCEN has also claimed that the reporting category increased awareness across multiple sectors of the industry, evidenced by how many firms incorporated elder financial exploitation into their suspicious activity and risk monitoring programs.

Despite some evidence that this new filing category has boosted awareness, one firm interviewed stated that SARs were ineffective at resolving financial exploitation at the individual level due to inaction by law enforcement following a report. This firm stated that the lack of response created a disincentive to file. Indeed, there has been little indication that regional SAR Review Teams (comprised of representatives from state and federal law enforcement agencies) have pursued elder financial exploitation cases. One reason is that such reports represent only a small proportion of total SAR filings. Moreover, SARs are considered highly confidential documents, and some local law enforcement agencies must request access to the data from their state coordinators, which may be the state attorney general, state police, or the department of public safety (FinCEN 2012). This process slows investigations and acts as a further disincentive for police to pursue these challenging cases.

Reporting to Adult Protective Services

In addition to SARs filings, required by firms across all financial service sectors, elder financial victimization reports to APS are mandatory for financial institutions in twenty-five states. In other states, such as Iowa and Virginia, financial institution employees are permitted to report abuse to APS but it is not mandatory (Comizio et al. 2015). Laws vary with respect to what financial service designations are included—broker-dealers, accountants, insurers, banks, etc.—and who at a company must report—a director or officer of the institution or any affiliated employee. Table 9.1 describes which states have mandatory reporting laws for financial institutions and who at the institution must file the report.

At the majority of firms interviewed, employees relay suspicions of financial exploitation or fraud to a supervisor or a manager. The supervisor can then escalate the case to an internal compliance department that decides whether to report to APS and/or law enforcement. Wells Fargo Advisors has created the Elder Strategy Group, a central intake office comprised of lawyers and paralegals who specialize in elder financial exploitation. This team receives reports from advisors and client associates located anywhere in the country, investigates the allegations internally, and will contact the APS office in the location where the client resides if the allegations need to be investigated further and if the client needs protection. Out of 1,860 incoming reports between January through December 2015, 818 cases were reported to APS or law enforcement. Approximately 32 percent of these cases involved suspected abuse by family members, 23 percent involved exploitation by third parties (caregivers, neighbors, and friends), and 10 percent were scams by strangers (Long 2015). Although not all states require elder abuse reporting by financial institutions, Wells Fargo Advisors considers itself a mandated reporter and will contact APS regardless of any particular state's requirements (Long 2016).

Many financial institutions initially opposed mandatory reporting laws because of liability concerns, fear of jeopardizing customer trust, and lack of confidence that their reports would be addressed promptly and effectively by APS (Swett and Millstein 2002). Some interview respondents argued that reporting could potentially increase client risk of harm by the

TABLE 9.1 Mandatory reporting laws for financial service institutions and employees by state (2015)

States without mandatory reporting	States with mandatory reporting (any employee)	States with mandatory reporting (financial institution)	States with voluntary reporting laws
Alabama	Arizona	District of Columbia	Iowa
Alaska	Arkansas	Hawaii	Missouri
Connecticut	California	Kansas	Nevada
Idaho	Colorado	Maryland	New Jersey
Illinois	Delaware	Washington	Vermont
Maine	Florida		Virginia
Massachusetts	Georgia		
Michigan	Indiana		
Minnesota	Kentucky		
Montana	Louisiana		
Nebraska	Mississippi		
New York	New Hampshire		
North Dakota	New Mexico		
Ohio	North Carolina		
Oregon	Oklahoma		
Pennsylvania	Rhode Island		
South Dakota	South Carolina		
West Virginia	Tennessee		
Wisconsin	Texas		
	Utah		
	Wyoming		

Note: Financial institution must report when it refuses to disburse funds based on a reasonable belief that financial exploitation of a vulnerable adult may have occurred, may have been attempted, or is being attempted.

Source: National Adult Protective Services Association Elder Financial Exploitation Advisory Board and EverSafe (2015).

perpetrator if they become aware of APS involvement; also, even if APS could help, the agency might be too understaffed and overwhelmed by the high volume of cases to quickly intervene. As a result, some of the firms we interviewed preferred to resolve the less serious cases internally, such as by helping to recover lost assets and getting other family members involved. Nevertheless, they recognized the importance of involving social services when clients were not safe.

Although many concerns were raised about the efficacy of mandatory reporting, it is clear that these laws have increased the total number of cases investigated by APS. After mandatory reporting laws were revised to include financial institutions in California, reports from financial institutions jumped from 127 cases in 2006, to 940 cases in 2007, representing a 640 percent increase (Navarro et al. 2009). There is still debate about whether mandated reporting is necessary to motivate financial professionals to report. According to one interview respondent, states such as Massachusetts and Oregon have been successful at increasing reports to APS despite not having laws that make it mandatory. To help address some of the current limitations in elder abuse response and to increase visibility around the issue, the Securities Industry and Financial Markets Association (SIFMA), a trade organization for financial advisors, has advocated increasing government funding to APS (SIFMA 2016).

Working with Law Enforcement

When financial exploitation has occurred, key priorities for financial institutions and victim advocates are to protect the older person and to recover assets. Other priorities are to ensure that perpetrators are apprehended and that appropriate legal and criminal justice outcomes are pursued. These solutions generally require law enforcement and APS involvement. We interviewed a financial crimes detective who shared a story about a local branch manager who called police immediately when an elderly customer requested an unusually large withdrawal and was shadowed by a stranger during a visit to her bank. A deputy responded immediately and arrested the suspect in the parking lot. The scam artist, who was also attempting to fleece other seniors in the area, could have continued with this scheme if law enforcement had not been contacted right away.

Criminal prosecution of those who exploit vulnerable adults is only possible through cooperation and information sharing with law enforcement. Contacting APS and law enforcement can prevent re-victimization and ensure client assets are protected. The financial crimes detective stated that banks and financial advisors must have contacts at local police or sheriff stations to advise and facilitate investigations of fraud and financial exploitation. To comply with investigations, financial firms can help law enforcement by promptly releasing client financial records and other supporting evidence such as ATM camera and CCTV footage that may help identify the perpetrator. The detective stated that, although banks have improved communication with police in recent years, more collaboration and cross-training is needed.

The Regulatory Puzzle

If clients are cognitively intact, financial professionals are obligated to execute their orders and protect their private information, even if they believe the clients are making poor financial decisions. Interfering with a transaction by placing a hold on the disbursement of funds or by disclosing information to third parties may result in lawsuits from clients and/or sanctions from regulatory agencies. Yet there is also pressure from these regulators to protect clients from fraud and financial abuse. The firms interviewed stated that the contradictory pressures from regulators places them in legal limbo, particularly when confronted with complex or ambiguous financial exploitation scenarios.

According to our interviews, firms wish to do more to protect older clients, and regulators agreed that more actions are necessary, but the complicated patchwork of state and federal oversight, shown in Figure 9.3, makes it difficult to have a consistent response to elder financial exploitation. For example, depending on their designations and certifications, financial planners are governed by different entities and different laws (US Government Accountability Office 2011). Registered investment advisors are regulated either by their state securities departments and/or by the SEC, depending on the size of their firms. FINRA, which is an independent self-regulatory membership-based organization (SRO), is empowered by the SEC to oversee broker-dealers. Although banks and financial advisors have similar rules governing customer privacy and reporting elder financial exploitation, banks are regulated by prudential regulators such as the FDIC, the Board of Governors of the Federal Reserve Board System, the Office of the Comptroller of the Currency (OCC), and also by the CFPB.

Privacy Concerns

The primary concern among interview respondents was violating regulations intended to protect customer privacy. The Gramm–Leach–Bliley Act (GLBA § 504(a) (1)) of 1999 requires financial institutions to inform clients about their privacy policies, describe the conditions under which they may disclose non-public personally identifiable financial information to third parties, and provide a way for clients to opt out of information sharing (US Government Publishing Office 1999). Without client consent, financial institutions cannot contact next of kin if they suspect cognitive impairment or exploitation. But a close inspection of the GLBA shows that there are important exceptions to these privacy rules (Hughes 2003). First, notification and opt-out requirements do not apply in situations where firms act to 'protect against or prevent actual or potential fraud, unauthorized transactions, claims, or other liability' (GLBA § 248.15(2) (ii)). Second, client information can be shared with local law enforcement agencies and federal regulators, and it can also be shared to comply with 'a properly authorized civil, criminal, or regulatory investigation, or subpoena or summons by federal, state, or local authorities' (GLBA § 248.15(7) (ii)). Accordingly,

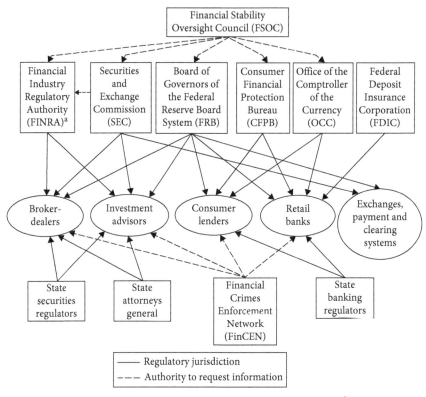

Figure 9.3. Regulatory oversight of select financial service providers[b]

Notes: [a] While the SEC is responsible for ensuring fairness for individual investors, FINRA is responsible for overseeing US stockbrokers and brokerage firms. FINRA is a self-regulatory organization (SRO), a non-governmental, membership-based organization that has the power to create and enforce security regulations and standards. [b] There are also other types of financial service providers—e.g., investment banks, commercial lenders, insurance companies—that are not depicted here. This figure excludes providers that do not offer direct services to consumers and their associated oversight agencies because these organizations are outside the scope of the chapter (FINRA 2011).

Source: Adapted from Murphy (2015: Table 2).

financial institutions and their employees have immunity from civil liability when reporting known or suspected financial exploitation, even if the allegations are ultimately not substantiated. This protection includes disclosing information to comply with voluntary or mandatory reporting laws and to file suspicious activity reports with FinCEN (Office of the Comptroller of the Currency 2013).

Statutory and case laws also protect personal financial information, but most have exceptions for disclosing financial records to APS and law enforcement.

Other than one state, South Dakota, APS laws provide immunity from civil and criminal liability to *any person* who reports elder financial abuse as long as they reported in good faith. One problem is that these laws do not specify whether 'any person' applies only to the individual employee or to the whole entity.

Additionally, the Right to Financial Privacy Act of 1978 (RFPA) protects confidentiality of personal financial records (US Government Publishing Office 1978b). Customers must be given prior notice and an opportunity to challenge the federal government's action in court before the government can obtain their private financial information from the firm. Nevertheless, the RFPA applies only to the federal government and not to state and local agencies like APS and police departments. These agencies can obtain customer financial records for investigative purposes. For example, if a bank teller in California suspected that a family member was manipulating an older client with dementia to withdrawal funds from his savings account, the bank can report concerns to APS and share the client's financial records with law enforcement when requested. None of these actions violate the provisions of GLBA or RFPA.

Rule Changes and Safe Harbor Protections

Several wealth advisory firms have stated that universal standards and safe harbor protections would enable them to do more to protect clients without fear of lawsuits and enforcement actions. Wells Fargo Advisors is taking a proactive approach, asking new clients to specify one or more 'emergency contacts' when they first open an account with the firm. The 'ICE' form (In Case of Emergency) authorizes the representative to contact the designated individual(s) if there are concerns about financial exploitation or fraud. Some emergency contact forms are modeled after advanced health care directives: they provide flexibility by allowing the client to specify what personal information can be shared with a specified contact and under what conditions. Unlike a power of attorney, the emergency contact form does not authorize the named individual(s) to transact business on behalf of the client, only to receive and share information related to the financial advisor's concerns.

Encouraging all new clients to name one or more emergency contacts will likely become a standard practice in years to come, but the forms have not been widely implemented and firms will be slow to collect this information from their existing clients. Financial institutions are already grappling with situations in which a vulnerable client has failed to provide authorization in advance, and where the client has no trusted friends or family members to name as emergency contacts. Financial advisors also fear that by delaying potentially fraudulent transactions, they may face liability for failing to follow through with the client's orders.

New legislation is being proposed to address these fears. In 2015, Missouri became the first state to pass landmark legislation, the Senior Savings Protection Act (MO Senate Bill 244/House Bill 636), that allows broker-dealers to breach privacy laws without being subject to civil liability suits as long as they have reason to suspect a client is being financially exploited. A qualified individual at the firm (a supervisor or compliance officer) is permitted to notify the client's legal representative or an immediate family member, such as a spouse, child, or sibling. The Act also allows financial advisors to hold a questionable disbursement for up to ten business days without penalty and report elder financial exploitation to the Department of Health and Senior Services and the Missouri Securities Commission. Washington and Delaware have similar laws, passed in 2010 and 2014, respectively, that allow financial advisors to pause a transaction if they suspect financial exploitation. This provides a short window to investigate the allegations before the client's money vanishes.

With support from their trade organizations, investment advisory firms from around the country encouraged NASAA and FINRA to follow these pioneering states and draft similar legislation. Both organizations issued proposals that give advisors safe harbor protections for intervening in cases of fraud and financial abuse, but there are important differences between the proposals. NASAA's Model Act permits firms to reach out to others if exploitation is suspected, but only if the client (age 60+) previously named emergency contacts. It does not provide legal protection if author-ization was not provided in advance. As a Model Act, NASAA's 2015 proposal will need to be enacted by individual states before it becomes law.

FINRA's rule proposals (amendments to rules 4512 and 2165) require that firms make *reasonable efforts* to proactively obtain contact information for a trusted person when an account is opened or in the course of updating account information, yet if no trusted person is listed on the account, firms would be permitted to breach privacy rules and contact an immediate family member of their choosing (FINRA 2015b). NASAA's proposal permits member firms to place a hold on the disbursement of funds or securities for up to ten days if they suspect exploitation *or* have concerns about diminished financial capacity, whereas FINRA's proposal allows a fifteen-day hold but only in response to suspected fraud or exploitation. Once the hold is in place, firms must immediately review the facts and circumstances that caused them to believe that exploitation is occurring, has been attempted, or will be attempted. NASAA's proposal mandates that all firms report to APS, but FINRA's proposal leaves APS reporting requirements up to the states. Because state securities regulators oversee more designations of financial planners than FINRA, which only has jurisdiction over its member broker-dealers, adoption of NASAA's proposal may have greater impact across the industry. The regulators we interviewed stated that they do not anticipate significant pushback from firms as they offer more flexibility and safe harbor protection.

Regulation S-ID: Preventing Identity Theft

In April 2013, CFTC and SEC issued a joint rule, Regulation S-ID under the Dodd–Frank Act, designed to protect consumers from identity theft. This rule also protects individuals from fraud and financial abuse because it requires broker-dealers, investment companies, and investment advisors to establish and maintain programs for verifying investor identities and detecting the red flags of identity theft. Many of these signs overlap with financial exploitation. The rule requires that firms monitor accounts for fraudulent activity, respond when altered or forged documents are presented to advisors, and determine the validity of address change requests. Firms must also have procedures for contacting the customer and/or law enforcement to report identity theft, and escalation procedures to refer cases to investigators. Institutions must train staff in implementing identity theft procedures and conduct ongoing assessments of program effectiveness. Firms are permitted to close existing accounts and can refuse to open new accounts if identity theft is suspected. Thus Regulation S-ID makes it harder for scam artists and opportunistic family members to gain access to an older client's accounts and to make unauthorized withdrawals.

Regulation E: Protecting Electronic Fund Transfers

Most cases of fraud and identity theft are perpetrated through electronic channels using an access device, such as when a caregiver steals an elder's debit card and pin number to withdraw funds from an ATM. The Electronic Fund Transfer Act, or Regulation E (12 CFR 205), protects consumers from losses associated with unauthorized ATM withdrawals, point-of-sale terminal transactions in stores, and preauthorized transfers to or from an account such as direct deposit of Social Security payments or automatic bill pay (US Government Publishing Office 1978a). When a fraudulent transaction occurs, losses to the account holder are limited to $50 as long as the customer informs his bank within two business days after learning of the loss. Customer liability increases to up to $500 (or up to the value of the stolen funds) after those two days. If the customer fails to notify the bank of the unauthorized charges after sixty days, the institution is no longer responsible for covering any portion of the loss and the customer is fully liable. Regulation E only protects consumers if the transaction is unauthorized. If an elder willingly gives his debit card and pin number to his caregiver to buy him groceries, and the caregiver drains his bank account, Regulation E may not apply.

Regulation E also does not cover transfers of securities purchased or sold through broker-dealers, wire transfers between financial institutions, or counterfeit checks, meaning that other mechanisms through which fraud and financial exploitation are perpetrated are not covered under the law. Furthermore, older customers with cognitive impairments may be unaware they have been victimized and may fail to report losses to their banks within the sixty-day period. These vulnerable consumers face the risk of losing their entire savings to fraud committed electronically.

Present Challenges

To improve the industry's response to elder financial victimization, a number of problems still need to be addressed. One wealth advisory firm stated that the three barriers to improving detection and response to financial exploitation are: (1) the high cost of implementing changes to policies and procedures, (2) restrictive legislation, and (3) insufficient personnel. The securities regulators we interviewed expressed concern that firms were not doing enough to protect their clients, but that allowing them to delay transactions and break privacy rules would give the financial industry too much control. They stated that financial victimization is hard to diagnose with absolute certainty. Without clear guidelines that specify exactly when financial firms are authorized to intercede, firms might lean in the direction of overprotection and interfere with their clients' liberty to make independent financial choices. They may also unintentionally disclose information to a perpetrator who is named as the client's emergency contact. Interview respondents recommended more rules and guidance to help firms decide what to do when faced with ambiguous situations.

We also found that there is considerable variability in how firms respond to elder financial exploitation, even within the same company. Although banks must adhere to many of the same reporting and privacy rules as broker-dealers, their protection practices vary. This lack of consistency is largely due to differences in the regulatory bodies that oversee these two financial service industry sectors and their different customer relationship models. Both companies would be better equipped to combat financial exploitation if they shared resources across departments and institutions. This would also help save on program development costs.

There are considerable barriers to resolving cases of elder financial victimization. According to our interview with a financial fraud detective, the policy of internally escalating cases of suspected financial exploitation to compliance officers is ill-advised. Law enforcement needs to be immediately informed of potential criminal activity to apprehend perpetrators, and APS workers also need to be notified to ensure client safety. When firms are slow to report, perpetrators have more time to spend older people's money and to cover their tracks.

Another challenge for detectives is obtaining client financial records to support criminal investigations, even in cases where firms do report directly to police. In 2007, FinCEN issued guidance on the legality of disclosing private financial information to investigatory agencies (FinCEN 2007). This guidance stated that, when an institution files an SAR, it must retain and provide all documentation supporting the SAR to law enforcement and/or to appropriate supervisory agencies upon request. This disclosure is protected by safe harbor provisions and no legal process is needed, yet some firms still require law enforcement to fax them a warrant from a judge before releasing information. Others require the warrant to be delivered in person. These procedural inconsistencies across firms create additional barriers to law enforcement officers who have minimal training in investigating complex financial crimes. As a result, perpetrators are rarely prosecuted for elder financial abuse (Navarro et al. 2013).

Representatives at the firms we interviewed agreed that collaborative partnerships with local law enforcement and APS agencies are needed. They suggested that law enforcement provide firms with regular updates on the progress of investigations and the outcomes of the case, yet detectives and APS workers are not legally permitted to share information about an open case. Premature disclosure could potentially compromise their investigations (Swett and Millstein 2002). This lack of communication between financial firms and local investigators may protect the privacy of those involved, but it also creates a disincentive to report as some private sector employees feel their concerns are ignored.

One solution to this fragmentation in communication is encouraging representatives at each firm to participate in local multidisciplinary teams that help coordinate inter-agency response to financial exploitation. Examples include Elder Abuse Forensic Centers and Fiduciary Abuse Specialist Teams. Member agencies generally include local law enforcement, APS, district attorneys, victim advocates, social services, legal services, and physical and mental health providers. These partnerships seek to ensure client safety, collect comprehensive and accurate information useful for legal proceedings (e.g., prosecutions and/or guardianship/conservatorship), and secure client property and assets (Navarro et al. 2015). Though confidentiality provisions differ across states, most laws permit team members to share information with each other without violating privacy rules.

Research shows that collaboration among stakeholders increases the odds of criminal prosecution of offenders and conservatorship of vulnerable adults who are victims of financial crimes (Navarro et al. 2013; Gassoumis et al. 2015). Elder abuse multidisciplinary teams could benefit from participation by financial service professionals with expertise in forensic accounting. Bridges between the financial service industry, the adult protection system, and the criminal justice system could also help financial firms. They benefit from greater community involvement, networking opportunities, and an improved understanding of investigation procedures.

Future Steps

Proactive strategies preventing elder financial exploitation and fraud can be a powerful business differentiator in a crowded financial services marketplace. Large firms have the resources to invest in training and consumer education programs to combat financial victimization, yet they also have less flexible response protocols. Community banks are more nimble and can adapt their protocols based on what services they provide, the regions they operate in, and the age of their clients, yet they also have smaller budgets to invest in such initiatives.

Trade organizations are supporting member firms by developing training resources and consumer education materials. SIFMA created an online *Senior Investor Protection Resource Center* where member firms can download free resources. Trade organizations have established partnerships with adult protection agencies, senior advocacy groups, and other professionals that work with vulnerable adults. For example, NASAA partnered with the National Adult Protective Services Association and physician groups to increase awareness. Moreover, aging and consumer advocacy groups can put pressure on policymakers to improve and clarify laws so that banks and wealth advisory firms are operating under the same guidelines. As part of its BankSafe initiative, the AARP Public Policy Institute conducted a survey and found that over 80 percent of adults age 50+ prefer to establish accounts at banks that offer services to protect them against financial victimization, such as extra account monitoring, phone calls to warn about suspicious activity, and having highly trained bank staff (Gunther 2016). Therefore, consumers can also motivate the industry by patronizing firms that offer more age-friendly services and that demonstrate a commitment to protecting them as they age.

There is tremendous opportunity for the financial service industry to engage with researchers to better understand elder financial exploitation, particularly in mapping patterns in customers' spending and saving behavior to proactively identify those most at risk, the mechanisms through which money changes hands, and possible touch points for educating customers on avoiding fraud and financial abuse. To our knowledge, there have been no studies evaluating the efficacy of different training programs to determine whether they increase identification and reporting of financial victimization. There is also scarce data on the total value of assets that have been protected or recovered using different prevention strategies, and whether customers are satisfied with their firm's response. Companies should turn to research before investing time and money on potentially ineffective programs.

Research in behavioral economics and decision neuroscience could also inform the industry about how age-related changes in decision making increase the risk of fraud and exploitation. Most decision research is conducted in laboratory settings where participants receive hypothetical endowments of funds and are instructed to make purchase decisions among a fixed set of options. Findings do not necessarily generalize to applied situations in which consumers are spending and investing their own money. This represents an enormous gap in the literature and highlights a need to develop protocols for how researchers can work with the private sector's data and clients without violating privacy laws or jeopardizing data security.

Conclusions

US financial services are changing rapidly with advances in technology. The personal relationships that financial firms have with their clients and customers will become less common as Millennials replace Baby Boomers as the primary users of financial services. New technologies are shaping how often and in what capacity customers interact with bank staff and financial advisors. While 89 percent of Americans age 50+ visit their bank in person (Gunther 2016), younger customers mainly rely on online banking to make transactions and view account balances (TD Bank 2014). Other new services include mobile apps for instantly transferring funds person-to-person, credit card readers that plug into cellular phones, and 'robo-advisors' that virtually select and manage investment portfolios without guidance from a personal financial advisor.

New access devices and increased automation will not stop fraud and financial abuse. These services may perhaps make the problem worse. As younger generations grow older, how will emerging technologies detect diminished financial capacity, undue influence, and other subtle signs of exploitation? While the financial industry is mobilizing to protect older clients today, it must also look ahead and invest in solutions that protect future financial services customers.

Acknowledgments

The authors acknowledge the interview respondents for their time and dedication to preventing elder financial exploitation within their organizations. They are especially grateful to Lori Stiegel, Liz Loewy, and others for their contributions, particularly their knowledge of state mandatory reporting laws and federal regulation. They thank Ronald Long, Lori Schock, Christine Kieffer, Gerri Walsh, Armand Abhari, Katie Libbe, Surya Kolluri, and Allyson Young for facilitating interviews with industry representatives, regulators, and law enforcement officers. They are grateful to Bill Stutts and Ken Scott for their expert knowledge of financial service industry regulation, and to Gary Mottola at the FINRA Investor Education Foundation for reviewing the manuscript. They thank Jilenne Gunther at AARP Public Policy Institute for connecting them to smaller financial institutions who helped inform this chapter.

Notes

1. Fraud prevention efforts by credit card companies, credit unions, insurance providers, money transfer businesses, and venture capital firms are not discussed in this chapter.
2. Interviews took place between September and November in 2015 and were conducted by telephone. Potential participants were identified through their sponsorship and collaborative relationships with researchers at the Stanford Center on Longevity (SCL) and SCL's Corporate Affiliates Program and Advisory Board. Interviews were arranged by the primary contact person at the institution or agency who assisted by selecting knowledgeable members who could discuss their company's financial exploitation detection and prevention programs and/ or who were familiar with regulatory policies governing the issue.

References

Acierno, R., M. A. Hernandez, A. B. Amstadter, H. S. Resnick, K. Steve, W. Muzzy, and D. G. Kilpatrick (2010). 'Prevalence and Correlates of Emotional, Physical, Sexual, and Financial Abuse and Potential Neglect in the United States: The National Elder Mistreatment Study'. *American Journal of Public Health* 100(2): 292–7.

Barbic, K. (2016). 'Safe Banking, Savvy Seniors'. *American Bankers Association Banking Journal* 108(1): 36–8.

Bonnie, R. and R. Wallace (2003). *Elder Mistreatment: Abuse, Neglect, and Exploitation in an Aging America.* Washington, DC: National Academies Press.

Button, M., J. Gee, C. Lewis, and J. Tapley (2010). *The Human Cost of Fraud: A Vox Populi.* Centre for Counter Fraud Studies and MacIntyre Hudson. <http://www.port.ac.uk/media/contacts-and-departments/icjs/ccfs/cost-of-fraud.pdf>.

Certified Financial Planner (CFP) Board of Standards (2012). 'Senior Financial Exploitation Study'. <https://www.cfp.net/docs/news-events—supporting-documents/senior-americans-financial-exploitation-survey.pdf?sfvrsn=0>.

Comizio, G., A. Kowalski, and L. Bain (2015). 'Elder Financial Abuse on the Rise: What Financial Institutions Can Do to Address Increasing Regulatory Scrutiny Designed to Protect At-Risk Customers'. Washington, DC: Paul Hastings LLC. <http://www.paulhastings.com/docs/default-source/PDFs/stay-current-elder-finan cial-abuse-on-the-rise-what-financial-institutions-can-do-to-address-increasing-regu latory-scrutiny.pdf>.

Conrad, K. J., M. Iris, J. W. Ridings, K. P. Fairman, A. Rosen, and K. H. Wilber (2011). 'Conceptual Model and Map of Financial Exploitation of Older Adults'. *Journal of Elder Abuse & Neglect* 23(4): 304–25.

Consumer Financial Protection Bureau (CFPB) (2016). 'Recommendations and Report for Financial Institutions on Preventing and Responding to Elder Financial Exploitation'. *CFPB* [website]. <http://files.consumerfinance.gov/f/201603_ cfpb_recommendations-and-report-for-financial-institutions-on-preventing-and-responding-to-elder-financial-exploitation.pdf>.

Cordray, R. (2015). 'Press Release: Prepared Remarks of CFPB Director Richard Cordray at the White House Conference on Aging Regional Forum'. Washington, DC, April 27.

DaDalt, O. and J. F. Coughlin (2016). 'Managing Financial Well-Being in the Shadow of Alzheimer's Disease'. *Public Policy & Aging Report* 26(1): 36–8.

Deem, D. (2000). 'Notes from the Field: Observations in Working with the Forgotten Victims of Personal Financial Crimes'. *Journal of Elder Abuse & Neglect* 12(i): 33–48.

Deevy, M. and M. Beals (2013). *The Scope of the Problem: An Overview of Fraud Prevalence Measurement.* Stanford, CA: Financial Fraud Research Center. <http://fraud researchcenter.org/wp-content/uploads/2013/11/Scope-of-the-Problem-FINAL_ corrected2.pdf>.

Enguidanos, S., M. DeLiema, I. Aguilar, J. Lambrinos, and K. H. Wilber (2014). 'Multicultural Voices: Attitudes of Older Adults in the United States about Elder Abuse'. *Ageing & Society* 34(5): 877–903.

Federal Deposit Insurance Corporation (FDIC) (2014). *2013 FDIC National Survey of Unbanked and Underbanked Households.* Washington, DC: FDIC. <https://www.fdic. gov/householdsurvey/2013report.pdf>.

Financial Crimes Enforcement Network (FinCEN) (2007). 'Guidance: Suspicious Activity Report Supporting Documentation'. FIN-2007-G003, Department of the Treasury Financial Crimes Enforcement Network. Issued June 13.

Financial Crimes Enforcement Network (FinCEN) (2012). 'The SAR Activity Review: Trends, Tips & Issues'. *BSA Advisory Group* 22: 1–60. <https://www.fincen.gov/ news_room/rp/files/sar_tti_22.pdf>.

Financial Crimes Enforcement Network (FinCEN) (2013). 'The SAR Activity Review: Trends, Tips & Issues'. *BSA Advisory Group* 23: 1–80. <https://www.fincen.gov/ news_room/rp/files/sar_tti_23.pdf>.

Financial Crimes Enforcement Network (FinCEN) (2016). *SAR Stats* [website]. <https://www.fincen.gov/Reports/SARStats>.

Financial Industry Regulatory Authority (FINRA) (2011). *2090 Know Your Customer SR-FINRA-2011-016.* FINRA Manual. Effective July 9, 2012.

Financial Industry Regulatory Authority (FINRA) (2015a). *Report on the FINRA Secur- ities Helpline for Seniors.* Washington, DC: FINRA. <http://www.finra.org/sites/ default/files/Securities_Helpline_for_Seniors_Report.pdf>.

Financial Industry Regulatory Authority (FINRA) (2015b). *Regulatory Notice 15-37: Financial Exploitation of Seniors and Other Vulnerable Adults.* Washington, DC: FINRA, 1–16. <http://www.finra.org/industry/notices/15-37>.

FINRA Investor Education Foundation (2015). *The Non-Traditional Costs of Financial Fraud: Report of Survey Findings.* Washington, DC: Applied Research and Consulting and FINRA Foundation. <http://www.finrafoundation.org/web/groups/sai/@sai/documents/sai_original_content/p602454.pdf>.

Gassoumis, Z. D., A. E. Navarro, and K. H. Wilber (2015). 'Protecting Victims of Elder Financial Exploitation: The Role of an Elder Abuse Forensic Center in Referring Victims for Conservatorship'. *Aging & Mental Health* 19(9): 1–9.

Gunther, J. (2016). *BankSafe: A Comprehensive Approach to Better Serving and Protecting Consumers.* Washington, DC: AARP Public Policy Institute.

Gunther, J. and R. Neill (2015). *Inspiring Case Examples: Age-Friendly Banking.* Washington, DC: AARP Public Policy Institute.

Heintjes, T. (2014). 'How We Pay: Results from the Federal Reserve's Latest Payments Study'. *EconSouth.* Federal Reserve Bank of Atlanta, January–April: 21–4.

Holtfreter, K., M. D. Reisig, D. P. Mears, and S. E. Wolfe (2014). 'Financial Exploitation in the Elderly Consumer Context'. Final report to the U.S. Department of Justice. Document No. 245388.

Hughes, S. L. (2003). 'Can Bank Tellers Tell? Legal Issues Relating to Banks Reporting Financial Abuse of the Elderly'. American Bar Association, Commission on Law and Aging. <http://www.americanbar.org/content/dam/aba/administrative/law_aging/2011/2011_aging_ea_bank_rpg_paper_long.authcheckdam.pdf>.

Jackson, S. L. (2015). 'The Vexing Problem of Defining Financial Exploitation'. *Journal of Financial Crime* 22(1): 63–78.

Joyner, E. (2011). 'Detecting and Preventing Fraud in Financial Institutions'. Cary, NC: SAS Global Forum, Paper 029-2011.

Lichtenberg, P. A. (2016). 'New Approaches to Preventing Financial Exploitation: A Focus on the Banks'. *Public Policy & Aging Report* 26(1): 15–17.

Little, D. and S. Timmerman (2015). 'Financial Incapacity and the Aging Baby Boomers: What is the Role of Financial Service Professionals?' Faculty Publications, Paper 317.

Lock, S. L. (2016). 'Age-Friendly Banking: How Can We Help Get it Right before Things Go Wrong?' *Public Policy & Aging Report* 26(1): 18–22.

Long, R. C. (2014). 'Elder Financial Abuse'. In *Elder Abuse and its Prevention: Forum on Global Violence Prevention.* Washington, DC: National Academies Press.

Long, R. C. (2015). 'Number of ECI Cases Opened by Type, January 2015–December 2015'. Presentation to Wells Fargo Advisors.

Long, R. C. (2016). 'Wells Fargo Advisors' Elder Client Initiatives: A Review of the First Year'. *Public Policy & Aging Report* 26(1): 34–5.

Marson, D. C. (2016). 'Commentary: A Role for Neuroscience in Preventing Financial Elder Abuse'. *Public Policy & Aging Report* 26(1): 12–14.

Marson, D. C. and C. Sabatino (2012). 'Financial Capacity in an Aging Society'. *Generations* 36(2): 6–11.

MetLife Mature Market Institute (2009). *Broken Trust: Elders, Family, and Finances.* New York: Metropolitan Life Insurance Company. <https://www.metlife.com/mmi/research/broken-trust-elder-abuse.html#findings>.

Murphy, E. V. (2015). *Who Regulates Whom and How? An Overview of U.S. Financial Regulatory Policy for Banking and Securities Markets.* Report R43087. Washington, DC: Congressional Research Service.

National Adult Protective Services Association Elder Financial Exploitation Advisory Board and EverSafe (2015). *Nationwide Survey of Mandatory Reporting Requirements for Elderly and/or Vulnerable Persons.* <http://www.napsa-now.org/wp-content/uploads/2014/11/Mandatory-Reporting-Chart-Updated-FINAL.pdf>.

National Center on Elder Abuse (NCEA) (1998). *The National Elder Abuse Incidence Study.* Washington, DC: NCEA. <http://aoa.gov/AoA_Programs/Elder_Rights/Elder_Abuse/docs/ABuseReport_Full.pdf>.

National Council on Aging (NCOA) (2015). 'Top 10 Financial Scams Targeting Seniors' [website]. <https://www.ncoa.org/economic-security/money-management/scams-security/top-10-scams-targeting-seniors/>.

Navarro, A. E., Z. D. Gassoumis, and K. H. Wilber (2009). 'Press Release: Los Angeles County Adult Protective Services: Trends in Financial Abuse Reports 2005–2008'. Los Angeles, CA: University of Southern California.

Navarro, A. E., Z. D. Gassoumis, and K. H. Wilber (2013). 'Holding Abusers Accountable: An Elder Abuse Forensic Center Increases Criminal Prosecution of Financial Exploitation'. *The Gerontologist* 53(2): 303–12.

Navarro, A. E., J. Wysong, M. DeLiema, E. L. Schwartz, M. B. Nichol, and K. H. Wilber (2015). 'Inside the Black Box: The Case Review Process of an Elder Abuse Forensic Center'. *The Gerontologist* [advanced online access].

Office of the Comptroller of the Currency (OCC) (2013). *Interagency Guidance.* OCC Bulletin, October 4. <http://www.occ.treas.gov/news-issuances/bulletins/2013/bulletin-2013-21.html>.

Oregon Bankers Association (2013). *Preventing Elder Financial Exploitation: How Banks Can Help.* Elder Financial Exploitation Prevention Project. Oregon Department of Justice, Oregon Department of Human Services Office of Adult Abuse Prevention and Investigations.

Pak, K. and D. Shadel (2011). *AARP Foundation National Fraud Victimization Study.* Washington, DC: AARP Foundation. <http://assets.aarp.org/rgcenter/econ/fraud-victims-11.pdf>.

Securities Industry and Financial Markets Association (SIFMA) (2016). 'Senior Investor Protection Resource Center'. *SIFMA* [website]. <http://www.sifma.org/issues/savings-and-retirement/senior-investor-protection/overview/>.

Senior Savings Protection Act (2015). Missouri Senate Bill 244/House Bill 636. Enacted August 23, 2015.

Survey of Consumer Finances (2013). *Federal Reserve Board* [data file]. <http://www.federalreserve.gov/econresdata/scf/scfindex.htm>.

Swett, L. and R. Millstein (2002). *The Philadelphia APS Bank Reporting and Loss Prevention Program.* Philadelphia, PA: National Adult Protective Services Association. <http://www.napsa-now.org/wp-content/uploads/2012/06/Phila-Project-Report-FINAL.pdf>.

TD Bank (2014). 'The Millennial: Financial Behaviors and Needs'. *Angus Reid Public Opinion.* <https://mediaroom.tdbank.com/surveys?item=34208>.

Titus, R. M., F. Heinzelmann, and J. M. Boyle (1995). 'Victimization of Persons by Fraud'. *Crime & Delinquency* 41(1): 54–72.

Triebel, K. L. and D. C. Marson (2012). 'The Warning Signs of Diminished Financial Capacity in Older Adults'. *Generation*, 36(2): 39–45.

True Link (2015). *The True Link Report on Elder Financial Abuse*. <https://www.truelinkfinancial.com/files/True-Link-Report-on-Elder-Financial-Abuse-Executive-Summary_012815.pdf>.

US Government Accountability Office (GAO) (2011). *Regulatory Coverage Generally Exists for Financial Planners, but Consumer Protection Issues Remain*. GAO-11-235. Washington, DC: GAO.

US Government Publishing Office (1978a). *Regulation E: Electronic Fund Transfers: 12 CFR 205*. Enacted by the 95th United States Congress.

US Government Publishing Office (1978b). *Right to Financial Privacy Act: 12 U.S. Code Chapter 35 § 3401*. Enacted by the 95th US Congress.

US Government Publishing Office (1999). *Gramm–Leach–Bliley Act Public Law 106-102*. Enacted November 12, 1999.

Chapter 10

Understanding and Combating Investment Fraud

Christine N. Kieffer and Gary R. Mottola

Despite the destructive toll that investment fraud can have on its victims, researchers have only recently begun to understand the mechanics of fraud and the characteristics of investment fraud victims. This chapter reviews investment and financial fraud victimization rates, examines the demographic and psychographic patterns associated with investment fraud victimization, explores the role of targeting in victimization, and explains how fraudsters rely on social influence tactics to defraud their victims. We find that about one in ten investors will be victimized by investment fraud over the course of their lives. Moreover, older people are targeted for investment fraud more frequently than younger people, but after controlling for the effects of targeting, older people are not more likely than younger people to be victimized by investment fraud. We conclude with a discussion of what is being done by consumer protection organizations and policymakers to protect investors from investment fraud.[1]

The Prevalence and Impact of Fraud Victimization

Investment fraud is a subset of financial fraud, and it occurs when someone 'knowingly misleads an investor using false information for the purpose of monetary gain' (Beals et al. 2015). Investment fraud includes scams like penny stock fraud, pre-IPO scams, oil and gas scams, Ponzi schemes, and high-yield investment program fraud, to name a few. More generally, financial fraud also includes other types of economic frauds, like lottery and sweepstake scams, as well as scams involving worthless or non-existent products, and services such as bogus weight loss products or fake memorabilia.

Obtaining an accurate estimate of fraud prevalence—whether investment fraud or financial fraud—has been hindered by a number of factors. Estimates vary, sometimes widely, due to inconsistent definitions of fraud, differences in the types of fraud examined, populations studied, under-reporting of fraud, and the method used to measure fraud, such as law enforcement records or surveys (Deevy and Beals 2013). As such, fraud prevalence estimates need to be considered in this context.

Although there are few estimates of investment fraud prevalence rates, one is that about 7 percent of older investors will be victimized by investment fraud at some point in their lives (Shadel et al. 2007). A calculation by the authors based on data from a 2012 survey puts the estimate at 10 percent of Americans age 40+ (FINRA Investor Education Foundation 2013a). More common are prevalence estimates of financial fraud. Financial fraud prevalence rates as low as 4 percent and as high as 14 percent have been reported (AARP 2003; Anderson 2007), and recent work by the Federal Trade Commission (FTC) puts the estimated prevalence rate at 11 percent (Anderson 2013). These estimates are likely on the low side because fraud tends to be underreported. Victims are often reluctant to report fraud because they believe that reporting will make no difference, they are not sure where to report the crime, or they are too embarrassed to do so (FINRA Investor Education Foundation 2013a). From an international perspective, a study by the United Nations Interregional Crime and Justice Research Institute found that consumer fraud rates averaged 11 percent across twenty-nine countries (Van Dijk et al. 2007).

Regardless of the varying prevalence rates, these and other studies conclude that financial fraud is a significant and costly problem for Americans. For example, the Stanford Center on Longevity's Financial Fraud Research Center (FFRC) estimated that approximately $50 billion is lost annually to consumer financial fraud in the US (Deevy et al. 2012). And the UK's Financial Conduct Authority estimates that £1.2 billion is lost annually to investment fraud, with an average loss of £20,000 per investor (Graham 2014).

The full cost of financial fraud can also extend far beyond the amount of money lost. The $50 billion dollar figure noted above does not take into account indirect costs like legal fees, late fees, and lost wages—and importantly, it does not consider the non-financial costs of fraud, including stress, anxiety, and depression. One study that examined the broader impact of financial fraud among Americans age 25+ found that nearly two-thirds of self-reported financial fraud victims experienced at least one non-financial cost of fraud to a serious degree, including anger, stress, and psychological and emotional issues (FINRA Investor Education Foundation 2015). Beyond psychological and emotional costs, nearly half of fraud victims in that study reported incurring indirect costs associated with the fraud such as late fees, legal fees, and bounced checks. For example, 29 percent of respondents reported more than $1,000 in indirect costs, and 9 percent declared bankruptcy as a result of the fraud. A sobering insight from that study is that nearly half of victims blamed themselves for the incident, an indication of the far-reaching effects of financial fraud on the lives of its victims. These non-traditional costs of fraud are not unique to the American context: a study in the UK also found high levels of anger, stress, and emotional issues among fraud victims (Button et al. 2014).

Beyond prevalence rates, another way to think about financial victimization is to consider how many investors have assets at risk. Nearly seven in ten households in America own investments either through taxable accounts or retirement accounts like 401(k)s and various types of IRAs (Mottola 2015). Accordingly, a broad swathe of the population has assets that are potentially vulnerable to investment fraud. Moreover, even people without investment accounts could fall prey to investment fraud if, for example, a fraudster convinces them to pull equity out of their homes to use in a fraudulent scheme. Further, many Baby Boomers are entering retirement with significant assets (Lusardi and Mitchell 2006). Enforcement actions by financial regulators indicate that investors can be vulnerable to fraud at key 'wealth events' in their lives, such as when they face a decision about what to do with money arising from the sale of a house, an inheritance, or an IRA rollover (FINRA 2015). Protecting these assets—for Boomers and younger generations who face key wealth events—will be important to ensuring the financial well-being and retirement security of millions of Americans.

The Demographics and Psychographics of Victimization

As noted earlier, our understanding of fraud victimization prevalence rates is hampered by a number of methodological and practical issues, and these limitations apply to our understanding of how demographic and psychographic variables are related to fraud victimization. Yet a growing body of research has provided important insights, including the notion that no single stereotypical fraud victim profile exists: that is, targets and victims of financial fraud vary by scam type. Early research has found that investment fraud victims tend to be college-educated, financially literate men who are optimistic (Consumer Fraud Research Group 2006). Subsequent research supports this profile (AARP 2011; Graham 2014). This profile may be contrasted to that of lottery fraud victims, who are more typically single older female consumers and those with lower levels of education and income (Consumer Fraud Research Group 2006; AARP 2011).

Age and Fraud

Age is probably the most frequently researched demographic variable associated with fraud. There is a common belief that older people are more likely to be victims of financial fraud, but stereotypes about victims are not entirely supported by research.[2] Certainly, some studies report that age and fraud victimization are positively related. For example, one study found that people age 50+ make up 35 percent of the population but 57 percent of telemarketing fraud victims (AARP 1996). Another study found that Americans age 65+ were more likely to lose money to financial fraud than those in their 40s (FINRA Investor Education Foundation 2013a). Also, some researchers found that decreasing cognition associated with aging is predictive of future financial fraud incidence (Gamble et al. 2014).

Nevertheless, other authors have reported the opposite: that is, as age increases, fraud victimization decreases. The first widely cited study on fraud found that older consumers were three times less likely to be victims of personal fraud than younger consumers (Titus et al. 1995). Two Federal Trade Commission studies also showed that younger adults are more likely to be victims of fraud (Anderson 2004, 2007). Another recent study reported that the risk of fraud victimization decreased after age 50 (DeLiema 2015). In addition, researchers surveyed findings from fourteen different studies, and they concluded that there was no compelling evidence of a relationship between age and consumer fraud victimization (Ross et al. 2014).

The confusion arises for several reasons. Perhaps most important, as noted earlier, fraud profiles vary with the type of fraud, so research that looks at the profiles of victims by grouping all fraud types together may attenuate the relationship between age and fraud. Also, different conclusions may be reached depending upon the type of fraud examined. Moreover, some research suggests that older people are less likely to acknowledge fraud (AARP 2011), which would obviously impact associations between age and fraud. Results can also vary based on differences in the populations studied.

Despite the empirical uncertainty about the relationship between age and fraud, there is widespread belief that older people are more likely to be victims of consumer fraud (Ross et al. 2014). Anecdotally, researchers have pointed to the likelihood of seniors having more assets than younger adults, consequently making them better fraud targets. In addition, researchers have started to establish a link between cognitive changes associated with aging and susceptibility to at least some forms of fraud. For example, several researchers found that older people were more trusting of strangers' faces, and neurological evidence supports this association (Castle et al. 2012). This higher level of trust could reduce the ability to recognize red flags and lead to greater engagement with fraudsters. Social isolation can play a role as well. Increased isolation among the elderly may result in an older adult being more open to engaging with strangers to fulfill unmet social needs (Ganzini et al. 1990; Lee and Soberon-Ferrer 1997; Federal Bureau of Investigation 2014).

Other Demographic and Psychographic Variables

Beyond age, research also suggests that a number of demographic variables are related to fraud victimization, although these findings are also mixed. Sex, income, education, and marital status have all been associated with fraud to varying degrees. Victims of investment fraud have higher incomes and educational levels relative to victims of other financial fraud crimes (AARP 2011). They are also more likely to be married (Consumer Fraud Research Group 2006; AARP 2011).

A number of psychographic variables have also been associated with fraud victimization, among them, risk tolerance, perceptions of debt, impulsiveness, and financial literacy. Specifically, higher levels of risk tolerance and engagement in risky behaviors are associated with a higher probability of fraud victimization (Van Wyk and Benson 1997; Schoepfer and Piquero 2009), as are higher levels of debt (Anderson 2004; Kerley and Copes 2002). Using multilevel data (i.e., fMRI, survey, and demographic), analysts have compared investment fraud victims and non-victims, and they found that victims reported higher impulsiveness and demonstrated less cognitive flexibility. They also showed less ventrolateral prefrontal cortical activity, which is consistent with reduced impulse control (Knutson and Samanez-Larkin 2014). Somewhat counter-intuitively, higher levels of financial literacy have been associated with an increased probability of investment fraud victimization (Consumer Fraud Research Group 2006; AARP 2007) and consumer fraud victimization (AARP 2008).

What could account for this counter-intuitive relationship between financial literacy and fraud? One explanation might be over-confidence, a well-established bias in which a person tends to be more confident than correct; in other words, over-confident individuals overestimate the accuracy of their beliefs (Myers 1993). The idea that over-confidence can affect financial decisions is not new. In an important study of stock trading behavior, researchers found that over-confidence was associated with higher levels of trading and lower portfolio returns for online traders (Barber and Odean 2001). Other researchers also found that over-confidence was a significant determinant of risky financial behavior: over-confident individuals made larger contributions in an investment game and were willing to take greater investment risk (McCannon et al. 2015).

In some interesting analyses on whether over-confidence was related to fraud susceptibility, researchers found that over-confidence was a risk factor for financial fraud victimization (Gamble et al. 2014). Yet the researchers did not establish whether over-confidence mediated the relationship between financial literacy and financial fraud. That is, it is possible that as financial literacy increases, feelings of over-confidence rise as well. This over-confidence could yield feelings of invulnerability that, paradoxically, make respondents with high levels of financial literacy more susceptible to fraud. From this perspective, there is not a direct link between financial literacy and fraud susceptibility. Rather, over-confidence may mediate the relationship.

An inability to identify the 'red flags of fraud' (i.e., responding positively when presented with persuasion statements) provides another psychographic factor thought to be related to investment fraud victimization (AARP 2011). People's inability to identify the red flags of fraud is usually measured by showing marketing statements typically used by fraudsters which are inconsistent with ethical investment advertisements. For example, 'The lowest return you could possibly get on this investment is 50 percent annually, but most investors are making upward of 110 percent per year' is a red flag statement, as is 'There is no way to lose money on this investment.' If the survey respondent rates these statements and others like them as 'appealing', they are considered less able to identify the red flags of fraud. The lack of understanding of reasonable investment returns (FINRA Investor Education Foundation 2013a), and the desire for higher-than-average investment yields, leaves many Americans vulnerable to fraudulent investment pitches.

The Role of Targeting in Investment Fraud Victimization

While there is ample evidence that both demographic and psychographic variables are related to financial fraud victimization, another factor may also help explain the likelihood of being victimized by fraud: the number of times someone is targeted for fraud. For example, one demographic group may have low levels of fraud victimization because it is not frequently targeted; conversely, a group may have high levels of fraud victimization because it is frequently targeted. In other words, examining the relationship between age (or any demographic variable) and fraud victimization, without controlling for how often a person is solicited for fraud, could result in biased estimates of the relationship between key demographic variables and fraud victimization.

To better understand investment fraud victimization, we use a regression framework to examine, in particular, the relationship between age and investment fraud victimization after controlling for a host of demographic and psychographic variables and the likelihood of being targeted for investment fraud. We are able to conduct this analysis by combining two different datasets. In 2012, the FINRA Investor Education Foundation commissioned a study that examined the susceptibility of Americans to financial fraud (FINRA Investor Education Foundation 2013a). As part of this research,

2,364 adults age 40+ completed an online survey via a non-probability based Internet panel. The survey covered a wide range of measures of fraud susceptibility and exposure to fraud. More than three-quarters of these respondents were recruited from the panel that had completed the 2012 National Financial Capability Study earlier that year (FINRA Investor Education Foundation 2013b). The two survey databases were combined and the resulting dataset of 1,721 respondents aged 40 to 94 was weighted to match the US Census distributions for both age (40 and over) and ethnicity. Table 10.1 contains sample characteristics and the Appendix contains a description of all the variables used in the regressions. As shown in Table 10.1, the overall investment fraud victimization rate was 10 percent, the average age was 57, 73 percent of the sample was targeted for at least one type of investment fraud, and, on average, respondents received 1.8 solicitations (i.e., were targeted) for likely fraudulent investments.

Table 10.2 presents the results of a series of logistic regression models predicting investment fraud. After controlling for demographic and psychographic variables, these results provide some insight into the role that targeting plays in investment fraud victimization. The first regression (column 1) contains only demographic variables, where age is strongly associated with investment fraud victimization. As indicated by the odds ratio (OR), for every ten-year increase in age, the predicted odds of being an investment fraud victim is 1.31 times higher. This statistically significant effect is equivalent to a 31 percent increase in the odds of being a victim of investment fraud.[3] Household income is also strongly and positively

TABLE 10.1 Sample characteristics for data analysis

Variable	Statistic
Investment fraud victimization (dependent variable)	10%
Targeted for at least one type of investment fraud	73%
Household income > = $50,000	46%
Male	47%
College degree	31%
White	73%
Dependants	29%
Widow/widower	7%
Mean age	57
Mean financial literacy questions answered correctly	3.1
Mean risk tolerance	4.3
Mean perceptions of debt	3.8
Mean inability to identify the red flags of fraud	5.9
Mean number of targeted investment frauds	1.8

Source: Authors' calculations based on data from the FINRA Investor Education Foundation's Fraud Susceptibility Study (2013) and the 2012 National Financial Capability Study.

related to investment fraud victimization, as indicated by the highly significant OR of 1.58, so the odds of investment fraud victimization for individuals from households with $50,000+ in income were 58 percent higher than individuals from households with less than $50,000 in income. The odds of males being victimized by investment fraud are almost two times higher than females (OR = 1.72), and the odds of college-educated respondents are 42 percent higher than their less educated counterparts (OR = 1.42). Non-Asian minority status (i.e., black and Hispanic), marital status, presence of dependants in the house, and being a widow/widower were not related to investment fraud victimization.[4]

Column 2 in Table 10.2 adds psychographic variables into the equation including financial literacy, perception of debt, risk tolerance, and a measure of the inability of respondents to identify common red flags of fraud. These four variables are all significantly and positively related to investment fraud victimization. Including these psychographic variables eliminates the relationship between household income and fraud victimization, as well as gender and fraud victimization. Yet the age effect remains strongly related to victimization.

The third column controls for investment fraud targeting by adding a variable that is a count of investment fraud solicitations, and this variable is highly related to fraud victimization. For each additional investment fraud solicitation that a respondent receives, the odds of his victimization increases by a factor of 1.84. In addition, the inclusion of this targeting variable eliminates the significance of all other demographic variables, including age. However, risk tolerance, financial literacy, and the inability of the respondent to identify the red flags of fraud remain statistically significant.[5]

It is not our intention, however, to suggest that age does not play a role in investment fraud victimization. Rather, we believe that the positive relationship often found between age and investment fraud could be due, in part, to older people being targeted for investment fraud more frequently than younger people. Aging could still increase fraud victimization through natural cognitive declines associated with the aging process—and with our current dataset we were unable to examine this possibility. More work clearly needs to be done in this area, but these regressions provide evidence indicating that targeting needs to be taken into consideration to fully understand the nuanced relationship between age and investment fraud victimization.

While the targeting variable is the strongest predictor of investment fraud victimization, we still need to know: how common are investment fraud solicitations, and who tends to get targeted? Figure 10.1 shows a histogram of the number of different types of investment fraud contacts that respondents reported. It is evident that most respondents had been

TABLE 10.2 Factors associated with investment fraud victimization

Variable	1 Demographic variables only		2 Demographics and psychographics		3 Demographics, psychographics, and solicitations	
	Coefficient	Odds ratio	Coefficient	Odds ratio	Coefficient	Odds ratio
Age (10-yr)	0.27**	1.31	0.36**	1.4	0.15	1.16
	(0.09)		(0.10)		(0.11)	
Income > = $50,000	0.46*	1.58	0.17	1.2	0.05	1.05
	(0.19)		(0.20)		(0.21)	
Male	0.54**	1.72	0.24	1.3	0.02	1.02
	(0.17)		(0.18)		(0.20)	
Non-Asian minority	−0.11	0.89	−0.04	1	−0.23	0.8
	(0.22)		(0.22)		(0.24)	
Married	−0.05	0.95	0.02	1	0.19	1.21
	(0.20)		(0.21)		(0.23)	
Presence of dependants in household	0.29	1.34	0.23	1.3	0.17	1.18
	(0.20)		(0.21)		(0.22)	
College educated	0.35*	1.42	0.21	1.2	0.00	1
	(0.18)		(0.18)		(0.20)	
Widow/widower	0.35	1.42	0.57	1.8	0.57	1.77
	(0.34)		(0.35)		(0.38)	
Measured financial literacy			0.34**	1.4	0.17*	1.19
			(0.08)		(0.09)	
Inability to identify red flags of fraud			0.08*	1.1	0.07*	1.08
			(0.04)		(0.04)	
Too much debt			0.08*	1.1	0.06	1.06
			(0.04)		(0.04)	
Risk tolerance			0.18**	1.2	0.14**	1.15
			(0.04)		(0.04)	

(*continued*)

TABLE 10.2 Continued

Variable	1 Demographic variables only		2 Demographics and psychographics		3 Demographics, psychographics, and solicitations	
	Coefficient	Odds ratio	Coefficient	Odds ratio	Coefficient	Odds ratio
Investment scam contacts					0.62**	1.85
					(0.06)	
Intercept	-4.36		-7.42		-6.58	
	(0.56)		(0.78)		(0.83)	
Observations	1,573		1,573		1,573	
R-square	0.03		0.07		0.14	
Max-rescaled R-square	0.06		0.13		0.28	
Likelihood ratio	44.411 p < 0.0001		106.243 p < 0.0001		236.941 p < 0.0001	

Notes: A logistic regression was conducted; standard errors are in parentheses. ** p < 0.01, * p < 0.05. The likelihood ratio is the difference between the log-likelihood for the constant-only and full model. Due to missing data, 148 observations were dropped from the analysis. For reference, 10 percent of survey respondents in this analysis were classified as investment fraud victims.

Source: Authors' calculations based on data from the FINRA Investor Education Foundation's Fraud Susceptibility Study (2013) and the 2012 National Financial Capability Study. Both the regression output and dataset are available upon request.

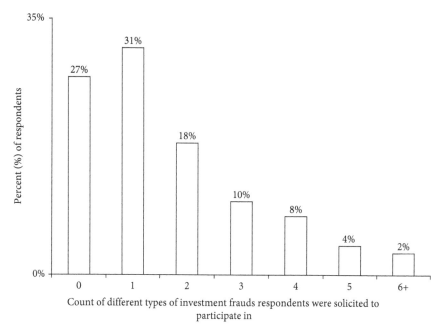

Figure 10.1. Number of different fraudulent investments that survey respondents were targeted to participate in

Note: Percentage of survey respondents by the count of different types of likely fraudulent investment scams that they were solicited to participate in (nine different investment frauds were examined).

Source: Authors' calculations based on data from the FINRA Investor Education Foundation's Fraud Susceptibility Study (FINRA Investor Education Foundation 2013a) and the National Financial Capability Study (FINRA Investor Education Foundation 2013b). Data are available upon request.

contacted to participate in at least one type of fraudulent investment, and many were contacted to participate in more than one. On average, respondents were contacted for 1.77 different investment frauds.

Table 10.3 shows the results of a negative binomial regression that predicts the number of times the respondents were solicited to participate in one of nine different likely fraudulent investments, using demographic information easily obtained by a fraudster. This analysis focuses on the targeting of investment fraud, so we only use variables in the model that can be known or easily obtained. Results in Table 10.3 show that, as age increases, the number of fraudulent solicitations a respondent received also rises. The incidence rate ratio (IRR) for age of 1.22 indicates that, for every ten-year increase in age, and holding other factors constant, the expected investment fraud solicitation rate is 1.22 times higher. Stated differently, a

TABLE 10.3 Factors associated with investment fraud targeting

Variable	Incidence rate ratio	Statistical significance
Age (10-yr)	1.22	**
	(0.03)	
Income > = $50,000	1.26	**
	(0.07)	
Male	1.36	**
	(0.07)	
Non-Asian minority	1.07	
	(0.07)	
Married	0.92	
	(0.06)	
Presence of dependants in household	1.03	
	(0.63)	
College educated	1.33	**
	(0.07)	
Widow/widower	1.08	
	0.10	
Observations	1,721	
Wald chi-square	230.77	**
Pseudo R-square	0.04	

Notes: A negative binomial regression model was used to model the count data; robust standard errors are in parentheses. (Poisson regression was not used due to overdispersion of the dependent variable, but both models yielded similar results.) ** $p < 0.01$, * $p < 0.05$.

Source: Authors' calculations based on data from the FINRA Investor Education Foundation's Fraud Susceptibility Study (2013) and the 2012 National Financial Capability Study. The regression output and dataset are available upon request.

ten-year increase in age is associated with a 22 percent increase in the number of investment fraud solicitations. Men are predicted to get 36 percent more investment fraud solicitations than women. Household income is also strongly and positively related to investment fraud solicitations, as is being college-educated. We conclude that older, affluent, college-educated males are most likely to be targeted for investment fraud, consistent with the AARP (2011) results.

Social Influence and Investment Fraud

While some demographic groups are clearly more likely to be targeted and become victims of investment fraud than others, anyone with access to capital could potentially be at risk. The ubiquity of fraud solicitations, coupled with the inability of many people to recognize the red flags of fraud, place a large number of Americans at risk of losing money to scams (FINRA Investor Education Foundation 2013a). Given that financial literacy appears to be positively correlated with fraud victimization, it is important to think beyond traditional financial education to address investment fraud victimization. Financial decisions have also been linked to emotions (Lerner et al. 2004); therefore, persuasion techniques that influence emotions can also impact decision making (Kircanski et al. 2016). Combating investment fraud thus requires an understanding of how fraudsters operate, as well as the techniques they use to separate victims from their money.

Social influence refers to the study of how people change the thoughts, feelings, and behavior of other people (Pratkanis 2007). The science of social influence offers insights into better understanding and preventing investment fraud. The Consumer Fraud Research Group analyzed 128 full-length transcripts drawn from undercover tapes of financial fraud pitches to identify the influence tactics used to perpetrate economic fraud crimes and to rank these tactics by frequency of use (see Figure 10.2). Their analysis included the seven most common scam types found in the database of tapes—including investment, coin, recovery room, credit card, sweepstakes, lottery, and travel scams (Consumer Fraud Research Group 2006).

Here we focus on five of the influence tactics identified in this research as commonly used in investment fraud. These include phantom riches (also called phantom fixation), scarcity, source credibility, social consensus, and reciprocity. Of course, influence techniques are not only used to defraud people: indeed, they are used in the marketing of a range of products and services every day. When fraudsters use these tactics for ill-intent, however, they cross an ethical line that can lead to long-lasting and potentially devastating consequences for their victims.

Planting the seed of 'phantom riches' is a common technique used by fraudsters and involves dangling the prospect of wealth by enticing a potential victim with something he wants but cannot have (Pratkanis and Farquhar 1992). An example of phantom riches used by fraudsters is a statement like 'The lowest return you could possibly get on this investment is 50 percent annually, but most investors are making upwards of 110 percent a year.' Survey research suggests that people are attracted to this type of statement (FINRA Investor Education Foundation 2013a), though it is not a responsible form of investment advertising, and returns of 50 to 100 percent per year are highly improbable.

The tactic of scarcity is applied when a salesperson creates a false sense of urgency by claiming there is a limited supply or limited time to act, or by claiming the opportunity is exclusive. This results in the product or service being perceived as more valuable. Worchel et al. (1975) demonstrated the influence of scarcity on perceived value in a simple experiment in which they asked subjects to rate the attractiveness of cookies. The experimenters manipulated the supply of the cookies by showing some subjects a jar with ten cookies in it, and other subjects a jar with two cookies in it. The cookies

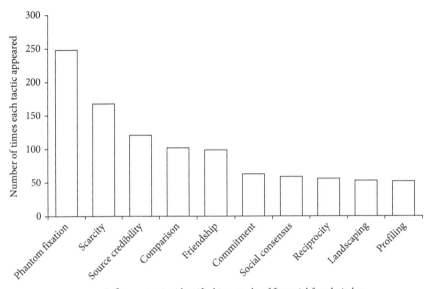

Influence tactics identified in a study of financial fraud pitches

Figure 10.2. Number of times identified influence tactics appeared in analysis of fraud pitch transcripts

Note: Analysis of influence tactics found in 128 full-length transcripts drawing from a total of 650 undercover tapes of financial fraud pitches. Seven common scam types were found in the database of tapes—including investment, coin, recovery room, credit card, sweepstakes, lottery, and travel scams.

Source: Consumer Fraud Research Group (2006).

were rated as more attractive when they were presented in the jar with two cookies. West (1975) found a similar increase in the attractiveness of cafeteria food, following a decrease in the availability of the food. Examples of how a fraudster might use scarcity include the following statements: 'This is an opportunity that is only available to a limited number of investors', or 'This offer is only good for today.' These are examples of scarcity based on supply and scarcity based on time, respectively.

The power of scarcity may be explained by Reactance Theory (Brehm and Brehm 1981). Reactance occurs when an individual is motivated to react against the impending loss of a behavior, item, or freedom. In terms of investment fraud, if a fraudster proposes that one could lose access to an investment by not 'acting today', one might react against this by wanting the investment more than one did before. Loss aversion may be related to scarcity as well. Loss aversion comes from Prospect Theory and posits that losing something is psychologically more painful than gaining something of similar value (Kahneman and Tversky 1979). In terms of its use by fraudsters, losing the opportunity to earn a big return on an investment may be painful enough to motivate a fraud target to go ahead with the investment, despite reservations.

Source credibility is a technique used by fraudsters that capitalizes on the finding that people are more likely to believe others in positions of authority, and to trust organizations that they perceive as legitimate. A classic example of the power of source credibility, although not an example of fraud, is Stanley Milgram's (1965, 1974) work on obedience. As is commonly known, that study showed the ease with which a researcher donning a lab coat and clipboard (to help establish credibility and authority) could compel study subjects to ostensibly shock confederates in another room, despite confederates pleading for the subject to stop the shocks (of course, no shocks were actually being administered). In fact, many subjects 'administered' shocks to a confederate even when they believed the confederate was unconscious. While Milgram noted that several factors contributed to the subjects' willingness to shock the confederates, he argues that authority must be established and perceived as legitimate.

Source credibility is used to build trust, and once trust is established between the fraudster and the potential victim, it becomes easier for the fraudster to perpetrate the fraud. Source credibility is also established by using professional credentials, whether real or artificial. An example of source credibility that an investment fraudster might use is a statement like the following: 'We are a highly regarded and profitable investment management company specializing in the foreign exchange markets, futures, options, commodities, stocks, bonds, real estate, business startup, and many other investments.' The appeal of this statement was tested among US adults age 40+, and 29 percent of the respondents found the statement appealing (FINRA Investor Education Foundation 2013a).

Fraudsters also use the tactic of social consensus (sometimes referred to as social proof) whereby the more it appears that everyone else is engaging in a particular behavior or holds a particular belief, the more likely it is that an individual will join and agree with the group (Pratkanis 2007). Social consensus is tied to social pressure and conformity. If everyone does something, not only must it be a good idea, but it can be difficult to go against group consensus. Solomon Asch (1956) famously demonstrated the power of the group to engender conformity in his classic line experiment. In this experiment, he used several confederates to provide obviously wrong answers about the length of a line on a card. The subject of the experiment, who answered the question about the length of the line last or second-to-last, often provided an obviously wrong answer as well, just to conform to the group.

Social consensus is often exploited by fraudsters to commit affinity fraud. This happens when a fraudster takes advantage of the trust inherent in groups of like-minded individuals, such as those who attend the same place of worship or social club. The fraudster, who is or pretends to be a member of the group, points out to potential victims that other members of their group have already purchased a particular investment. This implies that, if their friends and colleagues are involved, it must be a good investment. Further, among respondents to a study of investment fraud who indicated that they had participated in a fraudulent investment, 34 percent were introduced to the seller through a friend (FINRA Investor Education Foundation 2013a). Social consensus can even be effective with strangers. For example, a typical pitch from a fraudster is something like 'This investment made hundreds of people extremely wealthy.' With this statement, the fraudster is relying on the potential victim thinking that hundreds of people can't be wrong. In fact, research has found that such a statement is appealing to 30 percent of the respondents who rated it (FINRA Investor Education Foundation 2013a).

The norm of reciprocity is another technique that fraudsters rely on to convince potential victims to part with their money (Gouldner 1960). The norm is based on the notion that people should return help to those who help them, and the norm is found to be powerful and universal. The power of reciprocity has been demonstrated in a number of different settings, including charities (Cialdini 2001) and organizational/industrial settings (Rhoades and Eisenberger 2002). Given the effectiveness of reciprocity, it is not surprising that fraudsters use the technique. An example would be a fraudster giving you a 'break on his commission'. Similarly, free meal seminars are another common tactic that relies on the norm of reciprocity. A meal is provided, after which the fraudster expects that attendees will invest in his scheme in return for the meal. Not all free meal seminars are frauds, but a report by the Securities Exchange Commission, the North American Securities Administrators Association, and the Financial Industry Regulatory Authority found that, in half the cases they examined, the sales materials contained claims that were exaggerated, misleading, or otherwise unwarranted (Securities and Exchange Commission et al. 2007). Moreover, 13 percent of the seminars appeared to involve fraud, ranging from unfounded projections of returns to sales of fictitious products. While little empirical work has been done on the efficacy of free meal seminars, their ubiquity lends credence to their effectiveness: 64 percent of adults indicated that they were contacted to attend a free lunch sales pitch (FINRA Investor Education Foundation 2013a).

By its very nature, investing typically involves taking on some degree of risk, ranging from the risk of returns failing to keep pace with inflation, to the risk of incurring losses on investments, or even losing one's entire investment. Whether applied individually or collectively, these and similar tactics can greatly, and often subconsciously, impact the psychological and emotional state of the intended fraud target, which can affect perceptions of risk and lead to compromised decision making. For example, according to the risk-as-feelings hypothesis, emotional reactions to risky situations often drive behavior (Loewenstein et al. 2001). Newly emerging research has also found that inducing either a positive or a negative emotional state in older adults increased their intention to purchase items marketed with misleading advertisements (Kircanski et al. 2016). In short, social influence tactics may be effective because they can change a person's emotional state and, consequently, affect their willingness to take on risk and their ability to make sound decisions.

Combating Investment Fraud

Early campaigns to prevent investment fraud focused on warning investors about some perils associated with investing. One unintended consequence of warning campaigns, however, is that they may inspire fear in the target audience. And while fear has been identified as a powerful motivator—as explained in the examples of the scarcity tactic—it is thought to be largely ineffective in behavior change campaigns (Job 1988).

In recent years, investment fraud prevention campaigns have become more sophisticated and incorporate the knowledge and understanding of social influence tactics in an effort to empower consumers to spot and avoid fraud. As discussed earlier in this chapter, emerging research on social influence techniques employed by con criminals has revealed specific tactics that are used to harness emotion and ultimately influence their targets' financial decisions. Given this, some campaigns have shifted from warning investors about specific scams to educating investors about their vulnerability, the various social influence tactics that fraudsters use, and the types of resources they may use for vetting both sellers and products prior to investing.

This shift aligns with recommendations outlined in an Organisation for Economic Co-operation and Development review of anti-scam consumer behavior change campaigns (OECD 2005). The study concluded that a 'lack of data about the impact of anti-scam campaigns makes it difficult to be conclusive about the value of the campaigns that have been run to date'.[6] For this reason, the OECD examined a series of social marketing campaigns that did provide evidence of effectiveness. Through this analysis, the OECD concluded that successful campaigns must identify a clear target market; try to change behavior by specifying specific strategies and steps; use an authoritative tone; identify and communicate consumer benefits; tell stories; and engage partners. While information campaigns and targeted warnings have some utility, the OECD hypothesized that their value was limited by the reactive, specific, short-term nature of the prevention approach. They suggested that a more strategic, long-term, skills-based approach to tackling scams was required.

To combat investment fraud, organizations such as AARP, the US Securities Exchange Commission (SEC), the US Commodity Futures Trading Commission (CFTC), and the FINRA Investor Education Foundation have engaged in efforts that not only increase investor awareness of possibly fraudulent activities but also look to the science of social influence and the promise of social marketing to empower investors to resist fraud. The investor protection strategy of the FINRA Investor Education Foundation, for example, is built upon three key pillars: investors need to know that they are vulnerable; investors need to learn to recognize the red flags of fraud; and investors need to take simple protective steps, including asking questions and independently verifying answers.

Fraud prevention campaigns, like many other consumer protection campaigns, ultimately seek to change the behavior of consumers such that they may identify a scam prior to falling victim. Behavior change is rarely a discrete, single event (Zimmerman et al. 2000). An individual usually moves from being uninterested or ambivalent (the pre-contemplation stage), to considering a change (contemplation stage), to deciding and preparing to make a change. This can lead to the desired action stage, but often some type of maintenance and relapse prevention program is required to sustain the impetus to change (Zimmerman et al. 2000). Most individuals find themselves cycling through the various stages before the behavior change is ingrained.

During the pre-contemplation stage, in particular, many people may not see that advice on how to avoid investment fraud applies to them: that is, they have the illusion of invulnerability. This illusion poses a hurdle for investor protection efforts; consumers who do not believe the information applies to them are less likely to advance to the next stage, contemplation. Though some demographic groups are more likely to be victims of investment fraud, nearly everyone is at risk. If a person has money, he or she will likely come across someone who will try to coax him or her to 'get in on the ground floor of a great investment' or 'strike while the iron is hot'. In fact, one study found that over eight out of ten US adults age 40+ had been contacted in some fashion to participate in a likely fraudulent activity (FINRA Investor Education Foundation 2013a). Thus, campaigns that address the illusion of invulnerability and help investors recognize that they—like others—are at risk of falling victim to a scam may be more likely to succeed in moving investors to take action to prevent it.

Identifying the red flags of fraud is, not surprisingly, tightly linked with understanding the social influence tactics used by fraudsters. Accordingly, efforts to build the investors' skills to identify the questionable use of persuasion and influence have been undertaken. Influence techniques identified through social influence research in the context of financial fraud—including phantom riches, scarcity, source credibility, social consensus, and reciprocity (Consumer Fraud Research Group 2006)—are powerful in building emotion and convincing people to act without evaluating the risks of these actions. Teaching an investor to recognize these tactics is intended to heighten awareness of the emotional impact of the techniques, and consequently, to limit the impact of the techniques on financial decision making. In other words, by learning to recognize when decision making is clouded by emotion, investors may be better equipped to make less emotional, more cognitive decisions.

Beyond recognizing vulnerability and learning to spot persuasion, investors are encouraged to take specific proactive steps to protect themselves. One suggested step involves encouraging people to reduce their exposure to pitches. Some behaviors associated with fraud risk include openness to information and buying investments recommended by a friend, relative, co-worker, or neighbor (FINRA Investor Education Foundation 2007). As noted earlier in this chapter, targeting is highly predictive of investment fraud victimization. In reducing their exposure to pitches, investors may limit the number of fraud attempts to which they are exposed. Fraud prevention efforts also encourage investors to closely examine the background of those trying to sell them investments, and the legitimacy of the investments themselves. This step can assist investors in verifying whether the tactic of source credibility is being used in a deceptive manner. A legitimate securities salesperson must be properly licensed, and his or her firm must be registered with FINRA, the SEC, or a state securities regulator (depending on the type of business the firm conducts). FINRA's BrokerCheck provides information for investors checking the background of broker-dealers, and the SEC's Investment Advisor Public Disclosure (IAPD) database provides information on the background of investment advisors. The CFTC offers SmartCheck to help investors check backgrounds, as well. And each state has resources for helping investors research the background of investment professionals. The North American Securities Administrators Association (NASAA) is a one place to start to learn about state-level investment fraud prevention efforts.

Regulators also recommend that investors check to be sure the investment that he or she is being sold is properly registered with the SEC. Although not all investments are required to be registered, most investments are—and if they are registered they can be found in the SEC's EDGAR Database. Investors should be cautioned that there is an additional level of risk to investing in investments that are not registered with the SEC.

Evidence on the effectiveness of the fraud prevention education initiatives described above is limited and is difficult to obtain. The FINRA Investor Education Foundation and AARP conducted two rounds of field tests in an attempt to examine the effectiveness of a ninety-minute investor protection program. *Outsmarting Investment Fraud* (OIF), a program developed by the FINRA Investor Education Foundation and AARP to help investors resist fraud, was tested in a quasi-experimental fashion. The OIF program emphasizes the skills-building, investor protection strategy noted earlier in this chapter—accepting vulnerability, recognizing red flags, and taking simple steps prior to investing. Individuals who attended the OIF workshop were contacted three days later by a telemarketer who had experience with high-pressure sales, and the telemarketer asked if he could send the individual information about an oil and gas investment (oil and gas investments are often rife with fraud). To serve as a control group, the telemarketer also randomly contacted individuals who were registered to attend the OIF program the following week but had not yet been exposed to the program. The results showed that individuals who received the OIF training were significantly less likely to respond to a fraud appeal than individuals who had not received the training. Thirty-six percent of the control group agreed to send the telemarketer their contact information compared to 18 percent of the group that took the training—a significant improvement in resistance to high-pressure investment sales (Shadel et al. 2010). In short, the field test demonstrated that the OIF program—and the investor protection strategy on which it is developed—may change behavior and help protect investors from fraud.

   Outbound call centers have also been used to proactively contact people who might be at risk of lottery fraud and offer counseling to help the potential victim avoid victimization. A study conducted by AARP and the US Department of Justice (AARP 2003) found that the call centers were effective at reducing responsiveness to fraudulent pitches, and a follow-up field study conducted by Stanford University found similar results (Scheibe et al. 2014). Yet, neither of these studies focused specifically on investment fraud, so it is unclear if this approach would generalize to helping protect investors from investment fraud.

Conclusions

Our review of the literature suggests that investment fraud is a significant problem in America. It is also a problem that may become worse as the Baby Boomers retire and significant assets move out of their employer-provided retirement plans. While several demographic characteristics are associated with fraud victims (e.g., age, sex, and income), it is unclear whether certain demographic groups are more susceptible to investment fraud, more targeted by fraudsters, or both. Further, psychographic variables like risk tolerance, financial literacy, and the inability to identify the red flags of fraud are also associated with investment fraud victimization.

The science of social influence, which refers to how people change the thoughts, feelings, and behaviors of others through a variety of methods, has been used to help explain how fraudsters con their victims. Phantom riches, source credibility, social consensus, reciprocity, and scarcity are all among the social influence tactics commonly used by fraudsters, and their effectiveness at influencing behavior is supported by survey-based financial fraud research and experimental social psychological research. Educational initiatives aimed at getting people to understand the social influence tactics fraudsters use have been effective in increasing the ability of individuals to resist fraud pitches.

Given that the goal of many of the social influence tactics is to make potential fraud victims emotional, and that emotions have been tied to compromised financial decision making, one way to reduce the likelihood of falling victim to investment fraud is to wait a period, such as 24 hours, after being approached with an investment before making any investment decisions. This will enable potential victims' emotions to subside and give them the opportunity to discuss the possible investment with friends and family. Additional recommendations include checking the background of the person trying to sell you the investment and checking to see if the investment is a registered investment. Nevertheless, more work needs to be done to understand if these educational initiatives and fraud prevention strategies are robust across fraud types. In addition, policymakers and stakeholders may need to build a broader network of organizations to assist fraud victims—in part due to the high level of re-victimization (Hume and Canan 2016). For example, organizations such as the National Center for Victims of Crime are beginning to offer training to staff of adult protective services agencies, senior support groups, and other community-based consumer protection organizations, to build their capacity to assist fraud victims.

Research aimed at understanding the causes and consequences of fraud is in its early stages, so gaps in our knowledge exist. For instance, Deevy et al. (2012) posit a number of questions on a variety of topics that need to be addressed, including more accurately measuring the prevalence and costs of financial fraud, improving the reporting of financial fraud, assessing susceptibility to fraud, and identifying the motivations of fraudsters, to name a few. Since this list of research questions has been published, progress has already been made on more accurately measuring the prevalence and costs of fraud.

A collaborative effort of the US Department of Justice's Bureau of Justice Statistics, the Stanford Center on Longevity, and the FINRA Investor Education Foundation is trying to more accurately categorize and measure financial fraud. Working in coordination with other organizations and researchers, they have created a taxonomy of fraud that can be used to categorize the many different types of financial frauds including investment fraud (Beals et al. 2015). The goal of the project is to include a survey as a supplement to the Department of Justice's National Crime Victimization Survey, which would provide researchers, policymakers, and stakeholders with accurate baseline prevalence estimates of the various types of financial fraud and, potentially, an improved understanding of financial fraud. In addition, inclusion of fraud victimization questions in an upcoming wave of the Health and Retirement Study will provide researchers with a rich longitudinal data source to better understand the prevalence and predictors of financial fraud. The increased attention that these projects and others like them bring to the problem of investment fraud—and to financial fraud, more generally—offers promise that in the coming years researchers and policymakers will have a better understanding of investment fraud and effective interventions for protecting investors.

Appendix

This Appendix contains information on the variables included in the regression analyses that are reported in Table 10.2 and Table 10.3.

Dependent Variable

Respondents were shown nine descriptions of financial offers, all of which are known to be rife with fraud, but which were not identified as fraudulent in the descriptions—for example, lottery scams, oil and gas scams, and free-meal financial seminars. For each of these potentially fraudulent offers, respondents were asked whether they had ever been solicited with such an offer, whether they had engaged with the offer (e.g., made an investment or responded to the solicitor), and whether they had lost a significant amount of money after investing in the offer. Respondents who said they lost a significant amount of money investing in at least one of the nine offers were coded with a 1 to indicate they lost money in a potentially fraudulent activity; all other respondents were coded with a 0.

Demographic Independent Variables

The regressions included the following demographic variables.

   (1) Age—measured continuously
   (2) Household income—greater than or equal to $50,000 = 1 otherwise 0

(3) Sex—male = 1 and female = 0
(4) Education—college degree or higher = 1 otherwise 0
(5) Marital status—married = 1 otherwise 0
(6) Non-Asian minority—white and Asian = 0 otherwise 1
(7) Presence of dependants in the household—dependants present = 1 otherwise 0
(8) College educated—college degree or higher = 1 otherwise 0
(9) Widow—widow = 1 otherwise 0

Psychographic Independent Variables

The regressions included the following psychographic variables.

(1) Financial literacy—measured using a five-question financial literacy quiz of questions covering fundamental concepts of economics and finance that may be encountered in everyday life, such as calculations involving interest rates and inflation, principles relating to risk and diversification, the relationship between bond prices and interest rates, and the impact that a shorter term can have on total interest rate payments over the life of the loan.
(2) Risk tolerance—measured by asking respondents how willing they are to take investment risk (1 equals not at all willing and 10 equals very willing).
(3) Inability to identify common red flags of investment fraud—measured using a ten-point scale where 1 indicated that the respondent had no interest in a typically fraudulent advertising statement and 10 indicated extreme interest (the mean of six 'red flag' advertising statements was used in the regression).
(4) Perception of debt—measured using a seven-point scale where 1 indicated that they strongly disagreed with the statement 'I have too much debt right now' and 7 indicated that they strongly agreed with this statement.

Targeting Variable

The regression included a variable that quantified the number of different investment frauds that the respondent was targeted for. Targeting was measured in the same manner that victimization was measured—that is, by showing respondents nine descriptions of financial offers which are known to be rife with fraud. For each of these potentially fraudulent offers, respondents were asked whether they had ever received such an offer.

Respondents who said they did—regardless of whether or not they responded to the offer or participated in the solicited investment—were coded with a 1 to indicate they were solicited for the particular type of fraud being assessed, and 0 otherwise. The nine variables, one for each type of fraud, were then summed and the measure of fraud solicitation could range from 0 (never being solicited) to 9 (being solicited for all nine forms of investment fraud examined).

Notes

1. This chapter focuses on investment fraud, though much of the extant research examines more general financial fraud. Complicating the issue further, some researchers conflate the terms consumer fraud, personal fraud, telemarketing fraud, or fraud—often without providing explicit definitions. Research studies cited in this chapter cover all areas of fraud, but an attempt is made to focus on investment fraud. Further, when describing the results of a study, we typically used the same terminology that the authors use.

2. Financial elder abuse and elder financial exploitation are general terms that include the financial targeting of older people, often by someone in a position of trust. This chapter focuses on financial scams targeting all Americans, including the elderly, but does not focus specifically on older people or on different types of abuse by someone in a position of trust. See DeLiema and Deevy (Chapter 9, this volume) for more information on financial elder abuse.

3. Unlike marginal probabilities, odds ratios are invariant to the values of the independent variables (Liao 1994).

4. Survey respondents were asked if they were contacted to participate in or lost money in the following types of investment frauds: Cold Call Scam, Free Lunch Seminar, Oil & Gas Scam, Promissory Note Scam, Pump & Dump, Pre-IPO Scam, High-Yield Investment Program Scam, Multi-Level Marketing, and Digital Currency Purchase. For more information on the methodology used to collect these data, see FINRA Investor Education Foundation (2013a).

5. The results of these analyses are promising, but they suffer from two limitations. First, the survey methodology assumes that, in order to be victimized by investment fraud, the respondent had to be targeted or solicited to participate in a potentially fraudulent investment. As a result, respondents who said they were not contacted for fraud were not asked if they were ever victimized by fraud. Yet, it is possible that victims actually sought out interaction with the person who ultimately defrauded them. Second, the survey questions asked if respondents had ever been victimized by different types of investment fraud, so older respondents could have been targeted and victimized by investment fraud more often than younger respondents, simply because they had more time to be targeted and victimized. Nevertheless, research on memory decay suggests that respondents

cannot think back too far when recalling events, which may lessen the impact of this limitation (Jenkins et al. 2002).

6. The lack of evaluative reports might be attributed to the scarcity of time and resources for many of the campaigners, who likely have to focus on their other program activities instead of extensive evaluation. They may also lack the research expertise to conduct evaluations. Further, while academia has a high demand for publishing results, most non-profits have little incentive for making public any evaluations which they do complete. Notable exceptions came from evaluations of publicly funded programs, academic case studies, and professional associations working to improve best practices.

References

AARP (1996). *Telemarketing Fraud Victimization of Older Americans: An AARP Survey.* Washington, DC: AARP.

AARP (2003). *Off the Hook: Reducing Participation in Telemarketing Fraud.* Washington, DC: AARP.

AARP (2007). *Stolen Futures: An AARP Washington Survey of Investors and Victims of Investment Fraud.* Washington, DC: AARP.

AARP (2008). *Consumer Fraud: A 2008 Survey of AARP Colorado Members' Experiences and Opinions.* Washington, DC: AARP.

AARP (2011). *AARP Foundation National Fraud Victim Survey.* Washington, DC: AARP.

Anderson, K. (2004). *Consumer Fraud in the United States: An FTC Survey.* Washington, DC: Federal Trade Commission.

Anderson, K. (2007). *Consumer Fraud in the United States: The Second FTC Survey.* Washington, DC: Federal Trade Commission.

Anderson, K. (2013). *Consumer Fraud in the United States, 2011: The Third FTC Survey.* Washington, DC: Federal Trade Commission.

Asch, S. (1956). 'Studies of Independence and Conformity: A Minority of One Against a Unanimous Majority'. *Psychological Monographs* 70(9): 1–70.

Barber, B. and T. Odean (2001). 'Boys Will Be Boys: Gender, Overconfidence, and Common Stock Investment'. *Quarterly Journal of Economics* 116(1): 261–91.

Beals, M., M. DeLiema, and M. Deevy (2015). 'Framework for a Taxonomy of Fraud'. Working Paper. Palo Alto, CA: Stanford Center on Longevity.

Brehm, S. and J. Brehm (1981). *Psychological Reactance: A Theory of Freedom and Control.* New York: Academic Press.

Button, M., C. Lewis, and J. Tapley (2014). 'Not a Victimless Crime: The Impact of Fraud on Individual Victims and Their Families'. *Security Journal* 27(1): 36–54.

Castle, E., N. Eisenberger, T. Seeman, W. Moons, I. Boggero, M. Grinblatt, and S. Taylor (2012). 'Neural and Behavioral Bases of Age Differences in Perceptions of Trust'. *Proceedings of the National Academy of Sciences* 109(51): 20848–52.

Cialdini, R. (2001). *Influence: Science and Practice.* Boston, MA: Allyn & Bacon.

Consumer Fraud Research Group (2006). *Investor Fraud Study Final Report.* Washington, DC: NASD Investor Education Foundation.

Deevy, M. and M. Beals (2013). 'The Scope of the Problem: An Overview of Fraud Prevalence Measurement'. Working Paper. Palo Alto, CA: Stanford Center on Longevity.

Deevy, M., S. Lucich, and M. Beals (2012). 'Scams, Schemes and Swindles: A Review of Consumer Financial Fraud Research'. Working Paper. Palo Alto, CA: Stanford Center on Longevity.

DeLiema, M. (2015). 'Using Mixed Methods to Identify the Characteristics of Older Fraud Victims'. Unpublished dissertation. Los Angeles, CA: University of Southern California.

Federal Bureau of Investigation (2014). *Fraud Target: Senior Citizens*. Washington, DC: FBI.

FINRA (2015). *2015 Exam Letter*. Washington, DC: FINRA.

FINRA Investor Education Foundation (2007). *National Risk Behavior Study*. Washington, DC: FINRA Foundation.

FINRA Investor Education Foundation (2013a). *Financial Fraud and Fraud Susceptibility in the United States*. Washington, DC: FINRA Foundation.

FINRA Investor Education Foundation (2013b). *Financial Capability in the United States: Report of Findings from the 2012 National Financial Capability Study*. Washington, DC: FINRA Foundation.

FINRA Investor Education Foundation (2015). *Non-Traditional Costs of Financial Fraud*. Washington, DC: FINRA Foundation.

Gamble, K., P. Boyle, L. Yu, and D. Bennett (2014). 'The Causes and Consequences of Financial Fraud Among Older Americans'. Working Paper. Boston, MA: Boston College Center for Retirement Research.

Ganzini, L., B. McFarland, and J. Bloom (1990). 'Victims of Fraud: Comparing Victims of White Collar and Violent Crime'. *Journal of the American Academy of Psychiatry and the Law Online* 18(1): 55–63.

Gouldner, A. (1960). 'The Norm of Reciprocity: A Preliminary Statement'. *American Sociological Review* 25(2): 161–78.

Graham, W. (2014). *A Quantitative Analysis of Victims of Investment Crime*. London: Financial Conduct Authority.

Hume, C. and S. Canan (2016). *Older Consumers Targeted by Fraudsters Not Once, But Twice!* Consumer Financial Protection Bureau [website]. <http://www.consumerfinance.gov/about-us/blog/older-consumers-targeted-by-fraudsters-not-once-but-twice>.

Jenkins, P., G. Earle-Richardson, D. Slingerland, and J. May (2002). 'Time Dependent Memory Decay'. *American Journal of Industrial Medicine* 41(2): 98–101.

Job, S. (1988). 'Effective and Ineffective Use of Fear in Health Promotion Campaigns'. *American Journal of Public Health* 78(2): 163–7.

Kahneman, D. and A. Tversky (1979). 'Prospect Theory: An Analysis of Decision Under Risk'. *Econometrica* 47(2): 263–92.

Kerley, K. and H. Copes (2002). 'Personal Fraud Victims and Their Official Responses to Victimization'. *Journal of Police and Criminal Psychology* 17(1): 19–35.

Kircanski, K., N. Notthoff, D. Shadel, G. Mottola, L. Carstensen, and H. Gotlib (2016). 'Emotional Arousal Increases Susceptibility to Fraud in Older Adults'. Working Paper. Palo Alto, CA: Stanford Center on Longevity.

Knutson, B. and G. Samanez-Larkin (2014). 'Individual Differences in Susceptibility to Investment Fraud'. Working Paper. Palo Alto, CA: Stanford University.

Lee, J. and H. Soberon-Ferrer (1997). 'Consumer Vulnerability to Fraud: Influencing Factors'. *Journal of Consumer Affairs* 31(1): 70–89.

Lerner, J., D. Small, and G. Loewenstein (2004). 'Heart Strings and Purse Strings: Carryover Effects of Emotions on Economic Decisions'. *Psychological Science* 15(5): 337–41.

Liao, T. (1994). *Interpreting Probability Models: Logit, Probit, and Other Generalized Linear Models.* London: Sage.

Loewenstein, G., E. Weber, C. Hsee, and N. Welch (2001). 'Risk as Feelings'. *Psychological Bulletin* 127(2): 267–86.

Lusardi, A. and O. Mitchell (2006). 'Baby Boomer Retirement Security: The Roles of Planning, Financial Literacy, and Housing Wealth'. *Journal of Monetary Economics* 54(1): 205–24.

McCannon, T., C. Asaad, and M. Wilson (2015). 'Financial Competence, Overconfidence, and Trusting Investments: Results from an Experiment'. *Journal of Economic Finance* 40(3): 590–606.

Milgram, S. (1965). 'Some Conditions of Obedience and Disobedience to Authority'. *Human Relations* 18(1): 57–76.

Milgram, S. (1974). *Obedience to Authority.* New York: Harper & Row.

Mottola, G. (2015). *A Snapshot of Investor Households in America*, Washington, DC: FINRA Foundation.

Myers, D. (1993). *Social Psychology.* New York: McGraw-Hill.

Organisation for Economic Co-operation and Development (2005). 'Examining Consumer Policy: A Report on Consumer Information Campaigns Concerning Scams'. OECD Digital Economy Working Papers No. 103. Paris: OECD.

Pratkanis, A. (2007). 'Social Influence Analysis: An Index of Tactics'. In A. Pratkanis (ed.), *The Science of Social Influence: Advances and Future Progress.* New York: Psychology Press, pp. 17–82.

Pratkanis, A. and P. Farquhar (1992). 'A Brief History of Research on Phantom Alternatives: Evidence for Seven Empirical Generalizations about Phantoms'. *Basic and Applied Social Psychology* 13(1): 103–22.

Rhoades, L. and R. Eisenberger (2002). 'Perceived Organizational Support: A Review of the Literature'. *Journal of Applied Psychology* 87(4): 698–714.

Ross, M., I. Grossmann, and E. Schryer (2014). 'Contrary to Psychological and Popular Opinion, There is no Compelling Evidence that Older Adults are Disproportionately Victimized by Consumer Fraud'. *Perspectives on Psychological Science* 9(4): 427–42.

Scheibe, S., N. Notthoff, J. Menkin, L. Ross, D. Shadel, M. Deevy, and L. Carstensen (2014). 'Forewarning Reduces Fraud Susceptibility in Vulnerable Consumers'. *Basic and Applied Social Psychology* 36(3): 272–9.

Schoepfer, A. and N. Piquero (2009). 'Studying the Correlates of Fraud Victimization and Reporting'. *Journal of Criminal Justice* 37(2): 209–15.

Securities and Exchange Commission, North American Securities Administrators Association, and the Financial Industry Regulatory Authority (2007). *Protecting Senior Investors: Report of Examinations of Securities Firms Providing Free Lunch Sales Seminars.* Washington, DC: Securities and Exchange Commission.

Shadel, D., K. Pak, and J. Gannon (2010). 'The Effects of Investment Fraud Workshops on Future Investor Resistance'. Presentation at National Academy of Sciences meeting on Elder Mistreatment and Abuse and Financial Fraud, Washington, DC, June 22.

Shadel, D., K. Pak, J. Mathisen, B. Carlson, and J. Edwards (2007). *Inside the Con Man Mind: Advanced Training for Fraud Fighters*. Seattle, WA: AARP.

Titus, R., F. Heinzelmann, and J. Boyle (1995). 'Victimization of Persons by Fraud'. *Crime and Delinquency* 41(1): 54–72.

Van Dijk, J., J. Van Kesteren, and P. Smit (2007). *Criminal Victimisation in International Perspective: Key Findings from the 2004–2005 ICVS and EU ICS*. The Hague: Ministry of Justice, Wetenschappelijk Onderzoeken Documentatiecentrum.

Van Wyk, J. and M. Benson (1997). 'Fraud Victimization: Risky Business or Just Bad Luck?' *American Journal of Criminal Justice* 21(2): 163–79.

West, S. (1975). 'Increasing the Attractiveness of College Cafeteria Food: A Reactance Theory Perspective'. *Journal of Applied Psychology* 60(5): 656–8.

Worchel, S., J. Lee, and A. Adewole (1975). 'The Effects of Supply and Demand on Ratings of Object Value'. *Journal of Personality and Social Psychology* 32(5): 906–14.

Zimmerman, G., C. Olsen, and M. Bosworth (2000). 'A Stages of Change Approach to Helping Patients Change Behavior'. *American Family Physician* 61(5): 1409–16.

The Pension Research Council

The Pension Research Council of the Wharton School at the University of Pennsylvania is committed to generating debate on key policy issues affecting pensions and other employee benefits. The Council sponsors interdisciplinary research on private and social retirement security and related benefit plans in the United States and around the world. It seeks to broaden understanding of these complex arrangements through basic research into their economic, social, legal, actuarial, and financial foundations. Members of the Advisory Board of the Council, appointed by the Dean of the Wharton School, are leaders in the employee benefits field, and they recognize the essential role of social security and other public sector income maintenance programs while sharing a desire to strengthen private sector approaches to economic security. For more information see <http://www.pensionresearchcouncil.org>.

The Boettner Center for Pensions and Retirement Security

Founded at the Wharton School to support scholarly research, teaching, and outreach on global aging, retirement, and public and private pensions, the Center is named after Joseph E. Boettner. Funding to the University of Pennsylvania was provided through the generosity of the Boettner family, whose intent was to spur financial well-being at older ages through work on how aging influences financial security and life satisfaction. The Center disseminates research and evaluation on challenges and opportunities associated with global aging and retirement, how to strengthen retirement income systems, saving and investment behavior of the young and the old, interactions between physical and mental health, and successful retirement. For more information see <http://www.pensionresearchcouncil.org/boettner/>.

Executive Director

Olivia S. Mitchell, *International Foundation of Employee Benefit Plans Professor*, Department of Business Economics and Public Policy, The Wharton School, University of Pennsylvania.

MetLife, Inc.
Mutual of America Life Insurance Company
Ontario Pension Board
Pacific Investment MGMT. Co. LLC (PIMCO)
Prudential
Society of Actuaries
State Street Global Advisors
TIAA
The Vanguard Group
T. Rowe Price
Willis Towers Watson

Recent Pension Research Council Publications

Retirement System Risk Management. Olivia S. Mitchell, Raimond Maurer, and J. Michael Orsag, eds. 2016. (ISBN 978-0-19-878737-2)

Reimagining Pensions: The Next 40 Years. Olivia S. Mitchell and Richard C. Shea, eds. 2016. (ISBN 978-0-19-875544-9)

Recreating Sustainable Retirement. Olivia S. Mitchell, Raimond Maurer, and P. Brett Hammond, eds. 2014. (ISBN 0-19-871924-3)

The Market for Retirement Financial Advice. Olivia S. Mitchell and Kent Smetters, eds. 2013. (ISBN 0-19-968377-2)

Reshaping Retirement Security: Lessons from the Global Financial Crisis. Raimond Maurer, Olivia S. Mitchell, and Mark Warshawsky, eds. 2012. (ISBN 0-19-966069-7)

Financial Literacy. Olivia S. Mitchell and Annamaria Lusardi, eds. 2011. (ISBN 0-19-969681-9)

Securing Lifelong Retirement Income. Olivia S. Mitchell, John Piggott, and Noriyuki Takayama, eds. 2011. (ISBN 0-19-959484-9)

Reorienting Retirement Risk Management. Robert L. Clark and Olivia S. Mitchell, eds. 2010. (ISBN 0-19-959260-9)

Fundamentals of Private Pensions. Dan M. McGill, Kyle N. Brown, John J. Haley, Sylvester Schieber, and Mark J. Warshawsky. 9th ed. 2010. (ISBN 0-19-954451-6)

The Future of Public Employee Retirement Systems. Olivia S. Mitchell and Gary Anderson, eds. 2009. (ISBN 0-19-957334-9)

Recalibrating Retirement Spending and Saving. John Ameriks and Olivia S. Mitchell, eds. 2008. (ISBN 0-19-954910-8)

Lessons from Pension Reform in the Americas. Stephen J. Kay and Tapen Sinha, eds. 2008. (ISBN 0-19-922680-6)

Redefining Retirement: How Will Boomers Fare? Brigitte Madrian, Olivia S. Mitchell, and Beth J. Soldo, eds. 2007. (ISBN 0-19-923077-3)

Restructuring Retirement Risks. David Blitzstein, Olivia S. Mitchell, and Stephen P. Utkus, eds. 2006. (ISBN 0-19-920465-9)

Reinventing the Retirement Paradigm. Robert L. Clark and Olivia S. Mitchell, eds. 2005. (ISBN 0-19-928460-1)

Pension Design and Structure: New Lessons from Behavioral Finance. Olivia S. Mitchell and Stephen P. Utkus, eds. 2004. (ISBN 0-19-927339-1)

A History of Public Sector Pensions in the United States. Robert L. Clark, Lee A. Craig, and Jack W. Wilson, eds. 2003. (ISBN 0-8122-3714-5)

Benefits for the Workplace of the Future. Olivia S. Mitchell, David Blitzstein, Michael Gordon, and Judith Mazo, eds. 2003. (ISBN 0-8122-3708-0)

The Pension Challenge: Risk Transfers and Retirement Income Security. Olivia S. Mitchell and Kent Smetters, eds. 2003. (ISBN 0-19-926691-3)

Innovations in Retirement Financing. Olivia S. Mitchell, Zvi Bodie, P. Brett Hammond, and Stephen Zeldes, eds. 2002. (ISBN 0-8122-3641-6)

To Retire or Not? Retirement Policy and Practice in Higher Education. Robert L. Clark and P. Brett Hammond, eds. 2001. (ISBN 0-8122-3572-X)

Pensions in the Public Sector. Olivia S. Mitchell and Edwin Hustead, eds. 2001. (ISBN 0-8122-3578-9)

Available from the Pension Research Council website: <http://www.pensionresearchcouncil.org/>.

Index

Note: Tables and figures are indicated by an italic *t* and *f* following the page number.

AARP Public Policy Institute
  BankSafe 156, 178
  exploitation detection and
    prevention 156, 159, 178
  investment fraud, combating 202,
    203–4
  references 186, 187, 188, 189, 190,
    196, 204
Acierno, R. 154
active portfolio management 86
Adam, S. 47, 49, 52, 77n
Adult Decision Making Competence
    battery 15
adult protective services (APS), and
    exploitation 159, 160, 162, 163,
    168–70, 169*t*, 174
  challenges 176, 177, 178
  privacy issues 172–3
advance directives 6
advice, financial 8
  aging and likelihood of seeking
    advice 25–6
  assessment 38
  cognitive decline 34, 40, 43
  defined contribution plans 96–114
    automated 6
    demand and supply 98–100
    global financial crisis 103–4
    retirement age 101–2
    saving for retirement 97–8
    timing and patterns 104–9
  programs 10
  see also financial advisors; robo-advisors
Agarwal, S. 5, 6, 20, 24, 33
Age Discrimination Act (ADA, Australia,
    2004) 101–2
Age Wave 115–27

aging brain 7–8
  see also cognitive performance: trends
    over time
Agnew, J. 85
Ainslie, G. 97
Akerlof, G. A. 99, 103
Albert, S. M. 49
Allianz Life 161
Alzheimer's disease *see* dementia
ambiguity aversion 10n
American Bankers Association (ABA)
    Foundation 161–2
Americans' Perspectives on New
    Retirement Realities and the
    Longevity Bonus 115–28
Ameriks, J. 85
Anagol, S. 92
Anderson, K. 34, 186, 188, 189
Anderson, N. D. 47, 48
Angrist, J. D. 59
annuities
  guaranteed income 6
  options in public pensions 130–41,
    132*f*, 135*t*, 138*t*, 142–7*t*
Antolin, P. 6
anxiety 5
Appelt, K. C. 26
Area Agencies on Aging (AoA) 162
Arkes, H. R. 19
Arrow, K. J. 86
Asch, S. 199
assisted living, average age of entering
    (USA) 118
Association of Superannuation Funds of
    Australia 101
Atchley, R. C. 52
attorney, power of 159, 163, 167

Australia
   financial advice 111–12n
      defined contribution plans 97,
         100–1, 104–11
      global financial crisis 103–4, 105, 107
      labor force 102
      retirement age 101–2, 102t
Australian Bureau of Statistics 100,
      102, 103
automated advice 6
automatic defaults 10
   life cycle model of rational investor
      inertia 92
automatic savings and investment
      programs 1

Bäckman, L. 48
Ball, K. 23
Bank of American Fork 161
Bank of the West 162
banks, exploitation detection and
      prevention 156, 157, 178, 179
   challenges 176
   community outreach 162
   data-driven strategies 164–5
   federal reporting 166
   financial tools, products, and account
      features 164
   regulation 171
   training 159–61
   working with law enforcement 170
Banks, J. 48, 49
Barber, B. M. 35, 109, 189
Barbic, K. 161, 162
Barclays 160, 165
Baron, J. 97
Beals, M. 154, 185, 186, 206
Becker, G. 86
behavioral beliefs and preferences 4
Bekker, H. L. 25
Benjamin, D. 53, 77n
Bennett, D. A. 33, 36
Benson, M. 189
Bernard, T. S. 1
Bernartzi, S. 26
Besedeš, T. 18, 23

Beshears, J. 96
Better Business Bureau 161
Bianchini, L. 46, 49, 51, 52, 54, 55
Bilias, Y. 85
Bingley, P. 51, 54, 55, 56, 61
Binswanger, J. 24
blended families 122
blue-collar jobs *see* occupational
      characteristics
Blumer, C. 19
Boettner Center for Pensions and
      Retirement Research 213
Bonnie, R. 153
Bonsang, E. 46, 48, 52
   correlation between retirement and
      cognitive functioning 53, 54t,
      55, 56
   dataset, samples, dependent and
      independent variables 49, 50t
'boomerang' adult children 119, 122
Borella, M. 46, 49, 51, 52, 54, 55
Börsch-Supan, A. 77n
Bostrom, A. 27
Botti, S. 23
Bouchard, T. J. 48
Bound, J. 53
Bratman, M. E. 97
Brehm, J. 198
Brehm, S. 198
Brown, J. R. 49, 130, 148n
Brown, S. L. 122
Bruine de Bruin, W. 7, 15–32
Burks, S. V. 4
Button, M. 154, 187

Cahill, K. 148n
Caliński, T. 105
call centers, for combating investment
      fraud 204
Campbell, J. C. 96
Canan, S. 205
capabilities 5
   assessing 7
   cognitive decline 33, 34
   see also competence, decision making
Caplin, A. 111n

career intermission phase, new
 retirement workscape 123–4
Carman, K. G. 24
Carpenter, S. M. 24
Carroll, J. B. 77n
Carstensen, L. L. 21
Castle, E. 188
Cattell, R. B. 77n
Celidoni, M. 51, 54, 55
Certified Financial Planner (CFP) Board
 of Standards 34, 155
Chabris, C. F. 4
challenges for financial decision making
 at older ages 33–45
 cognitive changes 39–40
 data description and methods 36–43
 fraud 40–3
 overview of research findings 34–5
charitable donations and activities in
 retirement 124–7, 125*f*
Charles, K. K. 53
Charles, S. T. 21
Chen, A. 149n
Chen, S. T. 22
choice sets, reduced size of 23
Christelis, D. 49
Cialdini, R. 200
Clark, G. L. 8, 96–114
Clark, R. L. 8, 130–50
Cocco, J. F. 87
Coe, N. B. 46, 57
 correlation between retirement and
  cognitive functioning 52–3,
  54*t*, 55
 dataset, samples, dependent and
  independent variables 49, 50*t*
cognitive deliberation, and decision
 making competence 17*f*, 17–21,
 18*t*, 23
cognitive flexibility, and investment
 fraud 189
cognitive impairment 2, 5
 exploitation 159, 162, 163, 171, 176
 investment fraud 188, 192
 prevalence 1
 see also dementia

cognitive performance
 measurement 47–8
 and retirement *see* retirement: and
  cognitive functioning
 trends over time 7, 17–20, 48
 challenges for financial decision
  making 33–4, 35, 39–41, 43–4
 retirement, life priorities in 117
cognitive reserve 48
cognitive skills training 7–8, 23
Comizio, G. 153, 155, 168
Commodity Futures Trading
 Commission (CFTC)
 investment fraud, combating 202, 203
 Regulation S-ID 175
 SmartCheck 203
Community Commitment Awards 162
community outreach, exploitation
 prevention through 161–2
competence, decision making 15–32
 assessing 7
 cognitive deliberation 17–21, 23
 emotion regulation 20–1, 24–5
 experience 18–19, 24
 interventions 22–6
 limitations and next steps 26–7
 selective motivation 21–2, 25–6
 see also capabilities
confidence levels
 assessment 37–8
 cognitive decline 33, 34, 39–40, 43
 over-confidence *see* over-confidence
 under-confidence 16*f*
confidentiality *see* privacy issues,
 exploitation detection and
 prevention
Conrad, K. J. 155
Consumer Financial Protection Bureau
 (CFPB) 6, 156, 163, 164, 171
Consumer Fraud Research Group 187,
 189, 197, 198, 203
convenience accounts 164
Copes, H. 189
Cordray, R. 155
Cornehlsen, J. 6
corporate trustees 163

Coughlin, J. F. 162
Cowell, J. R. 8, 130–50
Craik, F. I. M. 47, 48
credit card readers 179
cross-sectional studies 26
crystallized intelligence 7, 47
  competence, decision making 18,
    19, 26

DaDalt, O. 162
Dave, D. 48
debit cards
  prepaid 164
  with spending limits 164
Deci, E. L. 25
decision choice architecture 6
decision making competence *see*
    competence, decision making
decision rules, applying 16*f*, 17, 18*t*, 18
decision tasks, age differences in 15, 16*f*
Deem, D. 154
Deevy, M. 9, 153–84, 186, 205, 208n
default setting 26
deferred annuity option, public
    pensions 136, 137–8, 138*t*, 140
defined benefit (DB) plans 3
  options 8
  retirement and cognitive
    functioning 48
  worker choices about payouts 130–41,
    132*f*, 135*t*, 138*t*, 142–7*t*
defined contribution (DC) plans 3
  advice 96–114
    automated 6
    demand and supply 98–100
    global financial crisis 103–4
    retirement age 101–2
    saving for retirement 97–8
    timing and patterns 104–9
  retirement and cognitive
    functioning 48
Delaney, R. 25
DeLiema, M. 9, 153–84, 188, 208n
Del Missier, F. 18, 20, 26
dementia 2
  concerns about developing 117, 118*f*

prevalence 1
recognition, by bank employees 161
and retirement 49
Dieckmann, N. F. 25
divorce between older adults 122
Dixon, R. 47, 48
Dodd–Frank Act (USA) 175
Dohmen, T. 53, 77n
Drexler, A. 24
Duckworth, A. L. 25

early retirement
  for health reasons 117
  Social Security (US) 139
Edey, M. 103
education factors, retirement and
    cognitive functioning 61,
    62*t*, 71*t*
Eisenberger, R. 200
Ekerdt, D. J. 52
Elder Abuse Forensic Centers 177
elder financial exploitation *see*
    exploitation
electronic fund transfers 175–6
emergency contact forms 173
emotions
  investment fraud 201, 203, 205
  regulation 5
    competence, decision making 17*f*,
      20–1, 24–5
English Longitudinal Study of Ageing
    (ELSA) 46, 49, 74*t*
    data description 64–5, 66
    dataset, samples, dependent and
      independent variables 50–1*t*
    disaggregating cognitive abilities and
      reconciling results 56
Enguidanos, S. 163
Ennis, G. E. 22
Ericsson, K. A. 24
Eslake, S. 103
Evans, D. A. 48, 53
EverSafe 165, 169
experience, and decision making
    competence 17*f*, 18–20, 19*t*,
      20*t*, 24

exploitation 9
  costs 154, 155
  definition 153
  financial service industry
      response 153–84
    analyses 155–7
    background and
      significance 154–5
    challenges 176–8
    findings 157–8
    future steps 178–9
    primary interventions 158–65
    secondary interventions
      166–76
  perpetrators 153
  prevalence (USA) 154
  see also fraud
extrapolation bias 4

family
  exploitation by 154, 163
    federal reporting 167
    reporting to adult protective
      services 168
  financial goals 127–8
  help with financial decision
      making 38
    cognitive decline 40
  as life priority in retirement 120–2,
      121*f*, 123*f*
family bank 121
Farquhar, P. 197
Federal Bureau of Investigation 188
Federal Deposit Insurance Corporation
      (FDIC) 159–60, 171
federal reporting of elder financial
      victimization 166–8, 166–7*f*
Federal Trade Commission (FTC)
      186, 188
fees
  financial advisors 88, 90, 92, 110
  plain-vanilla portfolios 92
  robo-advisors 90
  super funds 110
Ferrer, E. 77n
Fiaschetti, M. 8, 96–114

Fiduciary Abuse Specialist Teams 177
fiduciary responsibilities and
      compliance 6, 9
financial advisors 8
  choosing 85–95
    customized financial advice and
      simplified investment portfolios,
      comparison between 90–2,
      90–1*t*
    life cycle model of rational investor
      inertia 86–7, 87*f*
    when it makes sense 88–9, 89*t*
  defined contribution plans 96–7,
      100–1, 104*t*, 105–11, 106*f*, 108*f*
    demand for and supply of
      advice 99–100
  exploitation detection and
      prevention 156, 157, 179
  early financial planning 162–3
  regulation 171
  safe harbor protections 173–4
  training 158–9
  working with law enforcement 170
  fees 88, 90, 92, 110
  likelihood of seeking advice with
      increasing age 25
  use of 38
    cognitive decline 40
Financial Crimes Enforcement
      Network (FinCEN) 166, 167,
      168, 172, 177
financial driver's license 6, 10
financial education 6, 7
financial goals 8
  as life priority in retirement
      127–8
financial incentives, and selective
      motivation 25
Financial Industry Regulatory Authority
      (FINRA) 154, 174, 187
  BrokerCheck 203
  exploitation detection and
      prevention 156, 163, 171
  safe harbor protections 174
  free meal seminars 200
  Know Your Customer rules 163

Financial Industry Regulatory Authority
     (FINRA) Investor Education
     Foundation 34
  investment fraud 205
    combating 202, 203–4
    demographics and psychographics
      of victimization 188, 190
    prevalence 186
    social influence 196, 197, 199, 200
    targeting, role of 190, 191, 194,
      195, 196, 208n
financial literacy 2
  cognitive decline 33, 34, 35, 37, 39, 43
  investment fraud 187, 189–90, 192
    social influence 196–7
  saving for retirement 98
  variation in 98
financial mistakes 5, 7
financial power of attorney 159,
     163, 167
Finke, M. S. 5
Finucane, M. L. 18
First Financial Bank, Texas 160–1
flexible Social Security leveling option,
     public pensions 136–7, 139–40
fluid intelligence 7, 47
  competence, decision making 17, 19,
     20, 26
Fonseca, R. 7, 46–82
Forgas, J. P. 24
framing, resistance to 16f
Fratiglioni, L. 77n
fraud 9
  causes 35, 40–2, 43, 44
  common scams 153–4
  consequences 35–6, 42–3, 44
  costs 154, 155
  exposure to 6
  extent 34–5
  financial service industry
     response 153–84
    analyses 155–7
    background and
      significance 154–5
    challenges 176–8
    findings 157–8

future steps 178–9
  primary interventions 158–65
  secondary interventions 166–76
investment 185–212
  combating 201–4
  costs 186
  definition 185
  demographics and psychographics
     of victimization 187–90, 206–7
  impact 186–7
  prevalence 185–6
  social influence 196–201, 198f
  targeting, role of 190–6, 191t,
     193–4t, 195f, 196t, 207–8
perpetrators 153
prevalence (USA) 154
red flags of 188, 190, 192, 196, 202, 204
susceptibility to 35, 38–9, 41, 43,
     190–1
taxonomy 205–6
see also exploitation
Frederick, S. 53, 77n
free meal seminars 200
Fung, H. H. 26
future orientation 4, 5

Gabaix, X. 96, 97, 99
Galesic, M. 23
Gall, L. T. 52
Gamble, K. J. 5, 7, 33–45, 188, 189
gambler's fallacy 4
Ganzini, L. 188
Gassoumis, Z. D. 177
gender factors
  defined contribution plans, advice
     in 107–9
  global financial crisis, reaction to 104
  investment fraud 187, 192, 196
  retirement
    age (Australia) 102, 103t
    cognitive functioning 46, 48, 55,
      59–61, 59–60t
    giving opportunities 126
    health 117
    income, source of 100, 102
Germine, L. T. 5

Gerrans, P. 104
giving opportunities, as life priority in
        retirement 124–7, 125f
global financial crisis 103–4
    defined contribution plans, advice
        in 105, 107
    financial goals 127
Glymour, M. M. 53
goals, financial 8
    as life priority in retirement 127–8
Goda, G. S. 134, 139
Goetzmann, W. N. 35
Goldstein, D. 26
Gollwitzer, P. M. 25
Gouldner, A. 200
Graham, W. 186, 187
Gramm–Leach–Bliley Act (GLBA, USA,
        1999) 171–2, 173
guaranteed income annuities 6
guaranteed income products, whether
        and how much to invest in 4
guaranteed payment option, public
        pensions 132f, 133, 135t, 135,
        142–7t
Gunther, J. 155, 159, 160, 161, 165,
        178, 179

Hallett, M. 23
Halpern, D. F. 48
Hammond, B. 1–12
Han, S. D. 5
Hanoch, Y. 23
Hanrahan, P. F. 112n
Harabasz, J. 105
Hartshorne, J. K. 5
Harvey, N. 99
health
    how much to invest in 4
    as life priority in retirement 116–18,
        118f
    measures 66
    public pensions, worker choices about
        payouts 138
    uncertainty about 4
Health and Retirement Study (HRS) 46,
        49, 74t

correlation between retirement and
        cognitive functioning 53
data description 64, 65, 66
dataset, samples, dependent and
        independent variables 50–1t
disaggregating cognitive abilities and
        reconciling results 56
fraud 106
health insurance
    how much to invest in 4
    public retirement plans 130
Heintjes, T. 164
help with financial decision making see
        advice, financial
Hershey, D. A. 19
Hertzog, C. 47, 48, 77n
Hess, T. M. 19, 22, 25
Hira, T. 25
Hirshleifer, D. 21
Holtfreter, K. 154
home
    improvements 120
    as life priority in retirement 118–20
    moving, reasons for 119, 119f
    whether to sell 4
Hong Kong and Shanghai Banking
        Corporation (HSBC) 161
Horn, J. L. 77n
Huffman, D. 5
Hughes, S. L. 171
human capital 4
    financial advisors, choosing 88
    time cost of financial management 86
Hume, C. 205
Hutchins, C. 8, 115–29

identity theft 175
Imbens, G. W. 59
impatience 4, 5
impulsiveness 5
    and investment fraud 189
In Case of Emergency (ICE) forms 173
insurance
    goals 127
    health see health insurance
    long-term care 6

intelligence *see* crystallized intelligence;
    fluid intelligence
investment fraud 185–212
  combating 201–4
  costs 186
  definition 185
  demographics and psychographics of
      victimization 187–90, 206–7
  impact 186–7
  prevalence 185–6
  social influence 196–201, 198*f*
  targeting, role of 190–6, 191*t*, 193–4*t*,
      195*f*, 196*t*, 207–8
Investor Protection Trust 44
Isen, A. M. 24
Iyengar, S. S. 22, 23

Jackson, S. L. 153
Jacobson, D. 24
Jenkins, P. 209n
Job, S. 201
Johnson, E. J. 26, 35
Johnson, M. M. S. 22
Johnson, W. 48
Joint Academy Initiative on Aging 6
joint and survivor annuity option (J&S)
      131, 132*f*, 133, 135*t*, 135–6,
      142–7*t*
joint bank accounts 164
Joint Center for Housing Studies 118
Jorm, A. F. 52, 53
Joyner, E. 164
judgment tasks, age differences in 15, 16*f*

Kahneman, D. 4, 98, 107, 198
Kapteyn, A. 7, 46–82
Keren, G. 20
Kerley, K. 189
Kieffer, C. N. 9, 185–212
Kim, H. H. 8, 86–95
Kim, S. 21, 22, 25
Kircanski, K. 197, 201
Knoll, M. 149n
Knutson, B. 189
Kolluri, S. 8, 115–29
Korniotis, G. M. 33

Kotlikoff, L. J. 3
Kumar, A. 33, 35

labor earnings 87
Labouvie-Vief, G. 21
Lachs, M. S. 5
Laibson, D. 96, 97
Larrick, R. P. 19
Latimer, P. 112n
law enforcement, exploitation detection
      and prevention 170
  challenges 176–7, 178
  privacy issues 171, 172, 173
Lazear, E. P. 49
Lee, J. 188
Lei, X. 48
leisure 124
Lerner, J. 197
Li, Y. 5, 19, 20, 24
Liao, T. 208n
Lichtenberg, P. A. 155, 162
life cycle model of rational investor
      inertia 86–8, 87*f*, 92
  calibrated parameters 93–4*t*
Lin, I. F. 122
Lindeboom, M. 53
Lindgren, K. 112n
Little, D. 159, 163
Liu, L. L. 25
local average treatment effect
      (LATE) 59
Lock, S. L. 155
Loewenstein, G. 201
Loibl, C. 25
Long, R. C. 158, 168
longevity, uncertainty about 4
longitudinal studies 26
long-term care insurance 6
loss aversion 107, 198–9
lottery fraud 187, 204
lump-sum distributions
  private pensions 130
  public pensions 130, 131–2, 132*f*,
      135*t*, 135, 136, 142–7*t*
Lusardi, A. 1, 6, 24, 98, 187
Lutton, L. P. 92

Lyketsos, C. G. 49
Lyubomorsky, S. 24

McArdle, J. J. 77n
McCannon, T. 189
McFadden, D. 48
Malmendier, U. 33
Marson, D. C. 159
Martin, D. 111n
Martinello, A. 51, 54, 55, 56, 61
Mather, M. 21
Maurer, J. 48
Maurer, R. 3, 8, 86–95
maximizing strategies 22
maximum allowance 131, 132f, 133, 135t, 135, 142–7t
Mazzonna, F. 46, 48, 52
    correlation between retirement and cognitive functioning 53, 54t, 55
    dataset, samples, dependent and independent variables 49, 50t, 51t
Means, B. 24
Medicare 116
Mein, G. 52
Mercer, advice in defined contribution plans 100–1, 104t, 105–10, 106f, 108f
Merrill Lynch 116–27
MetLife Mature Market Institute 154
Midanik, L. T. 77n
Mikels, J. A. 21, 25
Milgram, S. 199
Millstein, R. 160
Milner, T. 25
Mitchell, O. S. 1–12, 24, 86–95, 98, 130, 187, 213
Mojon-Azzi, S. 52
mood inductions 24
Morrill, M. 149n
Morris, J. C. 47
Morris, M. 77n
mortgages
    paid off 119
    reverse home 6
motivation, selective 17f, 21–2, 21t, 25–6
Mottola, G. R. 9, 185–212

Moye, J. 5
Munnell, A. 123, 194n
Murphy, E. V. 172
Myers, D. 189

Nagel, S. 33
National Adult Protective Services Association 178
    Elder Financial Exploitation Advisory Board 169
National Center for Assisted Living (NCAL) 118
National Center for Victims of Crime 205
National Center on Elder Abuse (NCEA) 153
National Council on Aging (NCOA) 154
National Crime Victimization Survey 206
National Financial Capability Study 191
Navarro, A. E. 169, 177
Neill, R. 160, 161, 165
Neuman, K. 53
Nolen-Hoeksema, S. 24
North American Securities Administrators Association (NASAA)
    exploitation detection and prevention 156, 163, 174, 178
    free meal seminars 200
    investment fraud, combating 203
North, G. 96
nudge interventions 26

occupational characteristics
    classification 66
    and cognitive functioning 52, 55, 61, 63t, 72–3t, 76t
Odean, T. 35, 109, 189
O'Donoghue, T. 107
Office of the Comptroller of the Currency (OCC) 171, 172
old-age care
    long-term care insurance 6
    transition to 4

Olsen, A. 149n
optimism 4, 7
Oregon Bankers Association 160
Oregon Bank Project toolkit 160
Organisation for Economic
    Co-operation and Development
    (OECD) 49, 53, 69, 201–2
Outsmarting Investment Fraud (OIF) 204
over-confidence 4
  age differences 16*f*
  fraud victimization 35, 37, 41–2, 43
  investment fraud 189–90
over-optimism 4

Pak, K. 154
Park, D. C. 23, 24, 25, 47
Parker, A. M. 15
part-time work 124
Payne, J. W. 22
Pension Research Council (University of
    Pennsylvania) 213–16
  advisory board 214
  members 214–15
pensions 3
  private 130, 148n
  public 3
    retirement and cognitive
      functioning 48, 53
    timing of eligibility for 53, 69*t*
    worker choices about
      payouts 130–50
  retirement and cognitive
    functioning 48
  when to claim 4
  see also defined benefit (DB) plans;
    defined contribution (DC) plans
Peracchi, F. 46, 52
  correlation between retirement
    and cognitive functioning 53,
    54*t*, 55
  dataset, samples, dependent and
    independent variables 49,
    50*t*, 51*t*
personal relevance of information 25
Peters, E. 16, 18, 21, 23
Peterson, M. 48

phantom riches tactic, investment
    fraud 197, 198*f*
physical impairment 5
physically demanding jobs *see*
    occupational characteristics
Piquero, N. 189
Pischke, J.-S. 59
plain-vanilla portfolios 91*t*, 91
policy landscape 8–9
  exploitation detection and
    prevention 178
portfolio inertia 85–6
  life cycle model 86–8, 87*f*, 92
    calibrated parameters 93–4*t*
Poterba, J. 148n
Potter, G. G. 52, 53
Pottow, J. 33
power of attorney 159, 163, 167
Pratkanis, A. 197, 199
pre-retirement phase, new retirement
    workscape 123
privacy issues, exploitation detection
    and prevention 171–3, 174
  challenges 176, 177
  future steps 179
private pensions 130, 148n
prospect theory 4, 10n
  loss aversion 198
Prull, M. W. 47, 48
psychological theory on cognition 47
public pensions 3
  Australia 102
  retirement and cognitive
    functioning 48, 53
  timing of eligibility for 53, 69*t*
  worker choices about payouts
    130–50

Rabbitt, P. 77n
Rabin, M. 107
Reactance Theory 198
reciprocity tactic, investment
    fraud 198*f*, 200
re-engagement phase, new retirement
    workscape 124
regret 4

regulation
  ex ante 6
  exploitation detection and
      prevention 9, 155, 156–7,
      170–1, 172*f*
    challenges 176
    electronic fund transfers 175–6
    identity theft 175
    safe harbor protections 173–5
  financial advisors 92
    Australia 111n
Regulation E 175
Regulation S-ID 175
Reklaitis, V. 90
retirement
  ages 69*t*
    Australia 101–2, 103*t*
    public pensions, worker choices
      about payouts 133–4, 137,
      148–9n
  and cognitive functioning 46–82
    causality 52–6
    data description 64–6, 67–8*t*
    disaggregating cognitive abilities
      and reconciling results 56–61,
      70–6*t*
    measuring cognitive function and
      its determinants 47–8
    relationship between 48–52
  compulsory (Australia) 101–2
  definitions 65
    correlation between retirement and
      cognitive functioning 49, 52, 57
  and dementia 49
  duration 49, 55–6
  early
    for health reasons 117
    Social Security (US) 139
  honeymoon phase 52
  life priorities in 115–29
    family 120–2
    finances 127–8
    giving 124–7
    health 116–18
    home 118–20
    work 122–4

measures 65–6
  planning
    defined contribution plans 97–8,
      101, 104*t*, 104–10, 106*f*, 108*f*
    family support 121
    financial goals 127
    government information 96
    health care 116, 117
  saving for 97–8
  work after public sector
    employment 137–8
  workscape 123–4
reverse home mortgages 6
Rhoades, L. 200
Right to Financial Privacy Act (RFPA,
    USA, 1978) 173
risk-as-feelings hypothesis 201
risk behavior
  assessment 39
  fraud victims 35–6, 42–3
  investment fraud 189, 192, 200–1
risk perception, consistency in 16*f*
robo-advisors 179
  and customized financial advice,
    comparison between 90–1,
    90*t*, 92
Rohwedder, S. 46, 50, 52, 54, 55,
    56, 57
Rosenstreich, D. 25
Ross, M. 188
Roy, A. D. 107
Rush University Memory and Aging
    Project (MAP) 33–44

Sabatino, C. 159
Safe Banking for Seniors campaign 162
Safeguarding Our Seniors program 161
safe harbors 6, 10, 173–5, 177
Salthouse, T. A. 17, 19, 47, 77n
Samanez-Larkin, G. 189
Samuelson, W. A. 98
SAR (Suspicious Activity Report)
    filings 166–8, 166–7*f*, 177
satisficing strategies
  advice, search for 111n
  motivation 22

savings
how to draw down 4
for retirement 97–8
scarcity tactic, investment fraud
197–9, 198*f*
Scarmeas, N. 77n
Schaie, K. W. 26
Schaie, T. A. 47, 48, 77n
Scheibe, S. 204
Schoepfer, A. 189
Schooler, J. W. 18
Schreiber, P. 4
Schuth, M. 77n
Schwartz, B. 22
Schwartz, L. M. 21
Schwarz, T. 6
Securities and Exchange Commission
(SEC) 200
EDGAR Database 203
exploitation detection and
prevention 156, 171, 175
free meal seminars 200
Investment Advisor Public Disclosure
(IAPD) database 203
investment fraud, combating 202, 203
Securities Industry and Financial
Markets Association
(SIFMA) 170, 178
selective motivation 17*f*, 21–2, 21*t*, 25–6
self-control 4
self-employment 124
seminars 200
Senior Savings Protection Act (Missouri,
2015) 174
Serpell, A. J. 112n
Shadel, D. 154, 186, 204
Sharpe, W. F. 100
Sheeran, P. 25
Shefrin, H. 4
Shobe, M. A. 24
Shoven, J. B. 3, 139, 149n
Shumway, T. 21
Simon, J. D. 97
simplified investment portfolios 85, 91*t*,
91–2, 93
Skurnik, I. 20

Slavov, S. N. 3, 139, 149n
Slovic, P. 20
Small, G. W. 47
Soberon-Ferrer, H. 188
social consensus tactic, investment
fraud 198*f*, 199–200
social influence and investment
fraud 196–201, 198*f*, 205
combating 201, 202–3
social interaction, from giving and
volunteering activities 126
social isolation 5
investment fraud 188
social norms, recognizing 16*f*
Social Security benefits 3
when to claim 4
Social Security Leveling option, public
pensions 132*f*, 133–4, 135*t*, 136,
142–7*t*
flexible 136–7, 139–40
source credibility tactic, investment
fraud 198*f*, 199, 203
Spence, A. M. 99
Stanford Center on Longevity 205
stepchildren 122
Stern, Y. 48, 77n
Strough, J. 16, 20
Sturm, S. L. 24
Sun, Y. 22
sunk costs, resistance to 16*f*, 18–19, 19*t*,
20, 21, 25
Sunstein, C. R. 6, 110
super funds 100–1, 110
Survey of Consumer Finances 159
Survey of Health, Ageing and
Retirement in Europe
(SHARE) 46, 49, 74–5*t*
correlation between retirement and
cognitive functioning 52
data description 64, 65, 66
dataset, samples, dependent and
independent variables 50–1*t*
disaggregating cognitive abilities and
reconciling results 56
Sütterlin, S. 21
Swett, L. 160, 168, 177

Tabert, M. H. 49
Tanius, B. E. 23
Target Date Funds (TDFs) 85
  and customized financial advice,
      comparison between 91, 92, 93
TD Bank 179
technology
  exploitation detection and
      prevention 164–5, 179
  home improvements 120
  new retirement workscape 124
telemarketing fraud 188, 204
Thaler, R. H. 4, 6, 26, 35, 110
third-party account monitoring 164
time cost of financial management 86
Timmerman, S. 159, 163
Titus, R. M. 154, 188
tools 6, 8
Torges, T. M. 21
tournament strategy for decision
      making 23
training
  cognitive skills 7–8, 23
  exploitation detection and
      prevention 158–61, 178, 179
  investment fraud 205
Triebel, K. L. 159
True Link 154, 164
trust, and investment fraud 188, 199
trustees, corporate 163
Tufano, P. 8, 96–114
Tukey, J. W. 112n
Tversky, A. 4, 107, 198

UK Government 96
under-confidence 16*f*
United Kingdom
  ELSA *see* English Longitudinal Study
      of Ageing
  exploitation, financial service industry
      response 160
  global financial crisis 103
  investment fraud 186, 187
  workplace pensions and retirement
      account, relationship
      between 112n

United Nations Interregional Crime
      and Justice Research Institute
      186
United States Census Bureau 119
United States Department of Justice 204
  Bureau of Justice Statistics 205
  National Crime Victimization
      Survey 206
United States Department of Labor 9
United States Government
      Accountability Office
      (GAO) 171
United States Government Publishing
      Office 171, 173, 175
United States of America
  defined contribution retirement
      plans 3
  exploitation 9, 159–62, 179
    challenges 176–8
    future steps 178–9
    prevalence 154
    primary interventions 158–65
    secondary interventions
        166–76
  fraud 9, 34
    see also investment fraud *below*
  global financial crisis 103
  HRS *see* Health and Retirement Study
  investment fraud 185–208
    combating 201–4
    demographics and psychographics
        of victimization 187–90
    impact 186–7
    prevalence 186
    social influence 196–201, 198*f*
    targeting, role of 190–6, 191*t*,
        193–4*t*, 195*f*, 196*t*
  public pensions 3
    worker choices about payouts
        in 130–41, 132*f*, 135*t*, 138*t*,
        142–7*t*
  retirement, life priorities in
      115–28
Rush University Memory and Aging
      Project (MAP) 33–44
Social Security claiming ages 77n

United States Social Security
    Administration 3, 53
Utkus, S. 1–12

Van Dijk, J. 186
van Praag, G. 47
Van Putten, M. 25
Van Wyk, J. 189
visual aids for cognitive deliberation 23
voluntary activities in retirement 125–6

Waidmann, T. 53
Wallace, R. 153
Weber, M. 4
Wells Fargo Advisors 158–9, 165, 168, 173
West, S. 198
Westerlund, H. 52
white-collar jobs *see* occupational
    characteristics
Willis, R. J. 46, 50, 52, 54, 55, 56, 57

Wilson, T. D. 18
Winterbottom, A. 25
Wisconsin Legislative Council 131
Woodcock, J. R. 77n
Worchel, S. 197
work
    as life priority in retirement
        122–4, 125*f*
    see also occupational characteristics
World Health Organization
    (WHO) 1

Yang, J. 92

Zajonc, R. B. 20
Zamarro, G. 7, 46–82
Zeckhauser, R. 98
Zeldes, S. P. 85
Zikmund-Fisher, B. J. 23
Zimmerman, G. 202